Routledge Revivals

The Kurdish War

First published in 1964, *The Kurdish War* tells not only David Adamson's 200-mile journey on foot and horseback through the rebel mountains of Iraq but also of the circuitous route through the Middle East the author had to take to get there. For possibly 4000 years the Kurds have lived in the mountains between the Tigris and Armenia, owing fitful allegiance to many empires among them those of the Turks, Arabs, Persians, and briefly the British. Revolts against their overlords have been haphazard, bloody, and ill-fated. The one which began in Iraq towards the end of 1961 looked as if it would fall into the usual pattern, but in fact it was the deciding factor among the several which led to the overthrow of the late General Kassem.

In the summer of 1962 David Adamson was working in Paris for the Sunday Telegraph when he met Emir Bedir Khan, the doyen of the Kurdish nationalist movement. From that meeting sprang the discussion to try to enter the rebel held territory in the north-west of Iraq. In this book the author describes the leaders of the revolt and the aspirations, history, background of the Kurdish nationalists. This firsthand historical account is an essential read for scholars and researchers of Middle East history, Middle East studies, and history in general.

The Kurdish War

David Adamson

First published in 1964
by George Allen & Unwin Ltd.

This edition first published in 2022 by Routledge
4 Park Square, Milton Park, Abingdon, Oxon, OX14 4RN

and by Routledge
605 Third Avenue, New York, NY 10017

Routledge is an imprint of the Taylor & Francis Group, an informa business

© George Allen & Unwin Ltd,1964

All rights reserved. No part of this book may be reprinted or reproduced or utilised in any form or by any electronic, mechanical, or other means, now known or hereafter invented, including photocopying and recording, or in any information storage or retrieval system, without permission in writing from the publishers.

Publisher's Note
The publisher has gone to great lengths to ensure the quality of this reprint but points out that some imperfections in the original copies may be apparent.

Disclaimer
The publisher has made every effort to trace copyright holders and welcomes correspondence from those they have been unable to contact.

A Library of Congress record exists under LCCN: 65012426

ISBN: 978-1-032-32271-1 (hbk)
ISBN: 978-1-003-31423-3 (ebk)
ISBN: 978-1-032-32272-8 (pbk)

Book DOI 10.4324/9781003314233

1 *The great cave at Cham-i-Razan*

THE KURDISH WAR

DAVID ADAMSON

London
GEORGE ALLEN & UNWIN LTD
RUSKIN HOUSE MUSEUM STREET

FIRST PUBLISHED IN 1964
This book is copyright under the Berne Convention. Apart from any fair dealing for the purposes of private study, research, criticism or review, as permitted under the Copyright Act, 1956, no portion may be reproduced by any process without written permission. Inquiries should be addressed to the publisher.

© *George Allen & Unwin Ltd, 1964*

PRINTED IN GREAT BRITAIN
in 11 on 12 point Janson type
BY SIMSON SHAND LTD
LONDON, HERTFORD AND HARLOW

FOR BARBARA

NOTE

I have used pseudonyms to disguise the identities of some of the smaller fry who helped me in Istanbul, Persia and Iraq. I have also scrambled a few facts about those who helped me or talked to me about Kurdish politics on my way to Iraq, but they are very minor points and none of the essential details of what happened has been changed.

I have not given a bibliography, but I should like to acknowledge my indebtedness to two books, Mr C. J. Edmonds's *Kurds, Turks and Arabs*, London, 1957, and Mr William Eagleton Jr's *The Kurdish Republic of 1946*, London, 1963. Both are invaluable to anyone who wishes to study the history of the Kurds in the first half of this century.

CONTENTS

CHAPTER	PAGE
One	13
Two	26
Three	42
Four	56
Five	69
Six	84
Seven	100
Eight	113
Nine	126
Ten	141
Eleven	155
Twelve	169
Thirteen	178
Fourteen	193
APPENDIX	208

ILLUSTRATIONS

1 *The great cave at Cham-i-Razan*   frontispiece
2 *Ibrahim Ahmed*   facing page 32
   Mullah Mustafa Barzani
3 *On the Iraq-Persian frontier*   33
   On the way out of Iraq
4 *Colonel Akrawi*   96
   Kurdish soldier
   Mustafa Karadaghi
5 *The hospital in the cave at Cham-i-Razan*   97
   A mixed bag of prisoners
6 *Partisans at the Democratic Party headquarters*   112
   On the summit of Mount Sarband
7 *Refugee children outside their cave*   113
   Inside the cave

CHAPTER I

When I arrived at the Emir's diminutive flat near the Metro Dupleix I found that his wife was ill and in bed. She looked very oriental, I thought, and probably very Kurdish too, as she lay back among her pillows in the bed alcove, apologizing for not being able to cook lunch and thanking me for the pink azalea in a pot that I had brought. Afterwards I recalled it as a fine-boned, delicately featured face; but I must have been misled by the shadows of the alcove, for when I met her and her husband again nearly a year later I saw that it was a robust and cheerfully handsome face. Madame Bedir Khan, I discovered, is Polish; and the Emir, who teaches at the Ecole des Langues Vivantes, usually prefers to be known as doctor. This is not to demonstrate a type of disenchantment or that I went to Kurdistan with romantic ideas and came back with plain ones: merely that the Kurds are never quite what they seem, even the adopted ones like Madame Bedir Khan. The Kurdish war is a bit like that, too. The Arabs, Turks and Persians see it as an almost unbroken series of bloodthirsty, pillaging forays by wild tribesmen, but the Kurds (and on the whole I think they are right) look on it as a long national struggle which began in the second quarter of the nineteenth century.

The Emir (the title suits him better than plain doctor) Bedir Khan's great-grandfather, the Prince of Bhotan, was the first Kurdish national leader of any consequence; and apart from being somewhat blood-boltered by the massacre of 10,000 Assyrian Christians, he emerged with honour from his defeat by the Turks in 1847. He and his family went into exile in the following year, the Year of Revolutions, and if there was no immediate sign that what was happening elsewhere made any impact on them, the family was later to play an important part in promoting and keeping alive the idea of Kurdish nationalism. They published a newspaper, *Kurdistan*, which they

The Kurdish War

printed in a number of places, mostly in Cairo and once in Folkestone; and a Bedir Khan acted as adviser to Sheikh Ubeidullah, who founded a Kurdish League on the Turkish-Persian border, talked of autonomy, or internal self-government, and in 1878 wrote to a British vice-consul that: 'Something must be done so that the European governments having understood the matter shall inquire into our state.' The Kurds are still sending messages to European governments; I brought one home myself.

This is all by way of explaining why, in August 1962, when the *Sunday Telegraph* agreed with me that it would be worth looking into the possibility of visiting the Kurdish rebels in the mountains of northern Iraq, I went to see the Emir Bedir Khan. I was working in Paris at the time and I had seen various statements by him on the revolt and also knew that he had been to the United Nations in New York as a sort of unofficial Kurdish delegate. One energetic Swiss journalist, working from Beirut, had just come out of the rebel area and, the Emir told me, an American, the Beirut correspondent of the *New York Times*, was there now by invitation of the rebels. This worried me, not so much because others had got there before me as because it would be difficult to follow in their tracks. None of the other countries—Turkey, Persia and Syria—with Kurdish minorities has any love for the rebels and I felt there was a strong possibility that from now on any foreign journalist seen heading in the direction of Kurdistan would be turned back. However, the Emir said he would write to other Kurds who were better placed to give me introductions and advice and advised me to be patient. I went back to London at the end of August and waited, reading as much as the British Museum had to offer on the Kurds, about whom I knew nothing. I knew very little, in fact, about any of the peoples involved. Persia I had visited once, and then only briefly and as a tourist. The other countries of the Middle East were a blank in my experience and the only part of the Arab world I had seen was Algeria.

Looking at the confused and melancholy history of the Kurds in the last two centuries, it seems right that the Emir, the doyen of Kurdish nationalism, should have married a Pole, for the Kurds are, politically at least, the Poles of the Middle

The Kurdish War

East. They are crushed, as the Poles were, between more powerful neighbours. The tip of northern Kurdistan reaches into Soviet Armenia (not that the Russians have tried to suppress Kurdish nationalism; far from it), where there are rather more than 60,000 Kurds, and the southern edge of their homeland runs from Khanaqin, in Iraq, to Kermanshah, in Persia (I shall refer to Iran as Persia to avoid confusion with Iraq), a distance from north to south of over 400 miles. The Kurdish nationalists like to include the Lurs and Bakhtiaris in the south of Persia within their domain, but I am not altogether convinced that these tribes accept this. The nationalists, like nationalists everywhere, tend to exaggerate, claiming that Kurdistan stretches in a rough boomerang shape from the Gulf of Iskanderun, on the Turkish Mediterranean coast, to the Persian Gulf. The true western limit is probably about 100 miles from the coast, and the eastern limit 100 miles east of the Iraq-Persian frontier. The bulk of the Kurdish population lives in Turkey, where there are three to four million; next comes Persia with over two million, followed by Iraq, 1,500,000, and Syria, over 300,000. The total population is a matter of argument among interested parties. The nationalists claim that the governments' census-takers minimize their numbers, while the governments claim that the nationalists exaggerate. The true figure may be somewhere close to eight million, a figure in excess of official statistics but made probable by the extremely high birth-rate among the Kurds, particularly in Turkey.

Their homeland is a high, mountainous one, stark in most places but wooded and benign enough in others to make it one of the most beautiful places in the Middle East. There are thin woods, fields of tobacco and wheat in the valleys and fast rivers that never dry up. The Tigris and the Euphrates both start in Kurdistan. The mountains which breed them reach up to ten and twelve thousand feet, with Ararat, close to the Turkish-Russian border, the highest at over 15,000 feet. The Kurds claim that they have lived there for 4,000 years. They are an Aryan people, probably the same stock as the Medes, and more closely related to the Persians than to any other of their neighbours, although they have become very intermingled with others: Turks, Arabs and even the Mongols, who raged through the mountains in the thirteenth century.

The Kurdish War

You will find, for instance, that in Iraq a great many Arabs have Kurdish blood (the Arabs are less shy of admitting their mixed blood than similarly placed Kurds are of admitting theirs); Kassem, against whom the present revolt started in September 1961, was one of them. As well as blood, the Kurds have received much of their culture from their neighbours, the Arabs and Persians rather than the Turks. The Arabs have given them their religion, mainly Sunni Moslem, and the Persians their love of poetry and a vein of mysticism which pulses strongly through their religion despite a certain scepticism in their natures. They are Kurds first and Moslems second, and many look back with romantic nostalgia, rather as Irishmen mourn over the lost kings and myths of Ireland, to the pre-Islamic days (they were conquered and converted by the Arabs in the seventh to tenth centuries) when they were followers of Zoroaster, who hailed from Lake Urmia, on the Persian edge of Kurdistan. This mixture of races and cultures is one reason why they grasp at anything which seems truly indigenous, or at least dating from before the great conquests; the cult of the Kurdish Yezidis in northern Iraq, for instance, with its mixture of Mithraic and Zoroastrian beliefs.

It may be that this lack of strong cultural identification marks is one reason why the Kurds, and the Kurdish war, are so little known about in the West. There is no easily graspable aesthetic core to their revolt. To the British, blasé from years of warfare in the North-West Frontier of India, the revolt has never seemed much more than the squabbling of tribesmen. Our attempts after the First World War to give them some sort of self-government ended in failure and we washed our hands after that. They were the 'wild Koordes', and we accepted the stock Persian description of them translated by E. B. Soane who travelled through Kurdistan in 1908: 'Shedders of blood, raisers after strife, seekers after turmoil and uproar, robbers and brigands; a people all malignant, and evil-doers of depraved habits, ignorant of all mercy, devoid of all humanity, scorning the garment of wisdom; but a brave race and fearless, of a hospitality grateful to the soul, in truth and in honour unequalled, of pleasing countenance and fair cheek, boasting all the goods of beauty and grace.'

They are not as bad these days as the first part makes out,

The Kurdish War

but the essence of what the writer is saying is true; there is this curious duality in their nature. Sheikh Ubeidullah descending on the plains around Lake Urmia, driving the Persians back to Maragegh, and then pausing fatally to talk with an American missionary about saving the Christian communities at Rezaieh; Qazi Mohammad, the president of the brief Kurdish Republic founded at Mahabad in 1945, deciding to stay put and submit peacefully to the Persian forces; their extremely benevolent treatment of Arab troops captured in the present revolt. And the other, equally well-minted side of the Kurdish coin: the massacres of the Armenians and the Assyrians; the treachery and savagery of inter-tribal feuds; the murder in 1917 of the Assyrian Patriarch, the Mar Shimun XIX, at a parley.

Somewhere between these two aspects of the Kurds comes Mullah Mustafa Barzani, the leader of the 1961 revolt and several others as well. He is brave, loyal to his own, not very wise, obstinate and well used to strife and turmoil. When Qazi Mohammad surrendered so mildly, he and his tribesmen fought their way out of Persia, murdering eleven *aghas* of the Mamash tribe, and eventually struggled across the grain of the mountains, through Iraq, Turkey and Persia, to reach sanctuary in Russia in 1947. This is the great Kurdish epic, how Mullah (a first name, not a religious office) Mustafa and his 496 Barzanis trekked to Russia rather than surrender their leaders to the Iraqis against whom they had originally rebelled. No Kurdish leader has been so generally revered and his name has been put side by side (a bit incongruously in the circumstances) with that of Saladin, a Kurd of Arbil, who led the Arabs to victory over the Crusaders.

In a way the great march of the Barzanis and the legendary quality of their leader has harmed as much as helped the Kurds. They have been given a leader whose legend, if not his personality, has linked the politically-minded and the tribesmen, but it has also created an élite out of the most military and most hated of the tribal groups, the Barzanis. The leaders of the Democratic Party of Kurdistan may be the most vital force within Kurdistan and the true guides of the revolt, but they know that the revolt could not continue without Mullah Mustafa and the tribes grouped around him. They know, too, that he and his followers would be as unassimilable in any Kurdish state as they are in Iraq under the present constitution. Another effect of the Barzanis' march and exile has been to give the entire Kurdish movement a reddish colouring in the eyes of the West and the interested Middle Eastern governments; and this impression has been reinforced by the Democratic Party of Kurdistan's genuflexion in the past to Marxist-Leninist inspiration.

The Russians have long been interested in Kurdistan; twice they have penetrated it, during both world wars, and each time they have withdrawn without any glory. After Sultan Murad IV and Shah Abbas of Persia defined their frontiers in 1639, the Kurds were left with a considerable amount of autonomy within their tribal areas on the Turkish side. They were the guardians of the frontier and this rôle and their special status satisfied them until 1830 when the first of the series of revolts which went on until 1847 broke out in defiance of a weak Turkish Government which was attempting to reimpose its authority and collect taxes and enlist men for its armies. The Russians were later, as they tried to spread their influence through the Ottoman Empire and the Middle East to the Persian Gulf, to recognize the importance of the Kurds and to stimulate their ambitions, as they did those of the Armenians. Towards the end of the century a number of Kurdish leaders visited Russia and some of them were received by Tsar Nicholas II; and in 1908, when the Young Turks revolt had again raised Kurdish hopes, there seem to have been renewed contacts, this time between Russian agents and the chiefs in Southern Kurdistan where the Hamawand tribe, old-fashioned brigands rather than new-fangled nationalists, had been crushed by the Turks. In Constantinople in the same year the Kurdish exiles had founded the Kurdish Club, and with it the earnest-sounding 'Journal of Kurdish Self-Help and Progress'. Their slogan 'Kurdistan for the Kurds' stirred the tribes to a revolt which was crushed in 1913. The Hamawand, Jaff and Dizai tribes appealed for help to the Russians; and from the Mosul district several chiefs, including the Sheikh of Barzan, fled to the sanctuary of the Russian army in Azerbaijan, creating a precedent for Mullah Mustafa thirty-three years later.

The Kurdish War

The British with their stake in Middle Eastern oil and appreciation of the strategic importance of Mesopotamia to their communications with India, were also becoming interested in the Kurds, as they were in the other emergent nationalisms, Arab and Armenian, of the Ottoman Empire. The oilfields lay within the Mosul Vilayet, or province, and near Kirkuk, on the edge of the main Kurdish population. Their resources had not been exploited but their potential importance was well known; oil was becoming increasingly important as fuel for warships as well as for domestic purposes, and any new source attracted both capital and political attention. The British and Dutch held 75 per cent of the shares in the Turkish Petroleum Company and the Germans 25 per cent. But German influence, economic and political, was steadily gaining in the Ottoman Empire and they had brought off a major coup with the building of the Berlin-Baghdad railway. Soundings by the British of the strength of Kurdish nationalism and the attitudes of the tribes seem to have been made before the war, some of them possibly by Soane, whose precise reasons for the journey described in his book *To Mesopotamia and Kurdistan in Disguise* are difficult to fathom unless one assumes he went there as an agent.

The British entered southern Kurdistan in 1918 and found a territory whose life had been disrupted by two years of pillaging and murder by Russian troops. Most of the political officers who were sent there were from the Political Department of the Indian Government and so were familiar with similar mountain peoples. They preferred the Kurds to the Arabs, whom they distrusted, and at least one strong advocate of Kurdish autonomy was produced in the shape of Major E. W. C. Noel, whose lucid and sympathetic reports were for a time influential. On the other side of the frontier, in Persia, self-government was also in the air. In July 1918, the Kurdish chiefs met to discuss an independent state under British auspices and the idea was put to the British consul while he was on tour at Saqez in eastern Kurdistan.

If the Kurds failed to attain autonomy in what is now Iraqi Kurdistan in the years immediately after the 1914-18 war it was not entirely the fault of the British. They tried hard; and many Kurds who are not otherwise particularly kindly in their views of British motives, recognize this. Sheikh Mahmud, their first protégé, refused all restraints, placed the British advisers under house arrest and then ran up his own flag, a red crescent on a green background. The Treaty of Sèvres, signed by Turkey and the Western Powers in 1920 but never implemented, included, largely at the instigation of the British, terms creating a Kurdish state within what is now Turkey; the rise to power of Kemal Ataturk put paid to that. But as late as December 1922, the Kurds were still being told that 'His Britannic Majesty's Government and the Government of Iraq recognizes the right of the Kurds living within the boundaries of Iraq to set up a Kurdish Government within those boundaries. . . .' Their great difficulty was that there was no generally acceptable leader, and Major Noel in one of his reports quoted this verse current in Kurdistan at the time:

> 'If we had a king,
> He would be worthy of his crown;
> He should have a capital
> And we would share his fortune.
> Turk and Persian and Arab
> Would all be our slaves;
> But what can we do? Our market is dull;
> We have the goods but cannot find a buyer.'

Kurdistan became a pious thought and then not even that. Turkish patrols moved through the mountains of the Mosul Vilayet creating trouble and doubts; the French were said to be interested in the Mosul Vilayet too (even today they will in their sour fashion go out of their way to tell any Kurdish nationalist who happens to stray into the Quai d'Orsay how hostile the British are to Kurdish interests), and Arab opinion in Iraq had to be placated. By the beginning of 1923 it had been decided to exclude the question of the Mosul Vilayet, the only area in which the Kurds now had any chance of obtaining autonomy, from the agenda of the Lausanne conference called to draft a successor to the Treaty of Sèvres. Britain and Turkey were given a year in which to reach an agreement and if they were unable to do so, then the question was to go to the League of Nations; which was what hap-

The Kurdish War

pened. The League's commission listened and looked and in 1925 found that the best solution for the Kurds and the Mosul Vilayet was for it to be placed under British trusteeship with the rest of Iraq. National feeling among the Kurds was recognized, but . . . and that was that. In Turkey in the same year there was a widespread Kurdish uprising under Sheikh Said Pirani, one of many which erupted with as great or lesser intensity until the end of the 1930s.

In Iraq, the Baghdad Government and the British were always at loggerheads with the Kurds. But they were on the whole minor troubles; the Kurds of Iraq were better off than their brothers elsewhere and most of them knew it, except perhaps the Barzanis who were in a more or less continual state of mutiny from 1930 onwards. In the towns there was resentment that the agreement ending the British mandate (it ended in 1932) in effect handed over control to the Arab majority and there was the celebrated *Roja Rash*, the Black Day, when a number of Kurds on strike were killed in Sulaimaniya.

In the same town were detained several years later both Mullah Mustafa Barzani and his brother Sheikh Ahmed. Both had been exiled there since a rebellion in 1938. In their own barren territory in 1943 there was a serious famine; Government promises of help and oxen did not materialize and rebellion broke out. First Mullah Mustafa and then his brother, Sheikh Ahmed, slipped back to Barzan, fifty miles north of Arbil, to rally the tribes. The Baghdad Government does seem to have done its best to placate the Barzanis, appointing special liaison officers, conceding some points and in March 1945 granting an amnesty to Mullah Mustafa (who by now was in complete control of the Barzanis, the indecisive and unstable Sheikh Ahmed having been edged out) and the other rebels. But the obdurate impolitic streak in Mullah Mustafa prevented him from taking the only sensible course, which was to accept. The revolt spread, gathering up other tribes and stray nationalists, flared up seriously and was crushed by the RAF bombing the villages and the tribesmen and by the intervention of the Barzani's greatest enemies, the Zibaris.

To the east, in Persia, the war and British and Russian occupation of Kurdistan to safeguard the supply route from

The Kurdish War

the Persian Gulf to Soviet Armenia, had meant the disappearance of Persian control. In this no-man's land a Kurdish republic sponsored by the Russians was on the verge of being declared in Mahabad, not far south of the gloomy salt sea of Lake Urmia, by Qazi Mohammad, the Russian nominee for the presidency. Mullah Mustafa crossed the border with his Barzanis to become the defender of the new republic's frontiers. It was a mild, homespun régime, uncertain whether it was independent or autonomous and part of Persia. No one was shot for political reasons and there were two poets on the President's staff. The republic was declared on January 22, 1946, and ended in mid-December of the same year when the Russians withdrew from northern Persia and the Persian army was able to reclaim the national territory. Mullah Mustafa's flight to Russia I have already described. The story of the Mahabad Republic is a tragic one and its fate and that of its hanged leaders remains to haunt the memories of the Kurdish leaders in Iraq, particularly Mullah Mustafa who might well have died on the gallows in the Chwar Chira circle at Mahabad himself.

With this history of Russian support in the back of their minds, both the British and the Americans were uneasy when the Kurdish revolt in Iraq grew from largely tribal origins into something which by the spring of 1962 had taken on a much stronger political colouring. The main Central Treaty Organization defence line ran along the mountains of Kurdistan, and the Americans in particular (although they are not members of CENTO) saw the revolt as a threat to the region's safety. If a Kurdish state were formed, then it would be unstable and unworkable, a potential subject for Russian influence. The British, in their Asquithian way, were more prepared to suspend judgment and wait and see what happened. They did not believe, for one thing, that the Kurds would succeed, despite the military successes which had led to the eviction of the Iraqi army and the civil authorities from the mountains. And they argued, rightly as it turned out, that the revolt might lead to the downfall of the neurotic Kassem, who had destroyed the Hashemite régime imposed on Iraq by the British, and his replacement by a government friendlier to the West and less inclined to seek communist support.

The Kurdish War

Waiting in London, I heard nothing for over six weeks from the Kurds to whom the Emir had promised to write. When the letter came it was helpful in tone but naturally vague about a route into Kurdistan. I decided the best thing to do was to fly to Zurich and talk to Ismet Cherif Vanly, the Secretary-General of the Committee for the Defence of the Kurdish People's Rights.

I had no idea how I would enter Kurdistan, but middle European towns are wonderfully calming in the dead months of the year: Zurich in October was scented with woodsmoke, the shops were heavy with goods made for substantial people, and the lake was very still, with small gulls flying silently in the misty air above it. Ismet Cherif and another Kurd met me at my hotel and took me to the railway station, where we lunched in the first class dining room and were joined towards the end of the meal by a third Kurd who had either come from or was going to Vienna; I never found out which. The slight air of conspiracy was cosy and almost reassuring, the Zurich *Bahnof* as benevolently disposed towards us as we sat round our table like some splinter of the International as it must have been to all the other upholders of *isms* who have met there.

One of the wry points history, or perhaps more accurately the Turks, has scored against the Kurds is that many of their leaders have seen very little of Kurdistan. The Emir Bedir Khan has spent, I think, two and a half days there; and Ismet Cherif comes from Damascus, far away from Kurdistan. But exile has fed rather than stunted their zeal. The energetic and passionate Ismet, a former communist, represents the left-wing of the Kurds abroad, the students rather than the upper-crust of politicians, business men and diplomats, who regard him as too hot-headed and inclined to be impulsive. He earned their displeasure after the cease-fire in February 1963 when he, through the Committee for the Defence of the Kurdish People's Rights, attacked acceptance of the cease-fire, the negotiations for an autonomous rather than independent Kurdistan, and the decision of the chief negotiator, Jelal Talabani, to go to Cairo to talk to President Nasser. It showed, he said, a lack of character. So it was not altogether surprising that Ismet Cherif, although the accredited representative in Europe of Mullah Mustafa, was edged out of the diplomatic

The Kurdish War

offensive that was launched in the summer of 1963 by Jelal Talabani, by then the rebels' 'roving ambassador'. If it was intended to arouse enthusiasm for the rebels' cause, it failed. Talabani was refused a British visa and never came to London, the key city from the Kurds' point of view, since Iraq, by tacit agreement with the Americans, remains primarily a British sphere of influence. The British had by that time decided to support the Baath Party and were discreetly hostile to the Kurds.

It was unfortunate that while Talabani was applying for a British visa he should have made a broadcast for Radio Moscow and caused suspicion that he was visiting the Eastern bloc. In fact, the broadcast was recorded in West Berlin, but it was enough to arouse some of the old fears of communist influence among the Kurds. Matters were made even worse by the decision of Outer Mongolia to espouse the Kurdish cause at the United Nations assembly in September. The good done by an airing of the case might have outweighed the effects of Western suspicions, but just as the Kurds had got together a delegation to go to New York, Outer Mongolia decided to drop their resolution from the agenda, probably because of the Sino-Soviet dispute and a realization that championship of the Kurds would antagonize the Arabs at a time when the Soviet group needed friends.

Just as in the past the Kurds were nationalists before they were Moslems, so today they are nationalists before they are communists or even socialists. The appeal of the puritanical and militant Left is there and I should guess that a good many Kurdish students are or have been members of the Communist Party. But the party has not been a good friend of the Kurds and it would be wrong to lay too much emphasis on its importance.

It became obvious as I talked to Ismet and his friends that they could do nothing to plan a way into Kurdistan for me. Since the journey of the *New York Times* correspondent into Kurdistan, the route through Syria had been virtually closed as a result of Iraqi protests. The bridges across the Euphrates were now more closely guarded and unless I was prepared to swim the river, no doubt supported on inflated goat-skins like the Assyrian warriors in the British Museum's bas-reliefs, I

The Kurdish War

would be unable to enter the Kurdish area and pick up guides. Ismet Cherif suggested I should go to Istanbul and talk to Kurds there to see if they could help.

We met again at my hotel the next day. Ismet had sat up until three that morning writing letters of introduction in French, Arabic and Kurdish for me and lengthy despatches addressed to Mullah Mustafa or, in case I met him first, Ibrahim Ahmed, the Secretary-General of the Democratic Party of Kurdistan. Ismet wondered whether I minded carrying the Kurdish 'diplomatic bag' and I told him cheerfully that as the despatches were written on thin airmail paper I would if the worst came to the worst be able to eat them.

My plan had been to go to the Lebanon and Syria, but I changed this and booked on a plane to Istanbul. It was a hop into a void, really; no one in Europe knew much about the Kurdish marches. I hoped the *Sunday Telegraph* would be tolerant if the approach to Kurdistan took a long time.

CHAPTER II

I had placed the Kurdish 'diplomatic bag' in my breast pocket for safety's sake in case my grip was searched at the airport and the envelope, with Mullah Mustafa's name on it, spotted by a sharp-witted customs officer. But at one o'clock in the morning no one at Istanbul airport was examining baggage and I went through the customs and immigration check with all the speed of any accredited courier. The 'diplomatic bag', growing scruffier and scruffier in my pocket as the days went by, always lent me a slight feeling of panache, though, in my occasional dealings with the police; of black Russian cigarettes and vest-pocket pistols. But in fact, carrying it involved me in no risk and once inside Iraq it served as a useful passport and as such was probably as important to me as it was to the Kurds.

The airport minibus rattled along the dark road to Istanbul, through the walls built by Theodosius around the Byzantine city, over the Golden Horn by the inner bridge and up the narrow streets of Pera; past a night club whose patrons had just been turned out and were standing on the pavement, hands in pockets, hunched against the night chill and wondering sheepishly what to do next. The Istanbul Hilton, all air-conditioning and imminent Musak, was full, some conference of international agronomists or Middle-Eastern staff colonels having descended on it the day before. I set off to look for another hotel, rejected the taxi-driver's suggestion of a seedy-looking flop-house with an English name and found one that offered me not so much a room as a small dormitory with four beds. I locked the door and placed the 'diplomatic bag' under the pillow of the softest bed.

I moved in the morning to an hotel with rooms less reminiscent of a boarding school and began to consider how I should start the search for 'Mr Medes', the pseudonym of an important Kurdish nationalist. The first link, Mr Y, of whom some-

The Kurdish War

one, according to my introductory letter, had spoken highly of his '*grande enthousiasme*' for the Kurdish cause, was away when I rang his office. 'He should be back tomorrow,' said his secretary. I rang his home. An old, female voice replied in Turkish, via the hotel receptionist, that Mr Y was away. It seemed best to get in touch with the alternative link, a group of young Kurds. But when I showed the address to a taxi driver, neither he nor several passers-by knew where it was, for it did not give the district, and no one had heard of the street.

One can get an obsession with time on trips like this. Newspapers are after all commercial concerns with money at stake, and unseen pressures emanating from one's office create every day an arbitrary deadline for achievement of some sort; and a wasted hour can be an eternity of stomach-wearing frustration. I knew, too, from experience that one alteration of plans, as I had altered mine in Zurich, can multiply into innumerable big and little delays. I remembered guiltily that I had not cabled my address in Istanbul to the foreign news editor and hurried off towards the cable office.

Istanbul is a city of character but no great charm; too self-absorbed for charm, which gets lost among the hard-faced, unhappy masses of people and the battered dolmusses that scrape and lurch across the bridges and up the steep roads; everything hazed by the golden smoky dust that rises from Galata and floats gently over the city. When it is beautiful, it is beautiful as London is; either aloofly in panorama or almost palisaded off from the rest of the city. Sometimes it astonishes; for instance, a peacock carried by a man who smiles demurely to himself as the crowds go by unseeing or uncaring. Only in big cities lacking in leisure and self-indulgence can such incidents exist privately, and Istanbul, as I found when I set out to find the students, is vast, or at least gives that impression. And, moreover, a city without a street directory.

For over four hours I crossed and recrossed the city in a taxi, inquiring at the post offices, in shops and of passers-by until one bright housewife suggested I should try the central telegram office. I did and in a few minutes was given the district in which the street was. The taxi hurried me off to the suburbs, the driver stopping for final directions at a police station. I stayed outside wondering whether the Kurds were under any sort of surveillance, but the inspector came out with the driver and smiled benevolently at me as I stroked the station's yellow cat, victim like so many before him in old Constantinople of the gelder's knife.

We found the flat on the third floor of a modern house on a street corner, but there was no reply to the bell which rang in such a shrill neurotic tone that it set my nerves on edge and dissuaded me from trying it for too long. I tried the other flats and found someone in on the ground floor, a frail young Arab who stood defensively across his doorway, his wife just behind him against a background of diminutive stove and boiling pots. He spoke a little English and told me the young men had moved—where he did not know—but that the flat was now lived in by a relation of one of them and if I called back in —he looked at a large gold wristwatch, the strap tightened to the last hole but one on his bony wrist—in two hours' time then the relations would be in and able to redirect me.

But when I called again the relations were still out and the Arab invited me into his flat. He was wearing two thin woollen sweaters over pyjamas and looked pale and ill. A Turkish book on hydraulics lay open on the table and he told me he had been studying since six in the morning. Every so often a deep and dreadful cough welled up from somewhere within his board-thin chest and listening to it and seeing how tired he was I offered to go, but he asked me in an offended tone to stay and ordered his wife to make some coffee. 'My exams are tomorrow and I have read for too long,' he said, and shut the book.

He had many Kurdish friends, he said, as if to offset any disappointment I might have felt at not finding the Kurds. They were all brothers, as were the English, among whom he had friends too. His father had shot wild pigs for a British consul; and a Christian priest—he did not know what denomination—had told him about the Bible. 'I am a Moslem, but I study the Bible and the Torah because every man must have his own ideas,' he said primly but from a basis of that genuine spiritual tolerance—or at least interest in the religious ideas of others—which one can often find in the Middle East.

The Arab's wife came in with a kettle and a tin of Nescafé

The Kurdish War

on a tray decorated with a picture of two kittens in a box. She was Turkish, her husband said as if half explaining something, as she stood, tight-skirted and plump, on a chair to get the coffee cups from a cupboard. She made the coffee and then brought out from a drawer an old newspaper containing an account, with photographs, of the preliminaries to the hanging of Menderes. She shook her head and pursed her lips in an expression of coy sadness.

'She feels sorry for him because he had two sons,' explained the student. I asked why that should make her sorry, rather than the hanging itself. 'Because she has two sons herself by her first marriage,' and giving his wife a sharp look he tucked the newspaper out of sight and offered me as more salutary reading a magazine with an article on Kassem and an Egyptian pamphlet in English called *The Facts on Suez*. He didn't like Nasser or Kassem, he said, and he didn't blame the British or French for the Suez invasion. 'Every nation must fight for itself.'

I had watched an hour pass on his big gold wristwatch and I thought it would be best if I wrote a non-committal note for him to pass to the still-absent relation who could then deliver it to one of the young men. In careful block letters I wrote that their friend Ismet, now in Switzerland, had asked me to get in touch with them and I should be very glad if they would call on me at my hotel. I drew a little map showing the hotel in case in street-directoryless Istanbul they had difficulty in finding it. Thanking the Arab for his kindness and patience, I left. He was the only Arab I was to meet, apart from prisoners.

A team of Athenian footballers celebrating some victory over their old enemies, the Turks, made it a trying night, their slow, stamping dances shaking the hotel like a protracted earth tremor. And when in the morning I not very hopefully rang Mr Y's home and found to my surprise that he had returned, the footballers suddenly appeared *en masse* from the breakfast room carrying their overnight bags and boots and swarmed noisily round the reception desk and the phone box I was calling from. I could hardly hear Mr Y, who spoke halting French, above the row. He for his part seemed quite bewildered by my call but said he would meet me at his office that

The Kurdish War

afternoon. It struck me shortly afterwards that he might not have understood and I phoned him again when it was quieter, suggesting that as I wanted to discuss 'Mr Medes' it might be more discreet to meet him at his home, but he said, sounding peevish and even more bewildered, that the original arrangement should stand.

I decided in a cheerful moment to cross the Bosphorus to the Asiatic side and take the tram from Uskudar to Camlica Hill. The wind blew through the pines on the hill and the air was clear, but I could not see, as I had hoped I would, the Black Sea. The Sea of Marmora, like a vast pewter plate, and the crouching bulk of St Sophia on guard over the Bosphorus and the Golden Horn black with ships, had to be enough. Cuba was sending out its warnings of nuclear war, but knowing that island and its eccentric Marxists I could not believe the Russians would consider it sufficient of a symbol or a political investment to be worth mutual destruction. Later my wife was to complain that I sounded so casual in my letters while all the time she was sitting in a London suburb waiting for the rockets to drop, but really, reading the newspaper on Camlica Hill, away from the awful hysteria of England, the course of events seemed clear.

A note in an unknown language was waiting for me when I returned to the hotel. I asked the hotel manager to read it, but after pondering it he said he thought the language was Persian, though he wasn't sure. I guessed reasonably enough that it was in Kurdish and asked who had delivered it. A tall young man, said the manager, who did not want to give his name.

My letter to the young men had obviously been delivered promptly, but why they should reply to it in Kurdish I could not make out. Mr Y was also unable to decipher it when I met him at his office. He explained apologetically that he did not understand Kurdish and applied himself instead to the letter in French from Ismet which, for different reasons, was almost as bad.

Who was 'Mr Medes'? He had never heard of anyone of that name. A pseudonym, I explained.

'*Pourquoi il n'ecrit pas en clair,*' he muttered crossly.

Mr Y was old and rather deaf, but with one of those large,

expressionless faces lit by small eyes glimmering like nightlights which I have found often go with considerable shrewdness. I explained, with the few details I had, who 'Mr Medes' was. Mr Y's eyes glimmered a little brighter and he said he thought he knew who I meant. He read and reread Ismet's letter several times, whispering the words to himself, commenting aloud in a high-pitched voice at the more obscure parts, and then said he would get in touch with 'Mr Medes' and another Kurd who might be able to help me.

There was an air of suppressed curiosity behind the hotel reception desk when I returned. Two more mysterious young men had called, asked for me and left without giving their names. In my room ten minutes later the bedside telephone rang. All three of the day's callers were waiting below for me.

They sat together near the window; three young men in dark, well-cut suits, with grave, intelligent faces; Ishmael, Hamid and Abdul. They looked so tidy and politely earnest that for a moment I felt like a managing director about to conduct interviews for next year's batch of young executives. We went and drank Pepsi-Cola and Bubble-Up in a café while they questioned me (or rather Ishmael questioned me, for he was the only one who spoke good English) about the reasons for my visit to Istanbul. 'Mr Medes', they said, was not far away. Later, when it was dark, they hoped it would be possible to meet him. Ishmael explained that he had left the letter in case one of the others called at the hotel later in the day and did not know he had been there and missed me.

They began to emerge from the obscurity of their dark suits: Ishmael, authoritative and a little vain; Hamid, frivolous and amusing despite the first impression of gravity; Abdul, the odd man out, solemn and more kindly in his attitudes than the others. Held together by the strong thread of their nationalism, they expressed a left-wing empiricism that derived more from impatience than dogma. In fact, like most of the politically-minded Kurds I met, they detested labels. They must work out their own solutions, Kurdish solutions for Kurdish problems; a formula which, when adopted elsewhere, has delayed its adopters from facing the fact that there can seldom be agreement on what is a problem. One man's problem is another man's way of life.

The Kurdish War

Abdul had phoned a message to 'Mr Medes' to meet us in Uskudar, and we took a dolmus down to Galata, where the ferries leave for Asia. The ferry was crowded, heeling over wearily as it began its swinging journey into the fast Bosphorus current, but we found seats in an ancient, timbered saloon with sloping deckheads and converted oil lamps; and, in a corner, a glass-fronted cupboard full of yellowed linen swabs and glass-stoppered bottles labelled Alkohol and Sal Volatile.

Next to Kurdish independence, sex was the young men's main interest, and we amiably surveyed the girls set tantalizingly among the old, the ugly and the work-weary. No city has so many nubile girls as Istanbul. Dusky, plump, delicious; a rich and dedicated harem, if the young men were to be believed, among which they spent voluptuous nights, with Kurdistan no more than a puritanical forethought. 'Miss Turkey, 19—'; one could almost see them in their one-piece maillots; more welcoming than English girls, less of a packaged deal than French ones, and built more comfortably than those of New York.

'You see,' said Ishmael, 'what lovely girls we have. Where else would you find any so beautiful?'

The purity of the race, said the young men, a rumbustiously forthcoming trio, was their protection against the marriage-minded girls of Istanbul.

'Why won't you marry us?' the girls would ask.

'Because you are not Kurdish.'

'Then we will become Kurdish.'

'Ah! That's not good enough.'

Once when I crossed on the ferry alone with Ishmael a boy fell overboard and though it was accidental and the child was saved, the nearness of death drew from him a half confessionary, rather self-satisfied account of a girl he had known. He showed me a photograph of her; a surprised, imaginative face. She must have been about sixteen.

'I was going to marry her, but then I lost my temper with her one day, in Ankara, and said I didn't want to see her again. So she threw herself off a roof and was killed.'

In Uskudar we waited—the Kurds and I—in another café, drinking more Pepsi-Cola and Bubble-Up until it was time for Abdul to slip out and rendezvous with 'Mr Medes'. I half

2
*Ibrahim Ahmed,
Secretary-General of the
Democratic Party of Kurdistan*

Mullah Mustafa Barzani

3 *On the Iraq-Persian frontier looking into Iraq*

Near the Persian frontier on the way out of Iraq

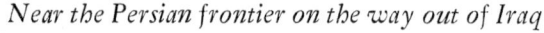

The Kurdish War

expected him to appear out of nowhere like a Middle-Eastern Harry Lime, perhaps walking along the tops of the houses. But he arrived very normally, smiling apologetically for being so long and waving a greeting at us through the café window before, his head bowed low to the whispered introductions, he sat down at the table.

A greying man with a defensive and nervous smile, as quick as a cat; an unwavering nationalist who had withstood prison, banishment from his home in the Kurdish mountains of Turkey, the ending of his career and the loss of most of the pleasant trivialities and easements of life which should have been his. A very brave man, I estimated later, who would willingly die for what he believed in. His type is almost incomprehensible to the conciliatory English who have not had any need for patriots of that kind since Hereward the Wake. Among the Kurds of Turkey his fellows had been shot and hanged in hundreds in the course of an oppression second only to that which destroyed the Armenians.

To find their kin in the British Isles one would have to search among the Sinn Feiners. As a child I had been romantically interested in the struggles of the Irish, stimulated by the recollections of my mother who is Irish and had been in Dublin at the time of the Easter 1916 rebellion; and by my father who was harried by the Sinn Feiners when he tried to practise dentistry in the west of Ireland after the First World War. So, at second hand, 'Mr Medes' had a certain familiarity.

He spoke with great fluency in Kurdish, gesturing like a Turk or a Greek (in contrast to the others who rarely gestured), turning every so often from Ishmael, who was translating, with a slow, lithe and slightly feminine movement of the head and shoulders to see how I was accepting what he had to say.

He spoke a little German and once quoted to me—from the Persian poet Firdausi, I think he said—that 'when part of a man is ill, then the whole man is ill'.

'*Das Teil ist Kurdistan, nichtwahr? Und der Mann ist der Naher-Osten.*'

We left the café and strolled through the mild, October suburbs in the dark. He placed his hand upon my shoulder and continued talking, like a sage to a neophyte. Hamid and Abdul

The Kurdish War

walked some twenty yards ahead, their hushed voices drifting back to us occasionally as 'Mr Medes', with Ishmael as interpreter, led me across the melancholy terrain where the Kurds and the Turks have mixed their blood and their history.

Until shortly before the last war the mountains around Lake Van, in Turkey, were the main centre of Kurdish rebellion against alien rule. Today they are subdued, the people detribalized, their leaders exiled or slaughtered and any potential militants kept down by a powerful army created to withstand the Russians and therefore well able to deal with the Kurds. An eighteen-kilometre-wide strip of evacuated and well-policed territory along the Turkish side of the frontier with Iraq prevents men, guns and passions from moving too freely from one side to the other; but nevertheless the revolt in Iraq has sent its shock waves through the Turkish Kurds, as it has through those of Persia and Syria. In Turkey their grievances, at their most mundane, are considerable: inadequate development lagging behind that of the rest of the country; poor primary schools with pathetically small staffs; the banning of the national costume, discrimination against the language and, generally, the campaign to make them into Turks. A situation perhaps comparable to that in the Highlands after the '45 when the kilt was banned and Gaelic discouraged.

The Turks, to be fair, are making attempts to improve educational opportunities for the Kurds and material conditions in Kurdistan. But despite the fact that the Turkish President, Inonu, is a Kurd, the concessions made to Kurdish nationalism after the Menderes régime was overthrown have been withdrawn. Kurdish language publications have been suppressed and nationalists, among them a number of students, arrested. Some students I met were by no means extremists, nor, so far as I could make out, had they ever been encouraged to be. For the Kurdish movement has differed from most national movements against colonial governments in that it has made little attempt to exploit the zeal of students. Those who offered to fight with the rebels in Iraq were told as a matter of policy to go away and finish their studies: 'Your country will need you later.' Mullah Mustafa is a firm believer in the virtues of education, although—or perhaps because—he had little himself.

The Kurdish War

'What will you do,' I asked the students, 'when you have graduated?'

'We shall return to help our poor people,' they answered stoutly. And then a bit later, in their contradictory Kurdish way: 'What chance is there of a job in London, Paris, New York?'

Some are sceptical about the loyalty of the Kurdish students, standing on the edge of a richer, larger and more glamorous world, to their poor and backward homeland. In favour of loyalty is the fact that the Kurds have never been great wanderers—despite the nomadic Kurdish tribes—or money-makers.

'Mr Medes' left the young Kurds and me at the ferry pier as he thought it best he should travel back to Istanbul on a different ferry. The secret police, he said, were sharp-eyed. We would talk about my route into Kurdistan tomorrow.

The young men were ready to make a night of it and wanted me to go up to a group of four giggling girls and ask 'Do you speak English?' a sure breaker, they thought, of ice that to me looked pretty well thawed already. I said I was tired and went back to the hotel.

But no sooner had I ordered myself a cup of coffee than the phone rang for me once again. A 'Mr Blankowitz' announced cryptically that he was coming round to see me right away and rang off. A few minutes later two men entered. One without looking right or left marched rapidly across to the far side of the hotel foyer and sat down; the other, after inquiring at the reception desk, came across to me and introduced himself as Mr Blankowitz. That was not his real name, but the ridiculous pseudonym will serve. I thought at first he was a policeman, but he said that Mr Y had asked him to call and he would be pleased to help me. He was aged about thirty, spoke good English and was considerably more sophisticated and knowledgable about the outside world than either 'Mr Medes' or the young men. The latter, when I told them I had met him, warned me not to tell him anything, particularly about 'Mr Medes'. He was a good Kurd, they said, but over-talkative.

Mr Blankowitz, who had summoned his friend with a jerk of the head, took me to a *boite* in Galata; a 'night club' too

The Kurdish War

shady for even the secret police, he said enticingly and dramatically. The Kurds, I was finding, had a not unnatural obsession about the secret police. We walked into the *boite* through a long corridor draped tent-like with red plush curtains hung here and there with photographs of diademmed dancers, their faces tilted provocatively and their bellies arched out. The music, at first muffled by the curtains, grew louder and finally deafening.

A Turkish band played on a foot-high stage in the middle of a crowded room proportioned like a drill hall. Men tilted back in their chairs shouting to one another above the band, their arms resting on the shoulders of girls, drinking beer, the empty bottles huddled on the tables in little amber flocks. We stumbled across the room, pistacchio shells crunching under our shoes, to the far end where there was a vacant table close to the wall. Mr Blankowitz's friend looked searchingly round the room and then drew his attention to a small, grey-moustached man who sat solemnly, an almost full glass of beer in front of him, a few tables away. A secret policeman after all, it appeared, but Mr Blankowitz decided he was off duty and would not want to admit, even for the sake of seeming exceptionally keen, that he frequented such low places. The policeman paid no attention to us and we no more to him.

I was not very much taken by Mr Blankowitz at first. He seemed too much like most of the other people one meets in night clubs of one sort or another, but he was in fact generous, helpful and, despite his worldliness, an innocent at heart, a point which explained the talkativeness of which the other Kurds complained. He, too, had been gaoled for nationalist activities, but he showed no obvious bitterness. The Turks, he admitted, were at last stirring themselves in Kurdistan and might conceivably win over the peasants one day.

Mr Blankowitz had travelled widely, left a wife behind somewhere, and had sopped up enough of the outside world to dilute the puritanism inherited from a sheikhly family; but still disarmingly priggish at times. I said, as he moved me closer to the belly dancers on the stage, that I liked the Turkish music; and he replied deprecatingly that he preferred Brahms. He had just furtively written out his address and made an assignation with a girl, so perhaps he did not want to give me

The Kurdish War

the impression that most of his entertainment hailed from such places as the *boite*. The next night he took me to a thoroughly respectable theatre, full of Istanbul's middle-class, and translated for me the jokes about Kochero, the Kurdish bandit whom the police were unable to catch. Kochero had offered his men to Mullah Mustafa—and been rejected, as Mr Blankowitz emphasized.

It was too noisy in the *boite* to talk coherently, but afterwards, walking towards a taxi rank, I asked Mr Blankowitz for his advice on a route into Iraq. He said the Syrian Kurds were very well organized and thought that through the Lebanon and Syria was therefore the best way. I told him what Ismet had said and he shook his head sadly and thought again. Turkey was impossible: too many police and soldiers. So there was only Persia.

'Mr Medes', when I saw him next day, agreed that Persia was the best way. Ishmael and I had travelled in an ancient train to a village station where he was waiting, a brief case under his arm. Together we walked down the railway line until after turning down an alleyway at the back of some gardens and walking for a quarter of a mile we came to a large wooden house, the home of Mr Y. He was waiting for us at the top of a broad flight of stairs; unshaven and wearing a camel hair dressing gown. He showed us into his study and seated himself behind a large desk piled high with Turkish paperbacks, folders and a dishevelment of old papers and documents. A round stove, with an ugly cream-painted pipe disfigured a pleasantly proportioned room.

It was largely a courtesy call since Mr Y had been kind enough to tell 'Mr Medes' about my arrival, although as it happened his help was not needed. I was warned not to be too communicative.

Mr Y, sensing an unwelcome discreetness although the conversation was polite, almost dowsed his night-light eyes. Had I found out yet who 'Mr Medes' was? he asked, although he knew quite well he was sitting opposite him.

I smiled and made a non-committal reply. 'Mr Medes' looked uncomfortable.

The door bell rang and a scholarly little man was shown up to the room. He had come to talk to Mr Y about some religious

The Kurdish War

question of interest to them both. Their high-pitched voices neighed at one another. 'Mr Medes' and Ishmael, both good agnostics, grew restless.

Mr Y's friend spoke a little English and he broke off his theological discussion to ask me what my profession was. A journalist, I replied, and heard 'Mr Medes' draw in his breath sharply at this indiscretion.

Ah! said the friend. He knew a gentleman on *The Times*, or at least had met him when he was in Istanbul. An elderly gentleman who walked with a stick. He could not remember his name, but surely I must know him. I had heard of him, I said tactfully, but like him, was weak on names.

More neighing wiffle-waffle from the friend until 'Mr Medes' could bear it no longer and stood up and said we had to go. Mr Y said a formal goodbye at the top of the stairs and did not come to the door with us.

'Mr Medes', Ishmael and I lunched in the open beneath the trees in a restaurant beside a smooth bay in the Sea of Marmora where a submarine nosed slowly up to a buoy. 'Mr Medes' had brought a German map of the Middle East for me so that we could study a possible route. Someone had already used it for a journey into Iraqi-Kurdistan, for a biroed line marked the way he had travelled through the south of Turkey, along the pipeline through Syria and then across the Tigris and into rebel territory near Zaccho.

My face was too round and my complexion too ruddy for me ever to pass for a Kurd, said 'Mr Medes' regretfully, so there was no possibility of disguise. We decided that the best course was for me to go to Erzerum by plane and from there on by bus through Bazorgan, on the frontier with Persia, and south to Rezaieh, near the western shore of Lake Urmia. There I would be in Kurdish territory and among those who would help me. Abdul would be my guide.

I was glad that it was Abdul who was to go with me rather than Ishmael who, while more astute and able to speak English, had the great disadvantage of a political face. An aware and rather arrogant face; the sort of person policemen in trouble-spots question out of instinct. Abdul, on the other hand, was, like me, unnoticeable.

'Mr Medes' said goodbye at the restaurant. 'Remember!' he

The Kurdish War

said. 'We are silent now, but it may not always be so. We shall see when Mullah Mustafa has finished with Kassem.'

He wished me luck and said he would change his pseudonym since his present one had become too widely known. The new one, which he confided in me, had a romantic ring suitable to the leader of an underground organization.

I had doubts about the route and, more particularly, the friends in Rezaieh. Were they sure, I asked, when Hamid and Abdul had joined us, that they would be willing and able to help? Oh, yes! they said. Were they not all Kurds with only one aim, the furtherance of their cause? And would Abdul be able to get a visa to travel with me in Persia? I asked. He had a friend in the Persian consulate, they said. I knew that I, as a foreigner, might have trouble travelling in Persian Kurdistan, since one was supposed to have a permit from Tehran, but I thought I might get away with it.

Of course when we met again the next day a crestfallen Abdul announced that he had been refused a visa and could not go with me. So I scrapped my plan to go through Erzerum and decided on grounds of speed to fly to Tehran that afternoon; got Hamid to write out letters of introduction to three people in Rezaieh, including an all-important sheikh. He even gave me an inch-square piece of paper on which was written in Farsi script some abracadabra which I had to show if any of the three doubted my *bona fides*.

I was more than a little doubtful about leaving Istanbul so suddenly on a Saturday as my office had asked me to stay on because of the Cuba crisis and repercussions in Turkey. But there was nothing I could do from Istanbul that our regular correspondent, who was in Ankara, the capital, could not do better.

The young men's thoughts were turning to more enjoyable weekend matters. Hamid had written another letter, this time to a girl who sat with her father on the other side of the room, and after making sure that she had noticed, crumpled it up and placed it in an ashtray where she could collect it. I declined an invitation to a tea-dance on the grounds that my only shoes had ribbed golf soles; took them for a farewell round of Pepsi-Cola to the Diwan Hotel of whose modest luxury they were contemptuous ('Women come here for a little cake just

The Kurdish War

so they can say they have had lunch at the Diwan,' said Ishmael) and then left them, a cheerfully waving group anxious to get away to their tea-dance.

I left a misleading message at the hotel for Mr Blankowitz, whom the others had made me agree not to tell where I was going, saying I would write to him from Beirut (I was supposed to see Mr Blankowitz that evening), cabled the office that I was leaving for Tehran and hurried out to the airport and on to a Pan-American Boeing full of American servicemen bound for Ankara. It seemed a good time to go to Kurdistan, when everyone was looking north.

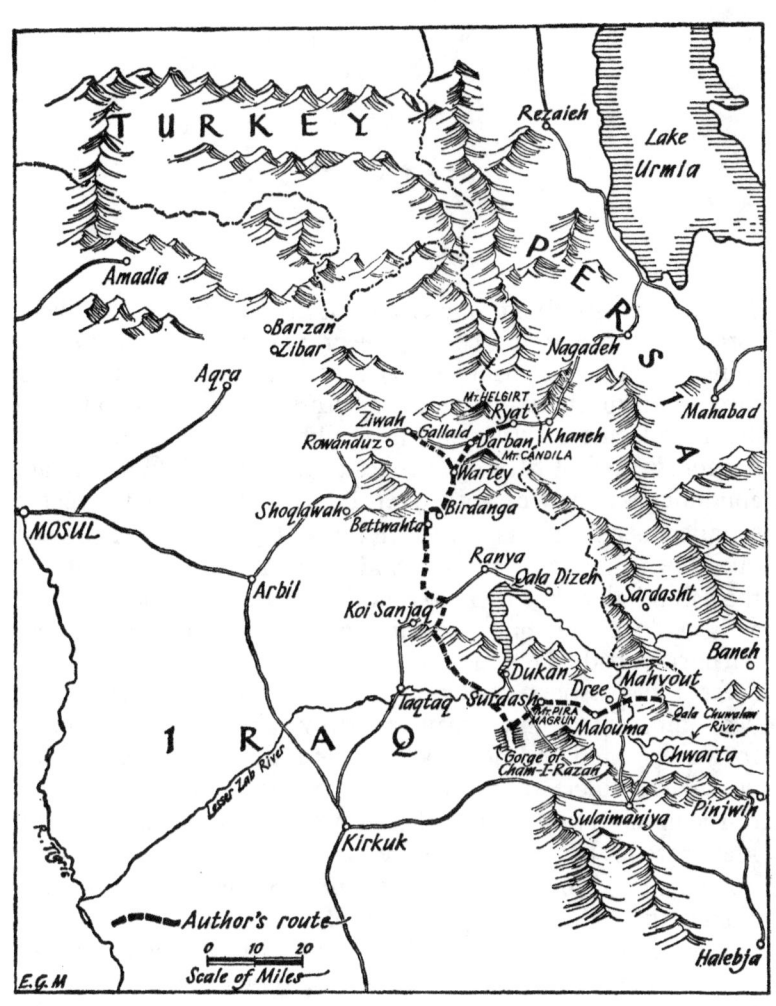

CHAPTER III

—◦❧❦◦—

The whole throbbing, quivering business of flying acts like a sort of vibro-massage, easing away anxieties like rheumatic pains; and I leaned back telling myself that the impetus of a three or four thousand mile trajectory would be enough to brush aside any reservations the sheikh might have on helping me across the last fifty or so miles to the frontier. The captain announced that we were over Lake Urmia and the name sounded as remote as a crater on a map of the moon. I pressed my face against the window and cupped my eyes to cut out the cabin lights, but there was nothing to be seen but stars and a tissue of cirrus; and presently we slid down to Mehrabad Airport, outside Tehran.

At the passport check an official raised his hand in a beckoning signal and a man in a grey raincoat came running forward, pencil and notebook in hand, dodging eagerly from one glass cubicle to another and peering over the shoulders of the immigration men to glean as much about me as he could. He wrote his last note hurriedly as I emerged, flipped his notebook shut and introduced himself as from the *Amir Hooshang Danai*, the General Department of Publications and Broadcasting. His department, as I no doubt knew, existed in part to serve visiting journalists. They would be only too happy to arrange any journeys or interviews I might wish to make during my stay in Persia. Where would I be staying and would 8.30 be too early for their Mr Cyrus to call me tomorrow morning? I had a swift vision of Mr Cyrus pondering doubtfully over my first request for an itinerary. I said irritably that I would make my own arrangements and anyway how did he know I was on the plane?

'We meet every plane,' he said, put out by my coldness. 'We are here all the time. I am not a policeman, you know.' And he showed me his card.

The Kurdish War

'Of course, I know you are not a policeman,' I said, feeling guilty, as the fumbling Westerner unable to distinguish between the genuine and the ingenuous so often does. We have a bad name, too, in Persia, we British journalists, for our rudeness; and it is no use explaining about our nervous dyspepsia, our foreign news editors and the awful archetypal images we have of thick, unimpassioned men in censor's offices snicking their scissors together impatiently as we explain the ethics of our trade. It means nothing.

I said I would be delighted to meet Mr Cyrus, or anyone else from the *Amir Hooshang Danai*, which, in fact, turned out to be a very useful and efficient organization and not at all intrusive or over-poweringly propagandist.

Mr Cyrus rang me promptly at 8.30 the next morning and I told him vaguely that I might tour a number of places: Persepolis, Isfahan, the Caspian shore and even Kurdistan. But first I wanted to see some friends and I would get in touch with him again later. He came round to the hotel shortly afterwards, carrying a bundle of travel brochures which we examined sitting on a sofa under the gaze of a sequinned portrait of the Shah.

After he had gone I made inquiries at a travel agency and found there was no plane to Tabriz that Sunday, so I booked a first class sleeping berth on the night train. I sat in my hotel room overlooking a row of private gardens jungled with peach and almond trees and wrote a cryptic letter to the office telling them my appropriate route. Everything, I said, with more confidence than I felt, was going well.

There seemed nothing much that could be done with the rest of the day. I had visited Tehran before and I recalled its intimidatingly dreary cake-grid of streets; so I settled for a dutiful but wearying hour of re-exploration and returned to the hotel with a guide book bought from the Persepolis Bookshop in the Takhte Jamshid. Rezaieh it described as a little resort near the shores of Lake Urmia where the Nestorian Christians made wine. It sounded pleasant; an oasis of festival on the approaches to austere Kurdistan.

The railway between Tehran and Tabriz is a single track draped over the high plateau of northern Persia, a piston-breaking drag which takes sixteen hours. It is, though, a com-

The Kurdish War

fortable enough journey provided you have a berth. The restaurant is good, serving excellent chelo kebab, a dish of grilled meat and rice mixed with butter and the yolk of egg, eaten with the huge slices of onion which are indispensable to any Persian meal. I ate with a lieutenant returning to his unit near the frontier. He was, I gathered, a sympathizer with the banned Tudeh Party (a communist organization) and was opposed to any involvement of Persia in a war over Cuba; but it was a delicate matter for one in his position to discuss with a foreigner and we turned instead to the English language and could I tell him the difference between ordnance and ordinance and which was which. Afterwards as I lay sleepless in my berth near the top of the hot and airless compartment I was not sure whether I had given him a correct answer and the matter nagged me off and on until I was able to get hold of a dictionary and check.

In the morning the other occupants of the compartment— an elderly Armenian, so round he could hardly stay on his seat, and a young Persian and his wife with their black-eyed baby daughter—made sure that glasses of tea were brought to me and offered me sticky cakes and fruit, including medlars with their squashy bruised tartness, a flavour which has almost vanished from Europe.

Those who have spent some time in Tabriz always tell me when I describe it in slighting terms that I am dreadfully wrong. The most interesting city in Persia, they say; a place seething with politics and intrigue, where contending puritanism and sensuality have produced attitudes as complex as those of a Presbyterian drunkard. 'Bring me my special white tea,' the Tabrizards are said to whisper to the waiter when they order their vodka.

To me, drifting briefly across its surface, it seemed a tawdry city full of shops selling transistor radios and old bicycle tyres. A Turkish city rather than a Persian one but reminiscent to me—in its social life as evinced in the dining room of the Hotel Metropole—of the cities of Calabria and southern Italy. In the evening when the Azerbaijani band plays selections from *South Pacific*, occasionally dropping with relief into its own gay vernacular of local music, there is a certain cautious pomp about the place; an impression of painstakingly noble faces

The Kurdish War

trying hard to suppress the twitches of financial and social gripe; of little communities of lost or abandoned souls, such as the band itself, in its corner alcove that looks as if it had been designed by some wandering master of the Locarno Ballroom period.

Tabriz was, and perhaps still is, the capital of dissent and separatism, the stronghold of the Tudeh Party on which the Russians after the war based their plans for an Azerbaijani state to which the satellite Kurdish state of Mahabad would have been linked in the south. It is a region of historic conflict between Persians, Turks, Russians, British and recently Americans. Through Turkey and the west of Azerbaijan the CENTO defence line sweeps southwards along the Kurdish mountains, protecting the oilfields of Persia and Iraq; a task that was once a British problem and is now a predominantly American one. The British consulate in Tabriz to which Qazi Mohammad, the President of Mahabad, sent a two-man delegation to ask for British recognition—which he never got—is gone and instead there is a young and knowledgeable American consul.

With Azerbaijan in friendly hands, the Russians might have been able to extend their influence into south Persia and the oilfields. As it is, their presence not far away is curiously pervasive, perhaps because of their powerful radio transmitters in Armenia and elsewhere in the Caucasus and the large numbers of Russian-built cars, these last a reminder of the growing trade links between Persia and Russia.

It was in Tabriz that I saw my first 'wild' Kurds, two lithe men in blue Kurdish dress, fringed turbans half veiling their eyes, and walking with that backward-leaning, heel-less tread so typical of the Kurdish peasant. They held hands and gazed at a shop full of galvanized bath tubs, their eyes full of the meek curiosity of bucolic window-shoppers rather than the rapture of potential looters.

I had decided that the best way for me to get to Rezaieh was to travel by bus through Marend and Khoy and then south through Shahpur and along the western side of Lake Urmia. The fact that I had no papers permitting me to move about the countryside, particularly in such a well-guarded area as Kurdistan, was a worry, but I thought that on a bus, lost in the midst of the *hoi-polloi*, there would be less chance of being noticed and questioned than if I went in solitary state in a taxi. As in most Middle Eastern towns, the buses, battered old Fords for the most part, seemed to start from anywhere which suited them, but I found that mine left from outside a respectable booking office close to the hotel. At five o'clock in the morning, said the clerk, marking my seat on a chart which he had in front of him.

The afternoon had drifted up and there was nothing to do. I visited a carpet factory where the workmen snarled like angry camels when I photographed them; looked at the tiles of a crumbling mosque and finally took a taxi to the Shah Goli where the breeze shook the whispy trees like prayer flags above the black water of the reservoir. The taxi driver came up the little slope from the village and with a bow and murmured expressions of politeness handed me two boiled sweets of the sort which have a shell-like exterior and an interior of fruity gum. He watched me with satisfaction as I ate them— although I loathe that sort of sweet—considering that I was now in his debt and he could overcharge me without having to face an effective protest, which was true.

I slept badly that night. The police suddenly demanded, via the hotel staff, that I should have a travel card, a document outlining my route and bearing my photograph. The language barrier prevented questioning and they made the card out, I discovered later, for a journey to Bazorgan, on the Turkish frontier, assuming that any European coming from Tehran would be heading in that direction. It was only a formality, but I realized how conspicuous and well-charted are the movements of a European anywhere outside the capitals in the Middle East. To the insomnia-making effects of this mild nervous shock, the dogs of Tabriz added by barking, snapping and howling endlessly at one another in the street below my bedroom from shortly after midnight until I got up at 4.30.

The street outside was cold and black beyond the cones of light thrown down by the street lamps and most of those who had already turned up for the bus were huddled inside a *chaikhaneh*, or tea shop, where the spirit lamp had not long been lit under the samovars. I went in and drank two glasses of hot milk.

Five-thirty came and went and at six there was still no bus.

The Kurdish War

A troop of tanks clattering down the street coincided with the street lights being turned off. Half-tracks carrying troops and towing field guns followed and then, a defiant gesture towards an era of megaton ripostes, a squadron of cavalry, the last troop mounted on pure white horses, the rearmost of them with a red hurricane lamp tied to its rump. The troops wore steel helmets and carried their carbines aslant their shoulders, bending forward in the saddles as the horses bunched together in an uneasy trot. In front, an officer peered anxiously into the blackness; and in the rear a tall, ungainly man wrapped in a greatcoat and a balaclava led a mule burdened with shovels and packs. The third world war, if it were to break out, promised some spectacular moments.

The bus left after seven and rumbled out dustily on to the plain around Tabriz, soon catching up with the cavalry which had spread out over the dark brown plough lands, the horses with their heads down plucking at the occasional scrub and tussocks of grass in a bored, dispirited way. Farther on, beside a spinney, the tanks had laagered with another squadron, which to judge from the tracks beside the road, had come from the opposite direction. There were troops on manoeuvres everywhere, it seemed; camping out in fox-holes under groundsheets or standing in small groups around officers who made sweeping gestures towards the horizon as if illustrating some grandiose tactical picture.

Lake Urmia is rarely more than fifteen feet deep despite its length of ninety miles, and most of the country to the north consists of shallow, dried-out lake beds from which red and grey mountains rise abruptly to points that, at that time, late October, had been foiled by a thin coating of the first winter snow. The villages appeared over the horizons as oases of fruit trees and poplar turning brown under the autumn sun. Beside the road farmers, sitting sideways on their little donkeys, jogged miles to their ploughs; and farther away, herds of cattle, sheep and camels grazed on the thin grass. We would stop every now and then either beside the road to repair a puncture or in one of the towns where the passengers could dismount and drink tea, buy fruit and relieve themselves squatting oriental fashion in the muddy courtyards behind the rows of single-storeyed shops built of mud bricks. There was

The Kurdish War

not much to choose between the towns. Each had identical *chai-khanehs* full of dour men drinking tea from their saucers and smoking hubble-bubbles. Each was the possessor of at least two grassed traffic circles, on one of which stood a bronze statue of the present Shah or his father. Khoy, with its string of dusty, broken down barouches—a reminder, perhaps, of more glamorous days as a Tsarist garrison town—was a little gayer than the rest.

Quite frequently we were halted while gendarmes made a perfunctory search for opium, or perhaps known opium smugglers, for this region provides a great market for the trade. Sometimes it is carried by day between the towns by individual carriers, but usually at night on strings of donkeys or camels, the smugglers relying on darkness and perhaps a bribe to the gendarmes so that they will remain in their huts when the string leaves the road and makes a tactful detour round the gendarmery post.

We passed through Shahpur and came in sight of the dead, blue waters of Lake Urmia, Shahi Mountain rising sheer from its far side twenty-five miles away. A white frill of salt edges the lake in which there are no fish and where, like the Dead Sea, it is practically impossible to sink because of the high salt content. Boats rarely sail on its desolate waters and the only creatures which make use of it are wildfowl. Despite the salt, the land on the west side is fertile; the orchards behind their high walls are plump with fruit in summer and the vines, tangled across ramps of earth that look a bit like potato clamps, produce good crops for the Nestorians' wine.

The Nestorians, followers of the heretical Nestorius, a fifth-century Patriarch of Constantinople, were once widespread throughout Asia, their creed as international as that of Catholicism today. In China it seemed for a while as if it might become the established religion; in India its communities were still in existence when the first Christian missionaries from the West arrived. In the Middle East, the conquests of Turks and Arabs destroyed its influence and power and it existed largely on sufferance. Nestorius's heresy lay in his insistence that Christ was two persons, one human and the other divine. The Virgin Mary was demoted from the position of Mother of God to that of mother of the human Christ. Endless and

The Kurdish War

destructive controversies over the nature of God split the Roman and Byzantine world at that time, when, according to Gibbon, 'A secret and incurable discord was cherished between those who were most apprehensive of confounding, and those who were most fearful of separating, the divinity and humanity of Christ.'

On the shores of Lake Rezaieh, in one of their last strongholds, they became a sort of ecclesiastical nature reserve. Visitors ranged from a delegation sent by the Archbishop of Canterbury to Dr Cochran, the American missionary, who played an incidental but important part in the defeat of Sheikh Ubeidullah in the 1880s. The sheikh had come from Turkish Kurdistan with a large force of men and in alliance with Hamza Agha of the Manghor tribe set out to avenge alleged Persian attacks on the Kurds. His forces found little to oppose them and they swept round Lake Urmia as far as Maragegh and Miandob, then turned their attentions to the western shore and gathered on the mountains near Rezaieh (or Urmia, as it was then). The town's officials knew that relief was on its way from Tabriz and if they could delay the onslaught for a few days they would be saved. Dr Cochran had a great deal of influence with Ubeidullah whom he had once cured of pneumonia and he, since he was concerned about what would happen to the Christians if the Kurds attacked, went to negotiate surrender terms. The sheikh delayed fatally, the relief force arrived and the Kurds were driven back into Turkey where Ubeidullah later surrendered to die exiled in Mecca.

But if the Christians survived then it was to face worse trouble during the First World War when the svelte and bloodthirsty Simko, of the Shikak tribe, moved into the vacuum caused by the Russian withdrawal from Kurdistan and Azerbaijan in 1917 and attacked the Assyrian Nestorians, many of whom had retreated there from the Turks. First Simko murdered the Assyrian Patriarch, the Mar Shimun XIX, at a parley called ostensibly to bring about a Kurdish-Assyrian alliance and then, with the help of the Turks, destroyed the Assyrian army of 6,000 riflemen. According to Mr William Eagleton, Jr, in his excellent *The Kurdish Republic of 1946* (OUP, 1963): 'Although it was not fully realized at the time, the Assyrian nation had been destroyed.' The remnants were resettled by the British in Iraq.

My neighbours on the bus, intrigued by me and my compulsory silence, tried to talk to me, pointing out the first Kurdish villages near Shahpur from where the road runs almost like a frontier between the Shikak and Herki Kurds, who have spread over the plains from the mountains to the west, and the Turkomans who inhabit the land between the road and the lake. They had kept a friendly eye on me for most of the way, shooing away a tattered old man who tried to sit next me in case he stole my money or gave me fleas or both; seeing to it in the *chai-kanehs* that I had an ash-tray and a spoon to stir my tea with, a politer method of sweetening it than sucking it through a sugar lump held between the teeth.

We half-circled a green island ringed with petunias and ornamented with a stone fawn frozen into a posture of alertness and we had entered Rezaieh. The Hotel Niagara, suggested one of the travellers, was the place for me and took me to it in a taxi: a white concrete building, its name in Farsi and Latin script on a board above the door. I had to stand in the large dining room on the first floor and shout for several minutes before a waiter carrying a white coat over his arm appeared from somewhere at the back and took me up to a room. He brought me some flat bread and cheese for a late lunch and I spent the rest of the afternoon in the room until it was dark. It had seemed, driving down the main street, a pleasant, relaxed little town, with a pretty mosque on one side and the entrance to a covered bazaar on the other.

I found my way in the dusk to the house of a man to whom Hamid had written a non-committal letter asking him to take me to Mr Begzadeh (I apologize for another pseudonym). The man knew no European languages and a spate of questions soon vanished in a dry silence. He walked with me to Mr Begzadeh's house, squinting at me out of the side of his eyes so that he could examine me without appearing rude.

Mr Begzadeh's house was set back from the road behind iron railings and a small garden. It looked a comfortable, well-built place, evidence that Mr Begzadeh was the sort of person who could arrange an interview with a sheikh. It was one of Mr Begzadeh's sons who let us in and showed us to the living

The Kurdish War

room where after a minute or two he arrived and welcomed me in broken French. I handed him my letter from Hamid which he read but said no more about until my guide left politely but still burning with curiosity after a stay of ten minutes or so. Mr Begzadeh had been travelling that day and looked tired. He was unshaven and wore a crumpled suit with a grey check pattern popular in that part of Persia. It was obvious that my arrival worried him considerably. He called his wife, a handsome woman with a strong personality; one of those formidable women that the Kurds talk about proudly, claiming that they are more intelligent, attractive and independent than women anywhere else in the Middle East. Among the tribes their status is not very high, but nevertheless considerably better than that of Arab women. They do not veil, although they will sometimes hide their faces from strangers, and they can sometimes assume the leadership of a tribe, as for instance the remarkable Adela Khanum, of the Jaf tribe, who ruled at Halebja and conferred her patronage on E. B. Soane.

Mr Begzadeh and his wife read and reread my letter several times and at the end Mr Begzadeh sat on the edge of a sofa, leaning forward with his elbows on his knees, clasping and unclasping his fingers, and said in a tentative fashion that he had had his difficulties with the authorities. *'Mais, je n'ai pas peur, je n'ai pas peur.'* But even if he was not afraid he was extremely reserved about what he could do to help me. I did not expect any promises of help at that point, for after all I had arrived out of the blue and all he had been asked to do was to take me to the sheikh and discuss with him my journey across the frontier. Nevertheless, his attitude struck me as uncomfortably cautious.

Did he support Mullah Mustafa and the rebels in Iraq? I asked him. *'Oui-i,'* he replied slowly, but with a curious and evasive lift of the eyes as if the question embarrassed him very much indeed.

A journalist in a situation of this sort is in a difficult position. Obtaining accurate information on great or small events is as important as the honest practise of the law, but he has no right to so to speak *sub poena* people to his aid. If he is honest, he can make no demands on their patriotism, loyalties or courage;

for specifically and immediately his aim is to create or satisfy curiosity for the commercial advantage of his newspaper. And no one can be asked to risk their livelihood for that. Certainly not Mr Begzadeh and I did not press him on his attitude. They had, his wife told me, a child in a clinic undergoing private treatment. She, I thought, as I talked to her had the child on her mind and what would happen if her husband's income was in any way jeopardized.

Begzadeh, after going out to make inquiries, could not find anyone reliable to drive me down to the sheikh's house, so I walked there with one of his sons as a guide. I had brought my camera thinking that not only would it be safer with me than in the hotel, but that it would make me look like a tourist with an obvious reason for being in Rezaieh. But Mr Begzadeh thought it made me look sinisterly like a journalist and told his wife to wrap it in newspaper for me.

They were genuinely alarmed at being associated with me, although there was really little or no reason for them to be. They did nothing wrong and what I wanted to do was in no way harmful to the interests of Persia, although it would have involved the technical offence of crossing and recrossing the frontier without permission. Perhaps it was memories of the Mahabad Republic of 1946 that stirred the Begzadehs to warn me how strict the police control was in Rezaieh. Mullah Mustafa had aroused old worries in the central government in Tehran. Mr and Mrs Begzadeh made their way separately by car to the sheikh and I walked close in to the shadows of the walls. Catching a little of the Begzadeh's fever I felt, absurdly, that any policeman who saw me would guess immediately that I was heading for the frontier and Iraq.

I had to wait for a minute or two outside the sheikh's house before a servant in Kurdish dress came out and signalled me to follow him into a darkened hall. The sheikh and the Begzadehs were waiting upstairs in a room in which the curtains had been drawn tight stretched across the windows but unfortunately did not meet, so that our meeting must have been quite visible to anyone who bothered to look up from the road. The sheikh was white-bearded, prophetic-looking. He sat bolt upright on his chair, his hands on his knees in the manner of a figure from Abu Simbel. He was polite but extremely guarded

The Kurdish War

and by no means welcoming. He puffed quickly at a cigarette after we had got over the formalities of introduction and I noted that his lips held it in a thin, nervous grip. I handed him the letter from Hamid together with the secret abracadabra on the little piece of paper and hoped for the best.

The sheikh read the letter quickly, dismissed the secret message with three quick puffs of his cigarette, and handed both back to me quickly with a stiffly outstretched arm.

Well, I asked in French, through Mr Begzadeh, would he help me?

Mr Begzadeh shrugged his shoulders in a slow, sad way and translated; then waited, his head bowed, while the sheikh replied in staccato Kurdish.

There were, said the sheikh, many difficulties. I had, he learned, booked in at the hotel where it was certain that my presence had been reported to the police who would wonder what I was doing in Rezaieh.

I interrupted to say that I was quite certain that I had not been watched or followed by the police. There was no reason why they should be suspicious of me.

The sheikh brushed this aside and said that the military and the police were very active in the hills between Rezaieh and the frontier, and as for my suggestion that I should go in disguise—he tittered slightly when it was translated to him—it was absolutely certain that I could never be made to look convincingly like a Kurd. Moreover, added the sheikh, the mountain passes were all at least a metre deep in snow.

This I felt angrily could not be true because I had carefully checked the snow levels on the mountains against my map, and found that there was none below 7,500 feet. Even though the mountains on the frontier went up to 9,000 feet there must be many passes no higher than 5,000 or 6,000 feet. I said this, but the sheikh shook his head firmly in contradiction and Mrs Begzadeh added mournfully that if I had only come a few weeks earlier they might have been able to help me.

The sheikh thought of another obstacle. There were, interpreted Mr Begzadeh, the *looses* to reckon with. '*Ils sont très feroces*,' he explained of his own accord.

I tried to think what a *loose* could be. '*Un chien sauvage?*,' I asked, thinking of *loup*. No. They shook their heads. Mr

The Kurdish War

Begzadeh described in words and gestures a huge growling creature with long arms, and I thought that perhaps I had stumbled on some beast out of the folk imagination of the Kurds; a Kurdish yeti called on wildly by the sheikh when I showed no sign of being impressed by his claim that the mountains were blocked.

Mrs Begzadeh had brought a French-Farsi dictionary and she looked through it until she found the word: *ours*. The bears would get me even if I did not perish in the snows.

The sheikh sat ramrod stiff in his chair, looking as if he were on some sedentary parade. It struck me that bears hibernate in the winter, but it hardly seemed worth saying. I jumped from my chair to look at a useless Persian map of Kurdistan and Azerbaijan, and the sheikh leapt politely to his feet so that his guest should not stand alone. He stood looking straight ahead, his hands by his side, only age slightly bowing his head. There were no alternatives and all the sheikh would offer was an invitation to a village of his near the frontier in the spring provided I had police permission to visit it.

It was futile to lose my temper or to argue, but I walked backwards and forwards in a furious agitation between my chair and the map and I found afterwards that I had made my lower lip bleed by biting it like some enraged sultan. My manners must have seemed appalling to the sheikh; and I committed solecisms such as pointing the soles of my shoes at him and speaking with a cigarette in my mouth. He sat rarely speaking, his mouth as thin as the back of a knife. The sheikh was no coward and he had been brought up in the traditions of the nationalist movement. His father was killed by the Turks and he himself is revered in much of Persian Kurdistan. He has, though, pursued a diplomatic course. He has never indicated any opposition to Persian rule and was not particularly enthusiastic when the Russians briefly considered him as a possible president for the Kurdish Republic. He was in any case dropped when his enemies alleged to the Russians that he was a British agent. And possibly also important, he had links with the Kassem régime through a son in Baghdad. And was there in any case any special reason why he should feel warmly towards Mullah Mustafa, whom he had never supported militarily or politically, or helped when his little army of Barzani tribesmen retreated through the sheikh's tribal areas from the wreckage of the Mahabad Republic towards the sanctuary of the Soviet Union?

No principle or friendship was at stake if he refused to help me; not even honour. And recognizing the weakness of my position I took my camera from its newspaper wrapping, hung it round my neck and prepared to leave. The Begzadehs and the sheikh exchanged alarmed glances, perhaps thinking that I was going to photograph them as evidence for goodness knows what. I said goodbye with unfair terseness to the sheikh and was let out into a side street, one servant keeping a cautious watch in the road to make sure I was not observed.

I had left my map at the Begzadehs' house and I walked back on my own to get it, my temper cooling gradually as I settled down to the business of thinking what to do next after two changes of plan and one collapse. The Begzadehs met me in the street, Mrs Begzadeh carrying my map neatly wrapped up in more newspaper. They said goodbye happily, Mrs Begzadeh inviting me back in the spring like a hostess whose guest has been disappointed by the weather. I looked round after we had parted and saw her leaning close to her husband as she talked to him, her hands clasped round his arm.

CHAPTER IV

Around a hawk's nest of gnawed chicken bones in the hotel dining room sat a group of half-drunk old rogues, happy in the patronage of a moon-faced lieutenant who, when he saw me in the doorway, shouted cheerfully and, raising a tumbler to eye-level, spun into it a silver thread of vodka from a bottle. 'Capital!' he cried, placing the tumbler on the table with a thump. A sophisticated greeting for Rezaieh, I thought as I sat down at his right on the chair he ordered to be brought for me; but in fact it was the brand name of the vodka, which he insisted on me drinking mixed with beer. Slyly he made it known that he knew my name and that I came from London; and the others laughed at my surprise, hooting delightedly when I guessed that the waiter had shown them my route card. 'Feesh and cheeps,' said a soggy old weasel on my right. 'London. Feesh and cheeps.' The waiter went out to fetch me some boiled chicken and flat chips. A pile of the latter, cemented together by fat, was already on the table and the lieutenant offered me some on a fork, pronged together like a kebab.

The lieutenant, who insisted that he was a colonel, was leaving in the morning to join his artillery unit at Khaneh, a large military depôt close to the frontier and on the only road between Persia and northern Iraq. I wondered as I chewed my chicken whether it might not be worth asking whether I could travel with him, although what I would do when I got there was hard to see. I might have tried to walk across the frontier, I suppose, if my map had been accurate enough to show where it lay. The lieutenant understood not at all my guarded questions about Khaneh, but placed an arm on my shoulders, tried to pour me some more vodka and, after much careful search for words, inquired whether it was true that most Englishmen were homosexuals. *Le vice Anglais* is known

The Kurdish War

about in remoter places than one would imagine.

There were two courses open to me, I thought. First, to try to obtain from the security police in Rezaieh permission to move around freely in Kurdistan. It was obvious that I would not get very much farther without this. Or secondly, I could return to Tehran and there follow a line which I had earlier rejected as being too faint and unpromising. There was one other possibility. I had a letter of introduction from Ismet Cherif to a man who lived well south of Rezaieh, but I had been told by Mr Begzadeh that he was hostile to Mullah Mustafa, and I saw no reason to disbelieve him. The last thing I wanted to do was to embark on another wild goose chase which might end in me being expelled from the country. So I decided that first thing in the morning I would see the police. I doubted whether anyone in Rezaieh could give me permission to travel in Kurdistan, but it was worth finding out.

The police station was by one of the green traffic islands. A large building, with an imposing doorway guarded by a moustached and athletic-looking policeman of a type which must be either specially chosen or bred for the Persian police force: very broad shoulders tapering away to a tightly belted waist and slim hips; an almost balletic figure, anchored only by heavy black boots. Upstairs the plain clothes men into whose office I was shown were grappling sourly with the problems of a new day. Tea was ordered for me and one of the policemen puzzled over my route card. 'Bazorgan?' he repeated several times and after a while sent for another, who came slithering in, hands clasped in front of him like some obsequious genie out of a bottle. He looked hurt by the policeman's sharp questions and I understood him to ask me to confirm that I had arrived on the bus from Khoy. I nodded. 'Hotel Niagara?' he asked, brightening; and I nodded again. The seated policeman scowled down at my route card; the genie left, smiling gratefully at me over his shoulder. I managed to convey to the policeman that I wanted my card altered and he handed it back to me, saying that he would arrange for someone who spoke English to see me.

I was surprised that they were not more immediately interested in what I was doing in Rezaieh, but Europeans are not such exotic birds in that part of the world that every

The Kurdish War

telescope is trained on them. There are Americans attached to the army; foreigners from Tabriz occasionally; and French Lazarist missionaries. That day, in any case, it was the Shah's birthday, a day of celebration in the minor key; for dancing near the traffic island with the stone fawn and a speech or two. A manacled prisoner guarded by two policemen, one in front and one behind, walked down the white line in the middle of the road, the prisoner, head bent forward in shame, so precisely on it that it seemed like a protestation of future good intentions. Five minutes later came the mayor of the town, a distinguished old man with white moustaches, escorted by the chief of police and other dignatories spread across the road at a regular distance of two paces from one another. I took some photographs from the pavement and walked down to the island where men were dancing, their arms laced at shoulder level, to the music of a drum and an instrument like a child's trumpet.

I wandered back through the bazaar and out into the main street again, where a round-faced young man in a tweed jacket and a trilby hat approached me and asked for my route card. He was too well-shaven, his tie too carefully knotted, to be anything but a policeman, but as he would not admit that he was one I did not show him the card until he muttered something about Bazorgan. The summons to the offices of the town's security forces came shortly afterwards. They lay a taxi-ride from the centre of town, anonymous but with the unmistakable trade mark of a high metal gate decorated near the top by a few arabesques of wrought iron. A down-trodden soldier with a carbine slung over his shoulder opened the gate, directed me to a grill in the wall of a guard house and shut the gate again softly. The grill was opened, I was examined and the gate was unlocked again, the soldier looking down at his toes as if he had never seen me before. I waited for a few seconds just inside the gate in a little gravelled court with a flower bed whose occupants drooped wearily in the sun as if they had been grilled all night by some cruel Scarpia.

The internal security force, usually known as Savak, has the reputation of being the most efficient organization in the country. Its writ does not run through the whole of Kurdistan —the army controls most of the northern part of the region—

The Kurdish War

but it was at that time extremely well-informed both about its own Kurds and those in Iraq. It employs a number of able Kurds in its senior ranks and these seem to have kept in touch with the Persian wing of the Democratic Party of Kurdistan which, of course, has its main strength in Iraq. It has never minimized the danger of Kurdish nationalism once again becoming militant in Persia; but neither has it attempted to crush all signs of it. The policy seems to have been to prevent it at all costs from going underground and becoming unmanageable.

The security chief's office was a large hut. He asked me to sit down while he examined some papers and answered in a casual, uninterested tone the questions of an old woman who sat in a corner by the door. He was a youngish man of not much over thirty, I judged, but immensely large and fat, perhaps sixteen stone; dressed in a charcoal-grey suit and moving with surprising springiness in brown suede shoes. He could not understand, he said when he turned to me, why I was in Rezaieh and not Bazorgan. That, I said, was simple: there had been an error. The police in Tabriz had assumed I was going to Bazorgan. He did not seem particularly worried about me and I could tell from his manner and his questions that I had not been seen going to either the shiekh's or the Begzadehs' house. I asked whether my card could be amended to allow me to continue through Kurdistan, but he said that was impossible and I would have to get permission in Tehran.

It seemed best to make my retreat to Tehran as swift as possible, and once back at the hotel I arranged for a Russian Volga, the newest and strongest taxi I could find in Rezaieh, to take me back to Tabriz, where I hoped I would be in time to catch the late afternoon plane to Tehran. We started off well, the driver pushing the car hard on the dusty, rutted road; only stopping for more perfunctory checks for opium, to drink glasses of tea (which the driver insisted on paying for, perhaps out of kindness, perhaps on the principle that prompted the Tabriz taxi driver to give me boiled sweets) and to pick up hitch-hikers, including a quartet of gendarmes who wedged into the back, their rifles poking out of the windows. But we developed trouble with the oil filter and then with the carburettor and came to a lengthy halt in Marend, where we

The Kurdish War

pushed the car forward and then let it run down a little hill until the pop-pop-popping cough of the engine turned into a revving roar. So by the time we came to Tabriz airport the plane had gone and only a solitary policeman remained to tell me to come back tomorrow. We hurried to the railway station, but the night train had gone too, and there was nothing for it but to spend another night at the Hotel Metropole, listening to the little band and eating *chelo kebab*.

I could have spent the following day in Tabriz and caught the late afternoon plane to Tehran, but it seemed more interesting to get up early and take the bus. An exhausting, 400-mile journey in the back, for I was too late to reserve one of the better seats near the front where the bus does not pitch so much nor the dust curl in, powdering mouth and membranes like parchments. My neighbours were sick as children, red-eyed and shame-faced when they raised their heads from between their knees; staggering palely into the dark backs of the *chai-khanehs* when we stopped in the towns.

We had climbed over the 7,000-foot Shebli Pass, seeming almost level with the snow slopes of Kuh-e-Sahand, and then on through plough-land and red and white deserts until we reached the long valley stretching all the way to Qazvin; perhaps ten miles broad and bordered by companies of mountains as irregular in size and shape as conscripts, a processional way laid out by cyclopean contractors for a mocking descent into the earthquake-stricken region of Qazvin.

Once we stopped to mend a puncture and I walked off the road and sat on a stone among a huddle of others as slivered but roughly shaped as flint shavings. A scattering of grey rocks, until with a phenomenological twitch of recognition I realized that they were gravestones. Not an inscription on them; the dust piled on one side by the wind so that they looked a little like a wreck over which the tide is brushing. We like to pretend that our memory lives on in public view for at least fifty years, but here people were too realistic, or perhaps too poor, for conceits of that sort. And in any case, among all that dust, under a dusty blue sky, without even a tree to bring relief from the failed geometry of the landscape, it would be hard to pretend to any more identity than one of the donkeys being worked to death in the middle distance.

The Kurdish War

Each stone was for the next comer an intimation of ultimate insignificance, a moral hitching post for the hopeless and a stumbling block for the hopeful, reminding them to watch where they tread lest the earth swallow them up too soon.

Perched on one of these miniature sarsens as the bus driver and several helpers sweated over the tyre, I felt suitably gloomy myself. When I examined my chances and allowed myself to be coldly honest, there did not seem much likelihood that I would get across the border. Nevertheless, with a restorative flash of bloody-mindedness, I decided to hang on as long as I could in Persia. Even if the office would wear it, which I doubted, there seemed little or no point in going to the Lebanon and Syria. The prospects there looked no better than those in Persia. I should, I realized, soon be involved in a psycho-diplomatic struggle with the office, who would before long want to recall me. Going to Kurdistan was my idea, largely sponsored and pushed by me, and if I did not get there the blame would be mine, not theirs; which, humanly enough, would be one less impediment in the way of recalling me.

I stayed in Tehran in an hotel on the Takhte Jamshid, near the American Embassy, with a view of the Elburz Mountains which rise to over 15,000 feet behind the city. Autumn was giving way to winter and the snow on the mountain slopes seemed to play a game of grandmother's footsteps with me, coming lower in abrupt little leaps at night when my back was turned. I wondered what it would be like in Kurdistan where, I was told, it was colder than on the Persian uplands. It seemed immensely remote from Tehran, a world formed in my mind from the stone engravings in the archaeologist Claudius Rich's book, written in the 1820s, and forty-year-old photographs in the books of Englishmen who had worked in Kurdistan after the 1914-18 war. Unreal and romantic, lacking in definition; and for those reasons, perhaps, beginning to be obsessional.

I had to wait several days before I could see my faint chance, Mr N. Miraculously, it seemed, he thought he could help. More times than I can remember I sat in his comfortable office in one of his black chairs with yellow cushions while he walked backwards and forwards, head bent and sipping a cigarette as he discussed my problem in a gentle argument with himself. He had a very soft voice and a courteous but oddly elusive manner. At times I had the impression that he had vanished, leaving only a twist of smoke, but a refocusing of my hypnotized eyes and he emerged again, his quiet voice continuing, half heard by me. He was an extremely intelligent, astute person, not altogether rooted in Persia by culture or sentiment, I thought; a polygot Middle-Eastern cosmopolitan with all the comforting kindness that goes with the good manners of that type, and I placed myself almost entirely in his hands, feeling that there was nothing very much I could do except keep a check on what was happening and make sure that the plans did not create any new problems.

Tehran, as I have said, is not a very exciting or beautiful city, but in the late autumn it has some charm. The days are cool and bright, and in the evenings the hurricane lamps throw their platinum light on the stalls which sell cooked beetroot, grilled meat, yellowish sour oranges and many other semi-luxurious supplements to a thin diet. In the mornings there was the pleasure of going out to buy a newspaper and walking down Firdausi Avenue with its carpet and antique shops clustered near the one-time affluence and influence of the British Embassy compound, this mainly a large garden within a high wall and perhaps of more value nowadays as real estate than a symbol of imperial majesty. The British are still respected in Persia but our loss of power depresses our policies. British policy in Persia, in fact, is much the same as British policy anywhere else in the Middle East: fatalistic. The imperial responsibility of containing the Russians has been handed over to the Americans and we are left with oil and the memories of Abadan and Suez.

Once I went to Kermanshah, in the south of Persian Kurdistan, to watch the Shah distribute land title deeds to landless peasants. Land reform is the key to much that has happened recently in the Middle East. It was the spark that touched off the Kurdish revolt in Iraq; and in Persia, where it is being carried through by a stronger and more capable government, it has led to serious disturbances brought about by a combination of landlords, mullahs and the dissident Qash'qai tribe in the south near Shiraz. For political reasons it has been hurried through in Kurdistan; and, curiously enough, introduced peacefully. One would have imagined, on

The Kurdish War

the face of it, that there would be some repetition of events in Iraq; that the tribal leaders—immensely powerful in Persian Kurdistan—would attempt to capitalize on sentiments aroused by the uprising and rebel.

At Kermanshah it was easy to see one important reason why they have not: the almost hysterical popularity of land reform with the peasantry, Kurdish and Persian. Cries of 'Zindabad!' poetical orations, the nasal treble of a choir of little girls singing like a flock of lost and grounded skylarks in the vast emptiness of the airfield where the ceremony took place, the excitement of the crowd of peasants as the Shah hand-shook his way along their eager, overwhelmed fringe; all merged satisfactorily for the Shah into a great demonstration of gratitude and loyalty. Land reform in *his* programme and he reaps the credit for it; as he may also one day harvest the discredit if, as some believe, he proves to have forced too fast a pace for the good of the country's economy and political stability.

But apart from the natural popularity of a programme which breaks up vast estates and gives them to the serfs, there were other reasons why there was peace in Persian Kurdistan. The region (which is the only Kurdish area which is officially named 'Kurdistan') has always been regarded as a refuge for Kurds fleeing from the exactions of others. The Persians and the Kurds spring from the same stock and, perhaps because of this, their relations have usually been reasonably good and the Persian Kurds correspondingly less militant. Even in the days of the 1946 Mahabad Republic the Persian tribes were never very enthusiastic about defending the republic's frontiers. That was left largely to Mullah Mustafa's Barzani tribesmen from Iraq. The great tribal leaders, such as Sheikh Abdullah Effendi Djilani, stayed neutral. When the Mahabad Republic collapsed they believed they had taught themselves a valuable lesson: that Kurdish rebellion had no future.

In Iraq the politicians of the Democratic Party of Kurdistan had given tacit support to what began primarily as a tribal revolt. But if the tribal landlords in Persia had considered rebelling they would have had no support from the Persian wing of the party. They were intent on keeping on good terms with the central government so that there should be no danger

The Kurdish War

of the frontier being completely sealed or for that matter of the rebels finding themselves with a hostile and well-armed army at their backs. Moreover, the Persian Government's attitude to Kurdish aspirations has been fairly liberal. Kurdish dress, banned in the days of Reza Shah, is permitted, a Kurdish language newspaper is produced in Senna, nowadays the cultural capital of Persian Kurdistan, and there is a Kurdish broadcasting station. Both gave news of the rebellion in Iraq until the summer of 1963 when, partly at British instigation, the government adopted a slightly stiffer attitude towards the Kurdish revolt.

It would not be right to say that the Persian Government welcomed the Kurdish rebellion in Iraq. Like the Turks, it fears the long-term effects if it succeeds. But at least it made remote any danger of the left wing regicides of Kassem's government spreading their ideas across the frontier and was therefore not to be actively hindered. To have done so would in any case have stirred up Kurdish nationalism at a time when it was least wanted; and a policy that while non-committal was not actively hostile could reap its reward later in the form of a friendly guarantee against trouble being caused in Persia by an autonomous Iraqi Kurdish state. This non-committal passiveness was not, it should be noted, extended to Mullah Mustafa Barzani; only to the political elements in the south. He has not been forgiven for his part in the setting up of the Mahabad Republic.

I was to spend over three weeks in Persia following the retreat from Rezaieh. The *Sunday Telegraph*'s impatience was not allayed by optimistic letters from me and the deadline for my return and the completion of my arrangements for getting to the frontier coincided. I cabled London and back came a cautious reply saying that I must wait for a few days while they made up their minds whether they still wanted me to go. I guessed that the reason was because they had begun to wonder whether they would ever get me back once I crossed the frontier. Apart from any solicitude they might have felt for me, they had to weigh the possible cost in compensation to dependants of a lost correspondent. I sent off another cable saying no undue risks other than obvious hazards were involved. It sounded a bit heroic but I hoped it would prove

The Kurdish War

reassuring. Two days passed before I got a 'yes'. By that time my arrangements had lost momentum and I was still in Tehran three days after London thought I was on my way to Kurdistan.

'Mr Shikak', who was to take me to the frontier, seemed rather lethargic about starting but at last agreed it was time we went. I got up at 4.30 the following morning and put on my special Kurdistan rig: khaki shirt, sweater, green scarf, light slacks, green waterproof jacket, thick woollen socks and a pair of walking shoes. I had decided to take very little with me in the way of clothes or other equipment, as I expected to do a lot of walking, so all my rucksack contained was a white nylon shirt (for formal occasions at Mullah Mustafa's headquarters), a spare pair of socks, underwear, a very shabby raincoat, several notebooks and spare biros and pencils, film for the camera, a Pelican history of eighteenth-century England, 'Mr Medes'' map, towel, washing and shaving gear, a variety of medical equipment such as adhesive plasters and Entero-Vioform tablets, and lavatory paper.

Mr Shikak's jeep came down the road promptly at five, turned in an arc and stopped on the far side of the road. I hoisted my rucksack on my shoulder and went down, waking the doorman to let me out. Mr Shikak stood huddled in his overcoat, clapping his hands noiselessly against the cold. We greeted one another wordlessly with a handshake and drove off on the road to Tabriz. My 'mission', as Shikak liked to call it, had begun.

Shikak was plump, with round, large brown eyes like a baby's, his mouth pursed in an expression of seriousness to contain his exuberant jolliness. His laughter blew away the cold solemnity of the road. He saw me looking sombrely at the cemeteries beside the road and dismissed them with a cheerful shout above the jeep's roar of 'Dead mens!' We groaned up a hill and there appeared on the summit an old man praying, arms outstretched to the golden, dying sun, like some ancient Zoroastrian imploring his god for pity. Again Shikak's laugh and his splendidly deflating obviousness: 'He pray to God!'

We shared a room with a big stove in the middle at the Hotel Metropole. Shikak's brother, who lived in Tabriz, came and had supper with us, mainly to talk over family problems with Shikak, who was worried because he refused to go back to his wife and family in Tehran. The brother looked tired and resentful, a man of about fifty determined to live his own life; he had his own house in Tabriz and lived there without servants, not even a housekeeper. The Metropole band played its way through *My Fair Lady* and the Shikaks argued on, the brother leaving his food untouched and smoking all the time. Even Shikak hardly touched his *chelo kebab*, although it was a dish he said he was very fond of. Too fond of, for it made him fat and his wife complained.

We had meant to leave early for our frontier town the next day, but in fact we overslept and did not leave until it was quite late, after we had breakfasted comfortably on flat bread and goat's cheese and honey and it was gone nine o'clock. The first Kurdish houses began to appear near Miandoab, southeast of Lake Urmia, flat card-houses of golden brown mud, piles of straw and fodder rising above the roof level like enormous beehives. The country, despite the barren hills ahead of us and on our right, was well watered. A slow, reedy river wandered towards the lake and white herons fished somnolently in its dark waters, their reflections as precise as their hunched but neat selves.

We turned off at last from the good road south on to a jeep track which, despite its narrowness and stoniness, carried quite heavy lorries. The track lay between formidable mountains, the real Kurdistan at last, and the air gradually grew colder as we climbed to five or six thousand feet. Sometimes we had to stop to allow other vehicles to pass, their wheels crumbling the edge of the road above the ravine, or for a caravan of miniscule donkeys to have their nerves quieted and then be driven scurrying past with blows from heavy sticks.

Our town lay on a shelf among the mountains above and beyond some well-cultivated fields of tobacco. Before us on the road were two girls, beautiful as an oriental dream, struggling to control a mule which had pranced stiff-leggedly into a hedge. They wore the full Kurdish dress of baggy cotton trousers, skirt, bulging flowered cummerbund wound from hips to breasts, shawl and blouse decorated with gold and silver coins and, unusual in Kurdistan, a veil. One girl sat on the mule,

The Kurdish War

hunched forward as she pulled on the halter; the other held its head but turned to look at us as we passed, her eyes so dark and significant that Shikak made a joking pretence of bringing the jeep to a skidding halt and shouted: 'You stay here?'

We crossed a stream by a ford and drove quickly to a house on the outskirts of the town, where I was whisked inside and up to a warm upstairs room, where the owner soon arrived. He had, he said, been expecting us two days earlier: at which Shikak looked a little guilty. 'Mr Jaf' was a solemn, helpful man, dressed in semi-Kurdish dress of baggy trousers pegged just above the ankles and a tweed jacket. He thought it would be best to move me to another house where I could be more easily hidden. Disguised like some caricature of a secret agent in a pulled-down trilby hat and dark glasses, I was driven quickly to another house whose courtyard was sheltered by a high wall and heavy wooden gates.

I was looked after well and offered such comforts as a hubble-bubble pipe, which I found difficult to smoke with any satisfaction, and a bed on which to sleep away the afternoon. I read my history of eighteenth-century England and slept; the pale mountain sunlight which came through the open window hardly disturbed me. I remember particularly the quietness of the little town. The clucking of the hens and the occasional braying of a donkey seemed to be the only sounds in the still afternoon. It had the immaculate calm that only mountain places have, where noises do not stagnate as they do on the plains.

When it was dark Mr Jaf came in and said that later, after we had eaten supper, two Kurds who would take me across the frontier would come to see me. One had entered Persia from Iraq to buy certain provisions, such as cigarettes, and was now waiting to return to Mahvout, an important rebel base close to the banks of a tributary of the Lesser Zab.

The guides arrived and greeted me with murmured '*Salaam Alekums*', examining me as carefully as politeness would allow. Raschid, a Persian Kurd, was to go with me and the Iraqi Kurd, Ahmed, as far as the frontier. From there Ahmed would be responsible. Raschid had a long, pock-marked face and wore the semi-costume of tweed jacket and pegged trousers gartered at the knee by long woollen stockings.

The Kurdish War

Ahmed wore the full Kurdish dress of the south, double-breasted tunic instead of a jacket and a lengthly *pishten*, a waist-sash of printed cotton, through the folds of which a Kurdish dagger had been stuck. Both wore mottled grey turbans whose fringed ends hung loosely on their shoulders.

Together we worked out our route across the border and the time it would take from one village or hamlet to the next. Distance is never reckoned in miles or kilometres in Kurdistan but in so many hours' walk. A Persian map that showed the main towns and villages and the rivers was brought out and we found our goal, Mahvout. There, Ahmed assured me, there were many people who spoke English and would be able to take me to Mullah Mustafa's headquarters, which he said were near Rowanduz, as I had expected. I was not to worry about my safety, for he had a gun, a nine millimetre pistol of Belgian make, which he carried wrapped in a piece of red parachute cloth obtained after an ill-judged Iraqi supply drop to a besieged garrison. Nor should I worry about getting tired on the journey, for I would ride his horse. I had rather expected to walk into Iraq and had not as a result brought any thick trousers for riding. A man was sent out to get a pair of blue jeans which I could wear over my slacks and so avoid getting my calves and thighs pinched by the stirrup leathers. The guides left and I went to bed, the meek smell of the Kurdish cigarettes Ahmed had smoked hanging on the air like a gentle allurement to the journey.

CHAPTER V

I had wanted to leave at 5.30, but this was Kurdistan and the Kurds, unlike the Persians, are no nation of early risers. The day has to begin slowly, to be taken stock of over glasses of hot sugared water and tea and mouthfuls of pancake-thin bread and runny yoghourt. But as it was imperative that we should be well clear of the town before sunrise, I sent a man off at six to find out where the guides were. I felt a bit taut and unequable and passed the time by shaving by the standpipe in the cold and frosty yard, a Spartan and unsatisfactory operation. Afterwards, in the room, Shikak sat cross-legged on his quilts and watched me try on my blue jeans, which I wore over my khaki slacks. They were very tight and as they had no fly buttons or clasps I held them up with the cord from the top of my rucksack. The Persians have a custom of offering sweets and little cakes or biscuits to travellers before they start their journey, and Shikak produced a tin of *Yaz*, a brittle sweet rather like nougat, the best of it made in Isphahan. There was a brightly coloured picture of a peacock with its tail fanned on the lid and the sweets inside were each wrapped in greaseproof paper. It seemed somehow a very civilized and elegant thing with which to start one's journey into the mountains, and I was touched both by its incongruity as I placed it inside my rucksack and by Shikak's kindness in thinking of it.

The man I had sent to the guides came back and said they would be waiting near the town and we were to go to them in the jeep, which was outside the yard gate. I climbed into the front of the jeep and, at Mr Jaf's insistence, put on my disguise of trilby hat and dark glasses, although it was completely dark and no one at all seemed to be moving in the little town. We drove slowly through the streets and then along a track before lurching over a shingle bank and through a ford across the river which runs close to the town. On the

The Kurdish War

other side Ahmed and Raschid came out of the darkness to greet me. A third man was holding the reins of two horses which were sucking up water from a pool, their hooves scraping on the pebbles as they strained forward to get at the deeper, sweeter water. The stars, I remember, were burning with a last end-of-the-night brilliance and Venus, low over the mountain behind us, seemed only a mile or so high, her reflection striking arrows across the broken, black water of the stream. The best horse, the one belonging to Ahmed, was brought forward for me to mount. Ahmed had asked the night before whether I could ride and I had said 'yes', although it was about fifteen years since I had last sat on a horse. I put my left foot in a stirrup iron and found to my relief that my shoe was not too broad for it; a thought that had bothered me for some time was that Kurdish feet and shoes might be smaller than European ones and their stirrup irons made to match. But, grasping the pommel and the back of the saddle, I found that I could not hoist myself up. The distance was too great and my trousers too tight. Shikak and Jaf laughed merrily in the dark and came forward to heave me up. I felt a little less as if I were taking part in an oriental version of Commander Crabbe's last mission. Ahmed climbed on to the other horse and my rucksack and a white napkin containing a chicken and bread which Mr Jaf had brought for me were tied on to the back of my saddle, together with one or two oddments.

I said goodbye to Shikak and Jaf and we set off, Raschid leading, Salah, the man who had held the reins, next, then Ahmed, hunched in an Iraqi army greatcoat filched from some captured soldier, his stockinged legs dangling from the sides of a padded mule saddle, and lastly myself. We followed a track through the fields, past occasional groups of huts whose occupants were blowing the first crackle of flame into cooking fires and stoves. It was bitterly cold on the horse and I shrouded myself in my old raincoat and buttoned my waterproof jacket up to the neck. Riding level with Ahmed, I offered him a cigarette; then cigarettes to the other two. We grinned at one another. There was not a word we had in common, apart from a few Persian ones, such as *sard*, cold. Raschid, seeing my blue hands as I fumbled with a match, offered me his leather gloves, but I refused them and stuck my hands into my

The Kurdish War

pockets, with my left arm through the reins which hung loosely on the horse's neck. It was getting quite light, although the sun had not yet shown itself over the mountains. Two magpies crossed our path, swooping out of some fringing poplars in a low, dipping flight, and I took it as a good omen. Behind us, the town had raised a grey quilt of smoke over itself.

The cultivated land came to an end abruptly and we turned on to a mule track which crossed a rocky and wooded spur before continuing along the side of a deep valley, at the bottom of which ran a fast stream. Although it had shied once at some white rocks, my horse did not seem anxious to do anything more than plod ahead, concentrating on keeping its footing on a track that for most of the time seemed just large enough for a well-dieted rabbit. Red and orange bobbles swung on its bridal which, like all the Kurdish saddlery I saw, was stiff and cracked with neglect. The bits were never cleaned and the disc-like centres which lay on the animal's tongue gathered a ferment of froth and herbiage. My saddle at first seemed quite comfortable, although the stirrups hung straight down beneath my thighs, instead of in front as in European saddles. I had been taught to ride with heels down and knees in, and attempts to do this in Kurdish saddles caused me a great deal of pain from twisted knee joints before I learned that the best method was to ride with a long stirrup, the legs hooped round the animal, the toes pointing out and down. In front of the saddle was a hooked pommel, on which one could lean forward comfortably, the reins hooked round it; and the saddle itself was attached by a girth, a crupper, which held the animal's short, ragged tail in a jaunty arch, and shoulder straps; all very necessary in rough mountain country where a slipped saddle can drop the rider to a stony death in a ravine. The other unusual piece of the animal's equipment were its shoes, which were steel plates; this, presumably, to prevent the sharp stones of the tracks injuring the frogs of the hooves. None of the several horses I rode seemed to have any spirit at all, and I remembered reading somewhere that, although the original Kurdish horses were sturdy animals rather like North Country ponies, they had later been interbred with the more stylish Arab horses which, though good on the plains, were unsuited to the moun-

The Kurdish War

tains. All those I rode seemed to have had their spirits ruined by their harness and their strength sapped by the unending mountains, a poor diet and inconsiderate riders. Whenever I got off a horse to rest it someone would politely take the reins and then before long after offering it back to me, jump on its back. They were, however, very sure-footed; as good, I thought, as the much vaunted mules. The only beast that fell down under me was a mule.

The mountains around us were mainly forested with oaks, most of the trees old and all set far apart. The flocks of sheep and black goats had not only eaten the grass down to the roots, but had prevented any saplings from growing; and all the trees had been cut back for firewood and winter fodder for the goats. The cut fodder branches, with their golden leaves, were placed in the pollarded arms of the trees, where they looked like the nests of giant birds.

The morning traffic of people on their way to the town began to pass us, greeting us with polite *bekherbeys*, the Kurdish welcome; little caravans of donkeys laden with wood for the most part, although there was occasionally the more eccentric load such as an unpainted window frame, a luxury in villages where glass is usually for the rich. I was surprised how many people there were: on the mountain sides, smoke rose from shepherds' camps and in the valleys from many little hamlets, probably the homes of people driven across the border by the fighting. Movements of this sort, common in the troubled Kurdish highlands, and the nomadism of certain tribes who frequently cross the frontiers with their flocks, would fox any census-takers, even if they did not wish to minimize the Kurdish population, as the nationalists claim they do. Their task is made even harder by the tribesmen's association of censuses with taxation and enlistment. If the total population does come to seven or eight million, as I have suggested, it is larger than that of any Middle Eastern Arab country, apart from Egypt; a valid point for the nationalists to make when they claim the right to self-government.

Once we came close to a police post on the edge of a village, a small green, white and red Persian flag flying above it and the policeman's wife and three children standing on the beaten patch of ground in front, saying their morning prayers to-

The Kurdish War

wards the sun which had spilled its light over the mountains on to their end of the valley. My guides consulted and then made a detour which took us off the track and through some stripped tobacco fields, the stalks cracking under the horses' hooves as they plodded through the loose earth. I dismounted and led my horse down one steep bank at the top of which he had paused, but Ahmed kicked and, using the long plaited throng that ended his reins, whipped his horse down it. The going had become increasingly difficult and on one treacherous piece of steep rock his animal had stopped altogether when the saddle began to slip; until, clinging on sideways, he had made it hop up a three foot high step of rock with a great, reluctant lunge that threw him back to its haunches.

We came out of our narrow valley into a larger one where the river was broader and wider. Salah took the horse from me and watered it, whistling softly so that it would feel soothed and at ease while it drank. The tone of the whistling, used for watering animals, was always low; a mellow, gentle blowing of one or two repeated notes rather than a tune. The Kurds have little regard for their animals, except sometimes their dogs, which they prize, but I never heard them speak harshly to a horse or mule. They would generally encourage rather than shout, and never show impatience. Whereas my cries of 'Hatta! Hatta!', the Kurdish and Arab equivalent of 'Gee up!', always seemed to me to have a tone of brutal irascibility, theirs had the note of true understanding and confidence. The great days of the Kurdish cavalry, of the Turkish-enrolled *Hamadieh*, are long past (although the present régime in Iraq enlisted Kurds in its 'Horsemen of Saladin' to fight the rebels) but something of the traditions of horsemanship remain. They can ride fast and well through bad country, although neither a horse nor a mule can equal the speed of a man on the rocky mountainsides. I certainly found it hard to keep up on a horse or mule with those on foot and often it was more comfortable, particularly when coming down the mountainsides, to get off and walk rather than have to keep urging the animal on.

Salah and Raschid took off their shoes and stockings and waded across the river, lurching over the rocks, while Ahmed and I followed on the horses, which hated the fast current and round, slippery rocks. Two or three hundred yards up the river a party of about twenty men paused in their work on a bridge of poles to shout and stare at us. We did not answer but turned away from them and, after passing a settled, fertile area in a valley about half a mile across, climbed away from the mountain on a steep and at times dangerous slope.

Ahead of us, I saw, when we got to the top was a much higher mountain; part of a long wooded ridge that curved away north and north-west. The Kurds turned to me and said 'Iraq', gesturing up and over with their hands to show that it was on the other side of the ridge.

We stopped at the foot of this last mountain by a group of huts. Several small children came to the door and stared unsmilingly at us while their mother hung back in the shadows, replying querulously to Raschid's questions. After some argument she brought some chaff for the horses while we went and sat on the roof and Ahmed divided up the chicken which Mr Jaf had had wrapped for me. He had even provided a plastic salt cellar. The woman appeared again on the far side of the roof, which appeared to cover about four households, with a brass samovar. She refused to come any nearer than about twenty yards and, wrapping her head scarf over her mouth and averting her face, she scurried away. Salah carried over the samovar, at the base of which glowed some white-hot embers, and also a metal tray with Persian waisted glasses and a bowl of broken sugar and a teapot.

It was clear and pleasantly warm. I felt relaxed and at ease and passed the time by asking the name of various things. Kurdish is an Indo-European language, closely related in its words if not its grammar to Farsi. Many of the words crop up in Western European languages too. It has an archaic purity, so I am told, which is much admired by those who have studied it, but it is not particularly attractive to listen to:

> 'Arabic is sonorous,
> Turkish an achievement,
> Persian is sugar
> And Kurdish an unpleasantness.'

A few Western Europeans have studied it, among them E. B. Soane (*To Mesopotamia and Kurdistan in Disguise*), who

The Kurdish War

is supposed to have spoken it fluently, but gave his origins away when questioned by his Kurdish hosts at Halebja by using the English 'no' instead of the Kurdish 'na!'. The incident is a minor legend in the south. The language is divided into two main groups: Kurmanji, which is spoken by most of the Kurds including those of Turkey and Syria, the USSR and the northern part of Iraqi Kurdistan down to, roughly, the Arbil-to-Persia road; and Sorani, which is the dialect of the majority in Persia and the southern part of Iraqi Kurdistan. Apart from these, there are a number of dialects of minor importance such as Feyli (spoken among the Lurs, who are related to the Kurds), Gorani and Kelhori.

Much is made of the difficulty the Kurds have in understanding one another, but in my experience it is not particularly great. My interpreter, at a later stage, came from Sulaimaniya, where Sorani is spoken, and complained how hard it was to understand Mullah Mustafa, whose dialect is Kurmanji. But in fact, they seemed to have little difficulty and I cannot believe that language problems, caused by differing outside influences and the isolation of one group of tribes from another by the mountain ranges, would hinder the development of a Kurdish state.

I ran through a limited vocabulary with the three Kurds:

Nan—bread. The same as in Persian.

Elka—egg. *Hegg,* I discovered, in another nearby Kurdish dialect.

Qant—sugar. The same as in Persian and the origin of the English 'candy'.

Tchilka—spoon; or it may have been a twig. Further north, I noticed the word for spoon was much the same as the Persian 'qashug'.

Damancha—pistol, similar to the Persian word. Both Ahmed and Salah had taken their guns from the white napkin in which they had been hidden with the chicken and bread and strapped them on with belts.

Joz—walnuts, which Raschid had brought with him.

Sarbaz—soldier, Kurdish or Persian as opposed to 'Askar', for an Arab soldier.

Khatt—letter, as in Persian.

I had thought this a good moment to produce my letter from

The Kurdish War

Ismet to the 'Kurdish Commander at the Frontier'. Ahmed read it through carefully, folded it up precisely and replaced it in its envelope before shaking hands warmly with me, as if to welcome me here, on the border.

Ahmed folded up the remnants of the chicken in the napkin, although I indicated that they were not worth keeping, but he shook his head with a frugal pursing of the lips. Raschid was to leave us at this point, with the horse which Ahmed had been riding, and I said goodbye and thanked him as best I could.

We began the long climb up the mountain, which I estimated at perhaps 6,500 feet high. Ahmed insisted that I ride and he and Salah walked ahead, bent almost double at times, their hands clasped behind their backs and their feet placed wide on the track. Ahmed had long since taken off his greatcoat and it lay tied across the back of my saddle. His turban flapped loosely over his shoulders, giving him an oddly wild appearance. Salah wore a *claeatur*, the headdress of the Kurd who feels he wants something a bit more practical and military than a turban. The best *claeaturs* are made of goats' hair and come from the villages around Ryat, on the frontier with Persia, where they used to have a ready sale to Europeans who went there to ski on the long slopes of Hadji Moran. The style, though, varies from one area to another. I was told by one Kurd that the *claeatur* is entirely a recent invention, but in fact I have seen something remarkably similar worn by a Kurd in a photograph taken just after the First World War; and the Turkish troops in the same war used to wear a fatigue hat which though made of flannel or cloth, was roughly similar in design. One theory is that they derive from the hats worn by caravan escorts in winter and were first made at Urmia. The *claeatur* consists of a round cap with a bobble and a thicker projection at the back which covers the nape of the neck. From the back hang two long tassels, about two inches broad and a yard long. They are bound above the bobbles at the end by silver thread or coloured cotton. The colours of the wool vary from charcoal to white. They are worn either as a balaclava, with the broad tassels protecting the face, or with the tassels bound round the front of the hat and then tucked through so that they hang over the shoulders. The

The Kurdish War

latter method gives the wearer a ferocious, slightly Mongolian look.

A boy with an old musket guarded a flock of sheep and black goats and watched us as we neared the top. His young sister half hid behind some bushes forty yards away, but he came forward quite fearlessly when Ahmed called him and asked for news. In the polite Kurdish way, he hardly looked at me and asked and said nothing directed to me, apart from acknowledging my 'Salaam'.

We came at last to the top of the ridge, both Ahmed and Salah, particularly Ahmed, exhausted by the long climb. I had ridden the horse as easily as I could, crouching forward over its withers to take the weight off its back, and despite its snorting and plunging heaves it did not seem particularly tired, but munched placidly at the grass and bushes where I dismounted.

The ridge was a true frontier; a vast rampart stretching and curving far north in a line so clear that it must have made easy the work of the surveyors of the Sultan Murad and Shah Abbas when they agreed it should divide the empire of the Ottoman Turks from that of the Persians. Ahead, rounded greenish-brown mountains shouldered their way mile upon sunlit mile into Iraq as if hurrying to look at the wonders of Mesopotamia. Quite close, it seemed, a large mountain raised two peaks of close on 8,000 feet to keep an eye on what might come out of the east. It was immensely silent; no distant thump of bombs proved there was a war; nothing more than the wind rattling dry thorns, the horse shaking its bit as it tried to chump the grass and Ahmed clearing a throat dried by the wind and the steepness of the climb. I felt so exhilarated, triumphant and full of brilliant air and sun that I might have leapt to the nearest mountain. For whatever this tract without judges, cars, telephones, written laws and most of the amenities and obediences of a modern state might mean in terms of politics, for me it was at that moment a revelation of freedom. Except that I wanted to go on at once into its Arcadia of shaded green, rocks and streams, I might like some over-excited Victorian castaway reaching land at last have gone down on my knees and given thanks, though to what or whom I am not sure, unless it was the no doubt slightly bewildered news desk of the *Sunday Telegraph* and Mr N in Tehran.

The Kurdish War

Ahmed pointed the way we would go, towards Mahvout, the military headquarters on the Qala Chuwalan, a tributary of the Lesser Zab. We got to our feet and leaving Salah to lead the horse down the mountainside, Ahmed and I went on ahead, skipping downhill in the Kurdish way, which, sensibly, is to run rather than jolt stiff-legged in a walk. If you are fairly agile and are quick enough to see the footholds and avoid tripping, running is not only far less tiring than walking but quite enjoyable. After a while I could bowl downhill with the best of them.

Salah and the horse were soon out of sight and we ran on past a clump of trees around a graveyard with pieces of white cloth hanging from the branches and down behind some huts whose roofs jutted out of the hillside like shelves. Ahmed motioned to me to stay out of sight while he went and fetched a metal bowl of water which we drank from before walking on more slowly on ground that was fairly level. After a quarter of an hour or so, I looked round and saw Salah riding at a fast trot through the trees; and shortly afterwards there was the steady, heavy thump of a horse cantering and he caught up with us, riding loosely in the saddle, with my jacket, which I had given him to carry, across the pommel. I waved aside his offer of the horse and we crossed a stream and came to a group of huts where the head of the family, a lithe almost toothless man of about fifty, came out to give me a shifty-eyed and appraising welcome. His huts were built in split level fashion, stepped into the hillside, and we sat on the roof of the lower one in front of the top half. Rugs and a samovar were brought out; also Kurdish cigarettes. Behind us a tall, loose-limbed woman sat winnowing rice. His sons were prepared to make a feast of it and first one black goat which had wandered near was slaughtered, its hoarse baas ending as its throat was cut and the blood spurted three feet; then another goat, which had continued grazing a few feet away, was also killed, a group of four small children who had gathered to watch from a log clapping their hands with excitement and eagerly gather-up up the feet as they were cut off. The heads were left lying in the dust as the men began to clean and skin the animals. I had heard of the generous but awkward Kurdish custom of providing a feast for any guest and how one should try to

The Kurdish War

forestall it by stressing that one only wanted a light meal. I had hoped Ahmed would intervene (for goats are too valuable to the mountaineers to be slaughtered casually for no good reason), but he continued talking to the headman, puffing away at his cigarette, and seemed unperturbed.

Two horsemen with rifles appeared down the track behind the huts; fresh back from the war, I gathered, as they patted their rifles, one a good Czech carbine, and pointed them with puffing explosive noises and cries of 'Abdul Karim!' (Kassem) and pointed vaguely southwards. They had come from Sulaimaniya. Both were young, one with a sharply vain and intelligent face under his expensive grey and black silk turban.

This was the country of the Pizhdar; according to Rich, who visited them in the 1820s, 'real Kurds', and also a celebrated country for thieves. It might, I thought, have provided the source-landscape for an oriental Samuel Palmer. The travellers who in the past crossed from the Turkish empire to the Persian one through southern Kurdistan have all noted its beauty. I had hoped earlier that we might go to nearby Deira, which Rich wrote about: 'embosomed in a wood of the finest walnut trees I ever saw, which had a prodigious spread. Gardens, vineyards and cultivation surrounded the village in every available spot on the sides of the mountain. The vines in many places crept up the trees and extended from one tree to the other, forming festoons and draperies. Multitudes of springs burst from the sides of the hills and dashed over the trees in numberless little cascades. Nothing was heard but the murmurings of the waters.'

But we turned away from the lushness, the country growing bleaker, in places seriously eroded. The woods were left behind and instead there were occasional clumps of gorse, still with late yellow flowers on them. We followed a long ridge and near sunset, after about two and a half hours, crossed a broad and steep curtain of scree and entered a village.

The man who had come as a guide from the group of huts we had left had gone ahead with Ahmed and Salah and I rode into the village on my own. There were no paths through from side to side as the houses were all stepped one above another into the mountainside; a convenient method which saves having to build a back wall. I rode along the roofs, close to the walls of the houses above and then, whipping the horse up a steep incline of loose shale, arrived at the reception party. There were about twenty people standing by a long hut which overlooked the village, among them a tall young man in the white turban of one who has made the pilgrimage to Mecca and wearing a long blue gown. I made as if to shake his hand but judged from his slightly deprecatory smile that it would be more polite to dismount, and jumping off rather stiffly, greeted him and limped into the hut. He was, I thought, about twenty-seven. His lips were large and sensual and he had a whispy growth of beard and moustache.

A long evening was in front of me. I could do little but smile benignly at the obvious references to me as I sat in an honoured position on the best quilts at a point which combined distance from the door, close to which the *hoi polloi* gathered, and nearness to the warmth of the stove. I was encouraged to sit with my legs straight out in front of me and lean back on my cushions, although it was not considered good manners to be so relaxed—the sign of a weak, lazy man. Three major solecisms I had read somewhere, were to point the soles of your feet at others, fondle a dog and eat with your left hand, which is associated with less sanitary activities. However, the Kurds politely make allowances for Europeans when it comes to their posture, recognizing that their narrow trousers are not suited to cross-legged sitting. Watching them I noticed that they did not seem particularly worried about pointing their stockinged soles at one another, nor, when the meal arrived, did they discriminate between which hand they ate with. They used both. And neither then nor later did I ever get close enough to a dog to be tempted to fondle it. My left knee was still troublesome after some seven out of ten hours spent in the saddle and I compromised between good manners and comfort by putting that leg out straight and keeping the other tucked under me.

The area near the door reserved for those socially below the salt filled up, some kneeling because of the lack of space. It was a pleasant hut, about 25 or 30 feet long and perhaps 12 or 14 across, with smooth mud walls decorated in one place with a red check fablon material and in others by patterned reed mats; and several rows of coat hooks.

The Kurdish War

The oil lamps were lit and hung on the walls and three dignified middle-aged men who seemed to have come from nearby villages arrived. Two wore white turbans and long blue gowns, but while one at least was of more solid stuff than our *agha*, they did not seem to have his rank.

They read my letter to the 'Kurdish Commander' and also my letter of introduction to Mullah Mustafa; very slowly, their fingers underlining the Arabic script, the flimsy airmail paper held to catch the golden light of the oil lamps. They muttered the words to one another, as if having difficulty. Reading was made harder by the fact that the writing was on both sides and therefore, because of the thinness of the paper, often confused. Ahmed, who when I had shown him the letters, had read them through quickly and easily, watched them expressionlessly. Salah sat some three or four feet on the right side of the door, his mouth caught in an expression of slightly worried sobriety, the white of his dark eyes catching the light as he examined those who sat above the stove.

Neither he nor any of the others who huddled near the door, talked except when they tinkered with the samovar or brought in the great pewter trays for the meal. They listened gravely, absorbing it all. Several youths acted as servants, bringing bowls of water to drink, wood for the stove, or opening the window on my right at the end of the hut when the room got too hot, as it frequently did. One had been taught English at school and had his textbook with him, full of phrases about chairs and classrooms and animals. But he spoke no English apart from a few words. At supper, I had a tray to myself, unlike the others who shared either in pairs or in foursomes. All ate at the same time without talking. There was rice and chicken and flat bread and hard, flaked goat's cheese and a spicy gravy, a bowl of yoghourt of which the Kurds are very fond, followed by a drink of a salted curdled milk, which was very refreshing. We washed our hands again afterwards in a silver bowl with the aid of a new bar of white soap and a clean towel, then drank more tea and smoked more cigarettes. I never saw anyone smoke a pipe all the time I was in Kurdistan. Cigarettes, often held in foot-long holders of cane, were the rule.

The young *agha* would occasionally turn to me, thump his

right fist against his left hand and cry: *'Abdul Karim—kallas!'* Abdul Karim Kassem—finished. The village had been bombed and shot up by a government Ilyushin bomber and other aircraft and he ordered his men to bring in some cannon shell cases and also a solid cannon shot. Two of the shell cases were clearly British. Where did I think they came from? they asked me politely but accusingly. Czechoslovakia, I said, and saw Ahmed looking at me quizzically. I winked at him; it became a much-repeated joke of his later, how I had said the British shells were Czech. Photographs of Mullah Mustafa dating from Mahabad days when he wore a Russian general's uniform were brought out and one given to me; a youth brought a magazine and opened it to show me a photograph of Ismet Cherif Vanly.

Ahmed, who had several times explained my silence by saying that I, alas, spoke no Turkish, Arabic, Farsi or Kurdish —like many Kurds, a good linguist, he spoke all of them— dominated the conversation, answering questions from those sitting above the stove; the young *agha* leaning forward with a girlish smile and the senior of the three dignified men who had entered later, nodded gravely and fingered a string of amber beads, clicking one against the other as if engaged in an endless, automatic prayer. The talk was of the Democratic Party, of Kassem and even Castro. That they should have known about Castro and the Cuban crisis was not surprising since transistor radios are commonplace in the hills. After a rifle and a pair of binoculars, a transistor is the most treasured possession of any tribesman or Kurdish soldier. A man in a dun, vaguely military, version of Kurdish dress who wore a leather bandolier of cartridges sat next to Ahmed and appeared to have some sort of official rank. A Democratic Party policeman, I believed, since they have their men stationed, usually in groups of three, among the villages to maintain some form of law and order and also keep an eye on the villagers and see they pay their taxes promptly.

I wondered afterwards if these conservative and—apart from the voluble young *agha*—reserved village elders were alarmed by the danger that the Left-wing Democratic Party with whom they were allied would want to change their comfortable but archaic little world so radically that there would

The Kurdish War

be no more room for white-turbanned *aghas* who wished to spend their days and evenings telling stories and gossiping while their barefoot bondsmen brought them tea and stoked the stove. For some, a minority perhaps, there would be religious reasons for any fears, for this was the country of the Sufis and Dervishes with their insistence on a personal path to God, linking Islam with monastic Christianity, pagan Neoplatonism and vanished faiths. The agnosticism of the politicians would grind them to dust.

I was tired after the long day and the heat of the room made me droop, but not the Kurds, the only Orientals, as Rich noted, who sit up late at night and rise late in the morning. I thought at one stage, after the three wise men had made a grave, unsmiling departure, of writing my diary, but I saw from Ahmed's quizzical expression and a slight pause in the conversation of the young *agha*, who was speaking to Ahmed and the man with the bandoliers, that it would not be good manners to so obviously withdraw from the group, and I put it away. After a while Ahmed asked whether I wanted to go to sleep and I nodded gratefully. Extra quilts were brought and two men with an oil lamp were deputed to guide me to the bath-house, which had on the outside wall a white painted message saying 'DDT 1960'. This, a standard feature of most large villages, was a long building next to the young *agha*'s house and consisted of a row of sty-like lavatories, each with a long oblong hole in the middle and below, under the pole and mud floor, the cess-pit. At the back of the building water dripped slowly into a large tank for communal bathing.

I went back to the room and feeling a bit more awake after an ice-cold wash wrote my diary while the others were getting ready for bed. Salah had already huddled under his quilt, still wearing his *claeatur*. The young *agha* had moved in a flurry of his gown and with camp gestures to sit beside Ahmed and draw him close to him while he whispered, his mouth twisted in contortions of subtlety and secrecy. Ahmed seemed to be explaining again something which had been said. They were still whispering when I put down my diary and went to sleep.

CHAPTER VI

The room was deadly cold when I awoke. The sharp winter frost had claimed it during the night. The stove was out, but after a while there were muffled stirrings at the end of the room and a boy brought a bundle of thorny twigs and tinder to the grate; struck a match which showed his still sleepy face as he cleaned out the ashes and put in the firing. I went out into the cold dark, braving it in my thick khaki shirt. Another servant looked at me surprised when I asked for some water, which he brought me. I decided to shave and asked for a bowl with which, after clearing away the dead leaves on a pool in front of the bath-house, I scooped up some water. It was so cold that the shaving soap hardly lathered and my razor tugged and stuck on what felt like clumps of wire. I looked up and saw Ahmed in the grey, aquatic dawnlight. He asked me wonderingly whether it was not cold and I gave a brave shrug, feeling rather stupid. I dropped stoicism from then on and did as the natives do, which was to shave every three or four days in the warmth of a hut.

The young *agha* joined us for breakfast. He had slept elsewhere. And shortly afterwards the three wise men once again entered gravely and unsmilingly and we started breakfast: of bread, yoghourt, scraped cheese, rancid butter and for me, as a special treat, wild honey with flecks of the comb caught in it, gathered in all probability from a hollow oak tree, for the Kurds rarely domesticate bees.

It had become stuffy already, the stove glowing red hot in places from the heat of the fresh wood burning undamped by ashes, and the window was opened on the *agha*'s orders, letting in a cool draught which seemed to come straight from the pale blue sky outside. A tree, possibly a peach, grew close to the corner of the hut, and leaves that were long and brown —for it was autumn—moved gently across the window. We

The Kurdish War

had finished breakfast and Ahmed had distributed several copies of a Persian newspaper, printed in Kermanshah by the Khayan group, which carried an editorial on the war. They muttered the words slowly to themselves, nodding solemnly at passages of which they particularly approved. Their murmuring, the pale blue sky, the flickering leaves, the samovar huffing to itself: it was a moment in another world and quite suddenly the strangeness of it and my isolation—which I had to a certain extent refused to feel—merged into a sensation of detached happiness. A selfish happiness perhaps, for I was not of their world any more than they were of mine; and if theirs went, then I would not mourn too much, for it was already lost and gone and yet preserved.

For some reason they wanted to see again my letter to 'The Kurdish Commander at the Frontier' and as I took it out of my rucksack Ahmed noticed that I had another addressed to Ibrahim Ahmed, the Secretary-General of the Democratic Party of Kurdistan. Ismet, in Zurich, had written it for me in case I met him first, but I had more or less forgotten about it in my concentration on getting to Mullah Mustafa's headquarters; and in any case I had imagined that the President and the Secretary-General of the party would be close together, possibly living in the same place. But Ahmed said that Ibrahim Ahmed was only five hours away, whether travelling through the district or at a headquarters of his own I could not make out. It seemed a pity to miss the chance of seeing him and I told Ahmed we would go to wherever he was and miss out Mahvout, which I understood would be off our route. I knew nothing about Ibrahim Ahmed other than that he was alleged to be a communist and was said to have been dismissed from the secretary-generalship by Mullah Mustafa, a puzzling rumour about which more later.

The young *agha* insisted that I take photographs of him and his men before I left. He posed before the group, looking up slyly from a copy of the Khayan newspaper which he held in front of him as if he were reading from a battle order. We said our incomprehensible goodbyes and I shook hands with as many as I could see before we set off up the bare slopes again with two new guides carrying rifles. The rivulets flowing down the mountain had been banked in with stones and turf and guided beside or through little plots of land. Sometimes the Kurds walked along the smooth banks while I splashed the horse through the water, not wanting to spoil someone's hard work. We passed between the two high peaks I had seen from the frontier and came down through fields of tobacco and under high walnut trees hung, as Claudius Rich described them at Deira, with vines, from the stems of which the villagers make a cloth called *spee*. We followed a fast, sharply dropping stream lined with water mills, the leat cut close to the cliff and bringing the water to a metal funnel through which it rushed on to a horizontal (instead of vertical, as in Europe) millwheel. A Kurdish miller showed me one working elsewhere, its small paddles racing round. To produce fine grain they check the speed of the upper stone, and for coarse they let it run fast.

We turned through well cultivated ground and came to a well-built two-storey house. I waited outside until the guide, who had entered, came out to beckon me to climb some mud steps to the top floor where I was shown into a large room. I could not see for a moment in the semi-darkness and so did not notice the owner of the house, who was sitting in a corner near the window. Ahmed, who was close behind, made amends for me quickly and went over to him and shook hands and introduced me. He made as if to get up, but Ahmed put his hand on his shoulder and pressed him back and I saw that he had only one leg. He had a large round, good-tempered face and reminded me of the Emir Bedir Khan; the same broad forehead and gentle but shrewd eyes. It was a quiet, pleasant house, with an ordered relaxed air. The children, including a small girl, squatted near the stove breaking walnuts some of which the eldest boy brought me on a plate, sitting next to me and watching very closely while I ate them. I pushed the plate towards him but he refused to take any until he was sure I had finished, his father smiling approvingly at his good manners. The paper and cardboard *cartouches* of Kurdish cigarettes were filled with tobacco and distributed to us.

As we sat there was the sound of another horse being ridden up to the house and tethered beside ours, which was eating chaff by the wall. A tall man of about forty in a military light khaki Kurdish dress came in wearing a *claeatur* and bandolier

The Kurdish War

and carrying his rifle. He sat and talked for a while and then asked for a mat and said his prayers in front of the window, standing between the owner of the house and myself. He seemed unperturbed by my infidel presence and said his prayers in a deep, rapturous mutter, interrupted by prostrations and sighs. Perhaps they were thanks for a safe return from the front. The Kurdish forces are organized as a militia, so that a man after spending a month on duty will return for an equal period to his family and land.

We had a simple lunch of rice, cheese and yoghourt and then left, Ahmed persuading the one-legged man not to strap on a Long-John-Silver stump to say goodbye to us. We climbed steeply for a while until we reached the top of steep crags where the guides pointed out our way and then left us. I could see a broad, low valley in the distance with a river and a modern metal bridge some ten or fifteen miles away; the new Bridge of Qamish, with above, hanging on the steep hill on the far side of the river, a town which Ahmed said was Dree.

We left Salah with the horse and skipped down the mountainside, turning away from the direction of the bridge at first and then zig-zagging back so that the descent was not too steep. Occasionally we looked back to make sure that Salah was following and had not fallen with the horse, which had been stumbling and slithering badly. Ahmed's sharp and accustomed eye could always pick them out about three seconds before I could. We had a joint sense of pleasure in the scene. The Kurds love and are extremely proud of their superb mountains; and Ahmed pointed out to me a group of goats and sheep with their shepherds clambering round a bushy tower of white rock in search of grazing. To Ahmed it was summed up in a word that sounded like *Juaniya*. I asked what it meant and he half-closed his eyes and drooped his arms obliquely, palms forward, in an expression of ecstasy. The green land ahead was *Khoesha*, good and beautiful.

We came at last down to the river and I continued to walk for the sheer pleasure of movement and exercise; and with the same feeling of physical exhilaration, I picked up a stone and flung it far out into the river to a sardonic '*Zor Basha*', very good, from Ahmed.

At one stage we could see Mahvout ahead of us, a large

The Kurdish War

circle of houses well above the green bank of the Qala Chuwalan: the headquarters of a regional committee under the command of Ali Askary. But we turned away from the track towards the bridge, near which on one side was a ruined police post from which two Kurdish partisans emerged and stared at us curiously, their hands in their pockets. Below the new bridge was the old, humped Turkish bridge, the centre span of which has been destroyed. A beautiful example of its type which one day should be restored; but somehow, pessimistically, I feel that it never will be. No one has much regard for ancient monuments of Turkish origin. Behind the bridge the river plunged into a deep gorge, presumably a natural cleft, as the least line of resistance to the river would have been to the east. A motorable road crossed the bridge and another branched off from it to Dree. While Salah cantered the horse along the road, Ahmed and I took a short cut up the hill, meeting on our way a patrol of three more partisans on their way to Mahvout. They looked quite spruce in their *claeaturs* and dun coloured uniforms, with their rifles slung on their right shoulders. One, who spoke some English, told me that the valley, which stretched back to near Sulaimaniya, had been the scene of fierce fighting two months earlier when the army had come with tanks as far as the bridge before their infantry, which was taking the brunt of the battle, decided it was time to retire.

I mounted the horse and rode for a while behind a string of donkeys going up to the village, which I half hoped we would pass through, but instead we turned off the road, crossed a stream and went up a steep hill with thorny bushes carrying diminutive yellow berries, some of which Salah picked and gave me. They had a nutty, sharp-sweet flavour. Ahmed had done as I had asked and forced the pace so that we would not waste any time. He looked very tired and paused to rest on the hill. The five hours to Ibrahim Ahmed were already proving long hours. Salah grinned and pulled at an imaginary beard to show that he was getting old. I waited discreetly for a little while and then insisted that Ahmed ride. From the horse he tested me on the Kurdish words I had noted down and was glad to find that I had remembered.

'Adamson,' he called. And when I looked round, pointed

The Kurdish War

first to me and then to himself and said with a smile 'Kaka'. I did not know precisely what the word meant and repeated it questioningly. He put his forefingers side by side and said 'Bra', which I guessed rightly meant brother. 'Kaka', in fact, means literally 'big brother' and is used as a term of acceptance and respect; a cross between mister and 'mate'.

It became dark but as Ahmed said that Ibrahim Ahmed's headquarters were only another two or three hours away, we went on. It was a bad track which meandered past fields, up hillsides and through dark villages where no one came to the door; so we were all exhausted when we came to a shelf of rock above a sheer drop to a stream. Ahmed suddenly turned round and, pointing at a hollowed-out semi-cave in the rock, said 'Ibrahim Ahmed, *pinj sa-at* [five hours]' and made a gesture as if we should sleep there. Then he laughed and pointed to our right, where I could see the vague glow of a fire. It burned before the caves of Ibrahim Ahmed.

We made our way down from the rocky shelf and across a shallow stream and followed a track into a deep valley flanked by high mountains until the fire turned from a glow into leaping flames and I could see the figures of two men standing by it. We turned up the track towards them and they challenged us; were answered by Ahmed, who took me up the hill, past a hut and into a cave, the entrance to which was half blocked by screens.

Inside, in the yellow glow of oil lamps, sat a dozen men as surprised as schoolboys in their den are when the outside world suddenly manifests itself at the doorway. They sat on benches and tubular metal chairs round a stove, for this was a refuge from the cities rather than an outpost of the mountains where men still prefer to sit on the ground. They welcomed me warmly, one of them in hesitant English, and made room so that I could sit next the stove. Ahmed took the introductory letter and went through a narrow archway in the rock at the back of the cave. The man who spoke English told me that Ibrahim Ahmed was there and we talked a little vaguely about who I was and where I had come from. Tea was brought to me in an enamelled mug with a blue rim, like a quarter-size British army mug. They were, I found, the rule at the establishments of the Democratic Party of Kurdistan and were part of the booty captured from the Iraqi army. As we sat and talked I heard the confused buzz of a military wireless set and, looking behind a wall of cans and screens, saw a wireless operator leaning back on a blanket with his earphones on and beside him a medium-sized receiver and transmitter.

Some ten minutes must have passed before Ahmed reappeared and signed to me to go through the arch. It was a low, narrow entrance and I stooped and stumbled before emerging into a small cave, the walls of which were covered with maps and newspaper so that it looked a bit as if it had been made of *papier maché*. Ibrahim Ahmed greeted me in English and introduced me to the two men with him: Nuri Sadiq Showais and another whose name I did not catch but who I gathered was a member of the Party's Central Committee.

We sat down round a table, a bit cramped since the cave seemed as small as a yacht's cabin. Both Ibrahim Ahmed and Nuri Sadiq (an engineer who is very close to Ahmed) spoke English, but it was Ibrahim Ahmed who dominated the conversation, weighing my questions very quickly and speaking in the practised, semi-formal manner of a politician used to measuring the impact of what he is saying. He is a small and delicately built man in his early fifties, greying and with sharp features reminiscent of Field Marshal Montgomery's, and like the Field Marshal's, saved from being described as elfin by a firm mouth and quick eyes. The son of a middle-class Sulaimaniya family, he trained as a lawyer in Baghdad and was early involved in nationalist politics. His first serious brush with the authorities of the *ancien régime* came in 1937 when he was brought before the courts over a pamphlet he had written. From then on he was in more or less continuous disfavour, principally because of the Kurdish magazine *Galaweich* which he founded in 1939 and continued to direct until 1947 when he was accused of communism. He became Secretary-General of the Democratic Party of Kurdistan in 1952 after three years in prison and has held the post ever since.

With his air of austerity and brisk manner, he would easily pass for a north country headmaster, proud of his boys, impatient with the selfish materialism of their parents and strict with wrongdoers. I felt he could have sunk into an English

The Kurdish War

background quite easily; became a stalwart of the old-school socialist tradition, with his taste for Marx, Bertrand Russell, Shakespeare and Harold Laski. But before I go too far in 'westernizing' him, I should say that he favours Hafiz, the Persian poet, before Shakespeare, wears his *claeatur* at all times like any oriental who hates to go bareheaded, and has a sinuosity of mind not often found in Huddersfield.

That he is not a communist is not, I think, so much out of any basic disagreement with their aims as because his approach is pragmatic and above all nationalist. The communists regarded him and his party as bourgeois and too narrowly Kurdish in their outlook. They believed there should be a joint Arab-Kurdish struggle for a 'Popular Front' Iraq, and that this should come before Kurdish self-government. For the nationalist non-communist Kurds this was unsatisfactory: they did not trust them as communists or as a predominantly Arab party to look after Kurdish interests. When the rebellion started in 1961, the communist attitude to Kassem was uncertain. He had taken Iraq out of the Baghdad Pact and if he had not turned the country into a communist state, he had at least provided a terrain in which they could organize and prosper. After Kassem had in his turn fallen to a *coup*, many Kurdish and Arab communists fled to the hills to escape persecution. Common hardships did not, however, make for reconciliation. Some of the communists were gaoled by the Kurds at Mahvout.

I think, looking back, that it was significant that Ibrahim Ahmed should have used the word partisan to describe the Kurdish soldiers of the DPK, for Tito's puritan revolutionaries had much in common with them, even if they were powered by a more simply designed political engine. They fought in the mountains, had once been part of the Ottoman Empire, came from a background at once primitive and oppressed and yet with heroic traditions which were venerated. Their battle, too, was in part a civil war. By no means all the Kurds support the rebels, and the government's Kurdish militia, although never a very formidable body, numbered about 5,000 men at the beginning of 1962.

Their policy would be one of neutralism, said Ibrahim Ahmed, looking beyond the day of victory. They wanted no

The Kurdish War

allies and they wanted no enemies. Two things had been learnt by them from the collapse of the Mahabad Republic: not to rely on tribal support and not to hope for outside help. Whatever they achieved would be achieved by themselves alone [but by the middle of next year they had changed their tune and were hoping for Western diplomatic support]. They would be a one-party state and surely I would not object to that—I had made a muttered democratic quibble—since the only other party was the Communist Party, and they had opposed the rebellion.

This seemed to me to be going a bit beyond what I should have considered the bounds of autonomy, for autonomous states do not decide separate foreign policies, neutralist or otherwise, nor, I should have thought, can they exclude other parties from their territory. So I asked how he would define autonomy.

'We are often asked to define this,' he said expertly. 'But we have never given a definition. It depends on our strength and that of our enemy. We would be agreeable to something similar to the Swiss system.'

He added a little later, almost humbly, that really they demanded very little. 'We are not dreamers,' he said. But he also said they would fight to the end for what they wanted. When they did define what they wanted during the spring and early summer of 1963, the terms proved too steep for the government, who would offer no more than 'decentralization'. (See Appendix.) An ill-judged attempt to 'up' the demands to include a Kurdish state within the federation of Arab states proposed—and for a time accepted by Syria and Iraq—by President Nasser of Egypt, was claimed by the government to be one of the main reasons why it abruptly ended the cease-fire and attacked the Kurds. I believe that the Kurds would have been prepared to soften their terms, but to what extent is a matter for conjecture. The most disputed demands were those for a fixed share of the oil revenues and a separate Kurdish corps within the Iraqi army.

Ibrahim Ahmed objected to any attempt to label him as a socialist. He belonged to a progressive revolutionary party. Such matters as land reform, which figured largely on their programme, would be left until the wishes of the people had been tested by a referendum, and the Iraq Petroleum Company would be left alone. Why should they interfere with their country's main source of income?

We turned to the effect of the revolution on the Kurds living in neighbouring countries: would an autonomous Kurdish state in Iraq encourage similar revolts in Persia and Turkey? 'If the Kurds there want to rebel, that is their affair. We have not asked them to help us. We certainly do not want to engage in hostilities with Turkey and Persia. And do not forget that after two or three years of war our country here will be completely destroyed and we shall have to concentrate all our efforts on rebuilding it. We think the success of our revolution will affect the Kurds elsewhere. That is a fact and there is nothing we can do about it.'

We talked about the machinery of the revolution and their plans, the third man, who spoke no English, quietly leaving us after shaking hands. The revolution, so far as the DPK's share of it was concerned, was in the hands of a five-man political bureau [consisting of Ibrahim Ahmed, Nuri Sadiq Showais, Omar 'Dababa' Mustafa, Jelal Talabani and Ali Abdullah] which in turn was controlled by a central committee of twenty-one members. All the leaders of the partisan groups in the south are sound Party members but by no means all the men or all the senior officers (not an accurate description since until a change of policy in December 1963 they had 'responsibilities' rather than ranks) are members. The main strength of the army does lie with the Party, but in the centre and much of the rugged and unsophisticated north of Iraqi Kurdistan it is the tribes who have borne the brunt of the fighting. This explains the importance of Mullah Mustafa Barzani, adopted by the Party, of which he is President, and yet the champion of the *aghas* and chieftains. His Barzanis and the tribes allied with them form almost a political grouping in themselves. Among the politically sophisticated in the south there is already talk of him being the Ben Khedda of the revolution, giving way after it is won to Ibrahim Ahmed's Ben Bella. How can the two coexist? The DPK has two main functions: to win the war for Kurdish nationalism and then to reform Kurdish society, which means the end of feudalism and the destruction of tribal society. The Party has already taken over control of some of

The Kurdish War

the tribal areas in the south, and the young men who are accepted into its army are given political lectures, so that when they go home they spread their belief, presumably, in the new order.

I became suddenly and sharply aware of the depth of this rift between the old and the new when Ibrahim Ahmed later hinted delicately that I should be discreet and understanding in what I quoted of Mullah Mustafa's pronouncements on Kurdish aims and Kurdish problems. His call for American support, and offer to put the Kurds' military weight behind CENTO, had caused considerable embarrassment and anger when it appeared in Mr Dana Adam Schmidt's stories in the *New York Times*. It conflicted with the Party's neutralism and the Kurds' enemies had been given a propaganda gift: the hypocrites were angling for help from the imperialists. Mr Schmidt, he implied, had made too much of it. It seemed a curious request for a Secretary-General to make to a reporter who was going to interview his President, and I said it would be better if any appeal for discretion were made direct to Mullah Mustafa rather than to me. I wondered afterwards whether they feared Mullah Mustafa was hoping for American support (the Americans sent him a message after the February 1963 cease-fire saying they would aid an autonomous state if one emerged from the negotiations with the Iraqi Government) to strengthen his own position and that of the conservatives against the Democratic Party, which already outweighed his forces.

Why did you support Kassem and why did the war begin? I asked, wondering where their politics ended and their nationalism began.

'We were in a cage,' said Ibrahim Ahmed. 'That was before 1958 when Kassem came to power. We were surrounded by three countries, Iraq, Turkey and Iran, who were all members of the CENTO Pact, or the Baghdad Pact as it was then. We supported Kassem unhesitatingly because the Baghdad Pact was an anti-Kurdish League and we thought nothing could be worse than Nuri es Said (the Iraqi prime minister, who was murdered at the same time as the Hashemite royal family). We were the deciding factor in bringing Kassem to power.'

The Kurdish War

To begin with, Kassem must have seemed the sort of leader the Iraqi Kurds had dreamed of. He had Kurdish blood from his mother's side; he was left-wing, austere, and he spoke of Kurdish rights as if he meant what he said. The constitution which he produced seemed satisfactory if a little contradictory. Article 2 said that Iraq was a part of the Arab world, which was contestable from the Kurdish point of view; but Article 3 described Kurds and Arabs as equals within the state and recognized the Kurds' national rights.

'It was unspecific,' said Ibrahim Ahmed, 'and we said we should be allowed autonomy. We explained there were many multi-national states.'

There were definite gains. For the first time the Party was given permission to work openly in all parts of Kurdistan provided that it had its headquarters in Baghdad, where it could be kept under the supervisory eye of Kassem himself; and they were able to publish the Kurdish language newspaper *Khabat*, which means The Battle. It is still published clandestinely by the rebels. Mullah Mustafa was brought back from exile in Russia in 1958 and many Kurdish nationalists who had been imprisoned under Nuri es Said were released. But this relief allowed the Kurds not only the luxury of openly discussing politics; they disputed with the Arab socialist parties and also among themselves. What had looked like a left-wing common front was soon badly cracked.

The DPK had at one time been heavily infiltrated by the communists: *all* the main parties in Kurdistan were either communist, communist led or listing heavily in that direction. The DPK had fought the communists for the allegiance of the young by acknowledging its debt to Marxist-Leninist inspiration in its constitution; a gesture which may have made it more acceptable but also meant that it attracted many who were communists. *Khabat*, the Party organ, was edited by one, Hamsah Abdullah; and Mullah Mustafa, who had accepted the presidency of the Party from Kassem, believed that the Political Bureau was dominated by them. Mainly through Mullah Mustafa's efforts, the Party was purged in 1960, the reference to Marxist-Leninism struck out of the constitution and the editor of *Khabat* ejected from his chair.

During the two years from 1958 to 1960 the relations

between Kassem and the Kurds had gradually worsened. The Arab press attacked the Kurdish nationalists, and Mullah Mustafa, whom Kassem had brought back from Russia with a great fanfare for Arab-Kurdish brotherhood, became estranged from his benefactor. He was no longer to be seen on the Baghdad saluting bases and gradually he retired to his own bleak Barzani territory. There was a quarrel too about the name of the Party. Kassem objected to it being called the 'Kurdish' Democratic Party and after some argument it was tactfully agreed that it should be known by its present name, which Kassem felt gave it a regional rather than a purely national basis.

Despite its nationalism the DPK has never been racist. Its members talk frequently of Arab-Kurdish brotherhood and mean it. So it was possible, despite their differences, to keep some sort of link with the 'bourgeois' Arab parties, such as the Baath. When, for instance, some members of the DPK became alarmed in 1959 at the growth of communist influence in the country, they consulted with the leaders of the Baath Party. And it seems that even during the revolt against Kassem these links were maintained.

Like all the rulers of the Kurds, Kassem was alarmed by the dangers of the tribes confederating for war. The DPK did not worry him so much since it stressed that its approach to Kurdish autonomy and the advancement of the Kurdish people would be by legal means and not by revolution. There was no such guarantee of good behaviour from the sulking Mullah Mustafa, whose acceptance of Kassem's good intentions had turned to bitterness when he found that nothing was forthcoming in the way of the Kurdish independence for which he had fought and suffered for so long. He told me later that he considered Kassem was 'mad'; a man with whom it was impossible to make any agreement.

After the unsuccessful rebellion at Mosul in 1959 of the middle-of-the-road Colonel Shawaf (a rebellion which Kassem crushed with the aid of the communists and the Kurds), Kassem set up a politically reliable left-wing militia. Raschid Lolani, sheikh and religious leader of the Lolanis, objected to this on the grounds that they were communist and led his tribe into revolt. But Sheikh Raschid had no allies; he was opposed

4 *Colonel Akrawi* (on right) *returning from Ziwah camp*

Kurdish soldier

Mustafa Karadaghi

5 *The hospital in the cave at Cham-i-Razan*

A mixed bag of prisoners—Arabs, alleged spies and Kurdish militia

The Kurdish War

to Kurdish nationalism as represented by the Barzanis farther east and by the DPK, whom he considered were also communist. The tribe was soon driven across the frontier into Turkey, where they stayed for several months before Sheikh Raschid decided to come to terms with Kassem and sent him a secret message saying he was opposed to Kurdish nationalism and would not make any more trouble if he were allowed to return. Kassem agreed on condition that he was prepared to engage in tribal warfare to check the growing strength of the Barzanis. Lolani agreed and was given rifles, ammunition and money, as were the Zibaris, led by Mohammad Agha. The Zibaris are the southern neighbours of the Barzanis and their deadly enemies; the feud dates from before the beginning of this century. So tribal warfare, with the Barzanis as usual at the heart of it, started in 1959.

By the following year the situation had become so bad that between thirty and forty Kurdish chiefs came to Baghdad to ask Kassem to cease making trouble among the tribes and to halt the transfer of Kurdish government officials and police to places outside Kurdistan and their replacement with Arabs. They spent nearly twenty days in the capital and none of their requests was met. More bitterness was caused by the imprisonment of Kurdish nationalists and the recruitment of large numbers of spies and police informers.

At the end of 1960 Mullah Mustafa went to Moscow for three months at the invitation of the Russians. He is said to have asked the Russians to bring pressure to bear on Kassem to make him ease his campaign against the nationalists, but with no obvious results. A month after his return, in February 1961, Abbas Mahmand Agha, of the Arkou tribe—which is centred on Ranya, some forty miles north of Sulaimaniya—began to prepare for revolt. His reasons were largely opposition to land reform and new forms of taxation. He seems to have approached the DPK to see what their attitude was and the nature of the answer varies according to which side one talks to. The Arkou claim that the DPK let them down and did not come to their aid. The DPK says it made no promises and, in fact, tried to discourage them. At that time it was still pledged to legal means of obtaining self-government.

Full-scale fighting broke out on September 11, 1961, when

The Kurdish War

some 2,000 men of the Arkou attacked an Iraqi column on its way from Kirkuk to Sulaimaniya. The attack was a complete failure and the army decided to bring home the lesson to the Kurds by attacking the Barzani villages as well, although the Barzanis had not taken part in the rebellion. They had, though, mastered the régime's allies, the Zibaris and the Lolanis. The bombardment of the villages started on September 16th and the Barzanis were drawn into the fight together with some of the neighbouring tribes.

Ibrahim Ahmed had gone underground at the beginning of 1960 shortly after the murder of Sadiq Miran Osman, an important landlord and a supporter of Kassem despite his previous involvement in Nuri es Said's régime. Ibrahim Ahmed was falsely blamed for the murder. The Party's decision to stand out of the fighting was gradually changing; not only had it become the subject of increasingly repressive measures but it seemed fairly certain that the tribes would be crushed. If that happened they would be next on the list and the opportunities for Kurdish nationalism to continue the struggle would have been remote. When the Party came wholeheartedly into the struggle is not absolutely clear. It was probably a gradual involvement, with the initial decision to join the fight taken, as Ibrahim Ahmed said, in December 1961. Others, though, gave the date as the following March, and I wondered for a while later whether this was in any way connected with negotiations with Kassem's opponents, including the Baathists. There had been, Ibrahim Ahmed told me, several approaches made directly to the Party and to Mullah Mustafa; and all had been dismissed. However, after the February 1963 cease-fire, the Kurds were able to claim that they had been instrumental in the success of the *coup* and had known about it since the previous March. It was in that month that Taher Yahya, later to be Chief of Staff of the Army but then a colonel who had been dismissed by Kassem, made an approach to the DPK through a Kurdish officer. The rebels showed interest and the talks broadened to include the Baath Party, as I have said. There seems to have been some assurance that if the Kurds played their part and did not attack the army when it turned its attention to Baghdad, then they would be rewarded with autonomy and four places in the Central Government. There was no written agreement and the Baathists were later to claim that by autonomy they meant 'decentralization'. The Democratic Party were probably extremely unwise to be involved in any way in this, for Kassem's rule suited them; he did not press the war against the Kurds (he wanted it to continue because it kept the army occupied and out of Baghdad) and the army was unwilling to fight for him. Many Kurds (and all knew that a plot against him was laid) feared that his successor would be far worse and would be able to turn the concentrated force of the army and the air force against the rebels; and who could trust Arab nationalists to subtract a portion of their 'homeland' for the Kurds? Yet they had personified the result as a 'war against Kassem', not against their Arab brothers and were to some extent in a psychological trap of their own making. But at least the cease-fire enabled them to improve their political control over the rebellion, stock up with fresh arms and ammunition and get in the harvest without interruption.

We talked on until a long accumulation of tiredness made it practically impossible to absorb any more facts about a political world which seemed as strange as the landscapes and the tribal society I had just passed through. It was a new doorstep to sit on, the rooms beyond dark and curious, not altogether within the understanding of a transient journalist. If the furniture was a little scarce, then for the occupants there was room for manoeuvre, for their own subtle imaginations to grow and fill the spaces with divans, whole corridors of intrigue. Like some Parkinsonian law, machinations always grow in relation to the poverty of the region. The rich like security and openness when dealing with one another. Outside the cave in the starlight I listened to the wolves howling from above on the mountainside. From the hut below the cave entrance came a low murmur of talk. A metal bed with a mattress and blankets had been prepared for me; a bed with firm military springs that allow no undisciplined sag and trained the back like a cordon.

CHAPTER VII

In the morning a little man of about forty with a glaucous left eye and not much more than five feet tall, came and sat beside me on a green leatherette bench in the large cave and introduced himself. He was, he said, to be my interpreter on the journey north to Mullah Mustafa, which he understood I wanted to make as quickly as possible. He spoke English well and I asked him where he had learnt it. 'At Habbaniyah,' he said. 'I worked for the RAF for many years. I joined at the time of the Raschid Ali revolt in Baghdad during the war. The British took all the guns from the Arabs in the camp and gave them to the Assyrians and the Kurds, and then they killed thousands of Arabs near the camp.'

'Did you fight?' I asked. 'No. I stayed in the camp. I was very young and frightened.'

This was Amin: warily pacific, somewhat crafty at times, half-westernized, half oriental, unKurdish in his spurning of such manly virtues as carrying a rifle, Arabized in his sharp sense of humour and quickness of mind, European in his love of facts and technicalities. He wore a *klow*, the skull cap around which the turban is wound, on which had been stitched by an Arab prisoner in Arabic and Latin script: Biji Kurdu Kurdistan (Long live the Kurds and Kurdistan). For his tea he produced a large British army mug which he usually kept attached to his belt like any RAF 'erk'. He scorned the oriental habit of drinking tea in hot little glassfuls and preferred, he said, to have milk in it. Even more *evolué*, his beads consisted of a length of what looked like lavatory chain which he would play with, wrapping it round his fingers or concertinaing the links together like a trellis.

Amin was to be a rather difficult mentor, for he had a rough manner, an unobliging attitude towards the 'tribalists' of the north, whom he both despised and feared. He had just returned

The Kurdish War

from one long journey and understandably was a little weary at the thought of having to undertake another. Nevertheless, he never complained.

I walked around the camp in the morning, talking to Ibrahim Ahmed and taking photographs. Messengers bearing diminutive packets occasionally entered the headquarters, a little hot and breathless in the layers of clothing which Kurds always wear whatever they are doing and whatever the temperature. The messages, as well wrapped as their bearers, were as brief as telegrams and written in Arabic script. Everywhere I went there seemed to be a non-stop flow of them. They were the main means of sending information and orders, for the wireless system was usually reserved for less important news, since codes are easily broken. The Iraqi army relied heavily on its wireless communications, with the result that the Kurds, who had many former wireless operators among their men, were able to keep themselves well informed about the army's intentions. They claimed they could break any code within a few hours. The messengers were specially chosen for their stamina and speed. Many were extremely fast, but I dismissed as Kurdish tall stories some of their reputed feats, such as walking forty or fifty miles across the mountains in eight hours. Ahmed, Salah and I had, taking into account the twists and turns inevitable in mountain country, covered some fifty or sixty miles in twenty hours and I refused to believe anybody could have done the same journey in just over eight.

Fighting had been going on around Pinjvin, a small town on the border south-east of where we were, and the messages arriving by wireless and foot claimed that several hundred Iraqi troops had been killed for no Kurdish losses. It sounded an unbelievably high number to me, but Ahmed said that in one battle they had killed 282 soldiers for the loss of eight Kurds. In this and many other fights they had captured three-inch mortars, Russian automatic rifles, wireless sets; everything they needed for their type of war (not absolutely everything, for they had no weapons with which they could break the grip of the government's tanks on the lowlands).

Kurdish figures for government casualties are exaggerated; arithmetic, I have noticed, is not their strong point. But that the losses are high—much higher than those of the Kurds—is

The Kurdish War

indicated by the number of prisoners in Kurdish hands. In November-December 1962 these amounted to 2,000, about half of them Kurdish levies known to the partisans as *Jash,* little donkeys.

'Look,' said Ibrahim Ahmed, bringing me a copy of *Khabat,* 'here are our casualty lists for the whole war: 172 men. And no one has been taken prisoner by the enemy.'

That their losses should be low is not altogether surprising. Fighting from the edge of the mountains against badly led, not very enthusiastic or well-trained troops, a few men with rifles and plenty of ammunition can hold out indefinitely and kill many times their own number. Tanks and armoured cars are useless in the mountains and aircraft are of limited value against determined men. Sterner disciplines hold the Kurds together today than in the twenties and thirties, when quick and inexpensive victories over them could be obtained with a few bombs on the villages, a method for controlling tribesmen which was devised by Lord Trenchard, of the RAF.

I wandered round the camp, went down to the brook we had crossed on the previous night, perching my washbag on a stone. A dipper, a curiously homely bird for these parts, hopped close by, swaying characteristically backwards and forwards on a rock as it watched me with one eye. I could see why the site, which was near the large village of Malouma, had been chosen. Its approaches were narrow and easy to defend, attack over the tops of the ridges unlikely. Nearby there were villages to support it with food, although the headquarters had their own flock of goats and sheep.

The place reminded me of Greece; the air had the same brightness and spry, herbal quality. The Greeks would have made it into a shrine, to lame Hephaestus, perhaps, since there is iron in the mountain and smiths have used its caves as forges. It may become a shrine yet, of course, but with gods from a newer Olympus. There were a few bears on the mountain, but they rarely showed themselves, for when they did every rifle within reach was raised at them. Ibex, deer and wild sheep lived on the top, and there were jackals and the wolves I had heard howling. The Kurdish fauna was always difficult to identify. I was told once that there were tigers in Kurdistan, but these dwindled under cross-examination to panthers. And

The Kurdish War

on another occasion I heard of a huge, ferocious animal which not so long ago lived on Mount Karadagh; an elephant, my informant said. But since it had horns growing from the top of its head, that did not seem very likely. A suggestion that it was a wild ox was rejected, but a description of a rhinoceros tallied and this was accepted. The last one on the mountain had been shot within living memory.

On the roof of the hut outside the cave a tall man, elegantly supported on a thumbstick as if he had arrived from some rather exotic Rover moot, spoke to me in English. He had just walked in from Sulaimaniya; his English he had learnt in the course of nine years spent in a Baghdad prison following the collapse of the Mahabad Republic. His name was 'Smile', the Kurdish abbreviation for Ishmael, and his height, which Amin with his interest in statistics of any sort knew, was 6 feet 3 inches. It was a distinctive and distinguished face, with pale reserved eyes that seemed to fade away from the light. His manner was controlled and calm, and despite his long years in prison he was lithe and agile; a very remarkable person to have survived so much with such—I thought as I talked to him—obvious personal integrity. Some time later when I was looking at an East German book on the Kurds I came across a picture of him, anonymous but quite unmistakably 'Smile', with his long Kurdish face seeming even more enigmatic in those slightly puzzling surroundings.

The partisans guarding the Party's headquarters stood or squatted around on the roof, while below the cooks bent over their pots. We had potatoes for lunch. And if I make a point of this it is because when you wander in a culinary desert such as Kurdistan you begin to appreciate such things as potatoes; they are almost exotics. The poor live badly in the mountains, perhaps having meat once a week, and if the army does better (meat three times a week on average as a sort of mark of prestige and an inducement) it does so in quantity of protein rather than variety. This is not to seem ungrateful. But after a while there comes a wild desire for some frill, even if it is only a cummin seed cake or a hot sauce. Chicken one grows to detest, even the sight of them scraping about in the mud on their skinny, gristly shanks. I wished at times they would learn to fly and vanish in great clouds of brown feathers to the

The Kurdish War

mountain tops. The wolves would be glad of them. And having said that, I begin to recall, too, the brown, anxious eyes of my hosts, watching me carefully to see that I was enjoying my food, and I feel more than a little mean. Sauces are not part of the Kurdish way of life, any more than they are the British.

A mule was saddled for me after lunch and I went to put on my blue jeans and found that the cord from the top of the rucksack which I had used as a belt had gone. Good cord was short in Democratic Party circles, it seemed. But I had a belt of Argentinian leather which served as well and I was able to keep the jeans up as I walked, shaking hands as I went, down the slope to a rivulet where the mule, a plump bay, was waiting. Ahmed, the guide, said he hoped we would meet again when Kurdistan was free, and I said I hoped so and I would send him some of the photographs I had taken. Ibrahim Ahmed watched me amusedly as I clambered on, one man giving me a leg up and another holding the far stirrup, and wished me a good journey, 'Qa hafeece!' We started off west towards Cham-i-Razan, an important military headquarters. Ahead of me marched an escort of five, their rifles slung on their shoulders, and Amin in his European clothes, his grey jacket bulged out by a pistol. We climbed slowly out of Ibrahim Ahmed's valley and then down from a ridge towards agricultural land where there was the village of Malouma to the right of the track. Near the village a group of partisans were building a small depôt, digging into the hillside and diverting a brook. A hatchet-faced man who looked like a Pathan ('a madman', Amin told me) greeted the escort and me in particular with wild shouts, while the others giggled nervously as if expecting me to take offence. I was offered a bowl of muddy water and drank it more as a sign of affability than anything else. Amin would not tell me what Mr Daygal, for that was his name and Amin for some reason insisted on the prefix, was saying, but as we left with Mr Daygal still shouting after us, he told me that he was no respecter of persons and he had even heard him tell Ibrahim Ahmed: 'I will f — your mother,' a standard insult but not usually delivered to such as the Secretary-General of the Democratic Party of Kurdistan. 'And what did Ibrahim Ahmed say?' I asked. 'Oh, he laughed.'

The valley was long, bordered by a low, sharp ridge of

mountains one side and the bulkier slopes of Pira Magrun, an 8,600 foot mountain, on the other. There were many small villages and fields. Shepherds wearing long felt overcoats greeted us, the coats slung over their shoulders so that the short, stiff sleeves stuck out like those of a scarecrow. We came to the straggling town of Surdash as it was getting dark and had a sulky welcome from groups of men who stood around in the streets or on the tops of the houses looking down at us. We did not stop until we got to the far edge of the village, where we rested near a spring, the mule tugging at a thorn hedge which topped a stone wall. It struck me then, as it did later, that the partisans were not always popular with the villagers, who perhaps regarded them as peasants regard any army: as an imposition. A 10 per cent tax on their produce must have seemed heavy, particularly if they knew that the soldiers were eating meat three times a week while they had it once or less. But the army regarded itself as an élite, entitled to its minor privileges. The entrance qualifications are stiff by the standards of the country: a man with a criminal record is not eligible and only those who appear to have intelligence and courage are accepted. The Kurds have a sense of individual valour which has largely vanished from Western countries, who have learnt that the brave perish first and that in the end it does not matter very much in modern warfare whether you are cowardly or not. But the Kurds are always talking of someone or other being a brave man with lots of courage. Valour is rewarded with an extra fifty rounds to go in the soldier's bandoliers.

We moved out of the village, up a long slope, realizing when we were half way up that Salah and the youngest member of the escort, a boy of about seventeen or eighteen, were missing in the dusk behind us. We stopped and shouted until Salah called back that the boy was feeling ill and wanted to rest. I suggested sending the mule back to him, but Amin said it was better to go on. He did not seem particularly perturbed; like most Kurds he tended to regard occasional, even serious, illnesses much as a matter of course and was fairly indifferent to the illnesses of others. They were, a discovered, fairly frequent. People were always falling sick with some complaint or other and then recovering again after a day or two.

The Kurdish War

At the top of the slope we sat in the dark and called again for what seemed like ages before we heard Salah shout and then, after another ten minutes or so, appear out of the dusk with the boy, who walked stooping and holding his head. I insisted on him riding the mule and offered to take his rifle, but the others would not hear of it. His bandoliers of cartridges were shared among the escort and one carried the boy's rifle as well as his own. I was glad to walk as my knee had become stiff again and anyway it was dark. Soon we came to a rocky shelf where the boy had to dismount, as the rocks were slippery and there was a sheer drop from the ledge. 'A policeman was killed here,' said Amin. 'His horse fell over the edge with the policeman on him. There was nothing left but bits.'

We had set out late so that we could cross the road from Sulaimaniya to the Dukan Dam in the dark, when there was no likelihood of meeting an armoured patrol. As it was time for a meal we stopped in a village after many inquiries as to who was willing to feed us. Amin was a bit anxious, as he said the villages near the road were dangerous and subject to surprise raids by the army, but no one else thought there was much risk. We divided up between two families. The husband of our household had gone to Sulaimaniya to sell his tobacco, and his harassed wife scuttled about to get our meal. It was a bare, windowless room, with some threadbare carpets to sit on and a painted chest as the only furniture apart from a few covered pots. She produced bread and yoghourt and a hot mess of crushed wheat and maize which we ate with raisin syrup taken from one of the pots. The mixture was revolting. The father of the family and the eldest son returned with a string of donkeys while we were eating and the father sat opposite us, smiling a weary smile of hospitality. Trade, or really smuggling, went on as usual despite the war, for the Sulaimaniya cigarette factories needed the villagers' produce. I remembered Mr Shikak's tin of *Yaz* and produced it from my rucksack for the sake of the several pale-faced and sombre children who sat round in the pale lamplight on the other side of the room. I was going to pass the tin round, but Amin took it from me and said it was better to distribute the sweets as he did not trust them not to steal the lot. It seemed a little mean to me, since they had fed us, but I let him count out the sweets and throw them one by

The Kurdish War

one to the family, who chewed them noisily but with expressions of doubt, as if no foreigner could be relied on to produce wholesome sweets suitable for a Kurd. The sweets were very hard and brittle and Amin cut his finger breaking one.

The sick boy was still feeling very ill and I went along to see him, taking some Anadin tablets with me. He sat in a long, warm room a little apart from the others, a red band round his head which he bent over his knees, groaning slightly. I felt his forehead and decided his temperature was not very high. He complained of a bad headache in a querulous weak voice and said he also had pains in his legs, which were stiff. I thought of polio, but when Amin told me he had been swimming in the stream near the DPK headquarters, it seemed to me that he had probably nothing worse than a chill. I gave him two pills, the occupants of the house, a livelier lot than those who had entertained us, grinning as the boy swallowed them. Several pretty young girls hovered close to the wall at the end of the room, where there was a barricade of family boxes painted in colours and patterned a bit like those on canal barges and gypsy caravans. There was a discussion on whether to leave the boy in the village, but the majority decided he was well enough to come with us and that the risk of him getting worse was less than that of him being captured and shot in a surprise attack by government troops. I made him, despite his protests, ride the mule again, and we left the village to cross the road.

A little way out, we heard the sound of a horse coming towards us. With a great clicking of bolts and warning shouts to the oncomers, the leading members of the escort went swiftly forward. There were two men on foot and one, wearing a long cloak, who dismounted from his horse and spoke to me in French. He had come from Syria, he said, and was on his way to Ibrahim Ahmed's headquarters. His turban was spread wide over his head with the fringes tucked in and clear of his neck, unlike the turban style of the south. He had a gentle, rather refined expression, which remains oddly stamped on my memory as things seen by moon or starlight so often are, perhaps because of the element of mystery and the elimination of colour and detail. This man was a member of the Syrian branch of the Democratic Party on his way to a meeting of the Central Committee which—although Ibrahim

The Kurdish War

Ahmed had not mentioned it—was taking place shortly. Observers from the Persian branch also crossed into Iraq to attend it. I wondered later whether my guide, Ahmed, had in fact gone to Persia to pass on information about it rather than make the purchases (which I never saw) which were the ostensible reason for him being there.

We passed a deserted police post destroyed by the partisans. On our right I could see the bright floodlights along the top of the Dukan Dam some eight or ten miles away. It was strongly defended, but the partisans claimed that they had in any case no wish to destroy it as it was part of their 'national property'. At the road we paused slightly to make sure that there were no patrols—they were very rare, anyway—and then crossed into a small grove of trees and made our way over low country towards a nomads' camp which was supposed to be somewhere near. On a stony track we stopped to rest and smoke, the Kurds talking, while I lay on my back looking at the stars, which were exceptionally bright. Amin told me the names of some of them—he had studied astronomy and knew the Arabic names of many—and I tried to remember the English names, searching for the Plough, which at last I found, the shafts just jutting over the horizon. I felt immersed in stars; the stones of the track under me were more unseen stars, the murmuring of the Kurds no more than a cosmic burble; so content as I lay stretched out that I did not try to break the mood by talking or even moving as I felt myself getting cold. At last the Kurds got to their feet and picked up their rifles and I climbed on the mule which the boy would not ride since he claimed he got too cold sitting on it.

The nomads' camp lay in a little dip to the left of the track and we plunged over tussocky grass towards it, the dogs barking ferociously and the cattle and sheep jumping to their feet and getting swiftly out of our way; the dogs the escort swiped with their rifle butts or threw lumps of earth at. We came to the main tent, of black goats' hair, surrounded by a palisade of cane screens which, after much shouting, the owner pulled aside to ask who we were and what we wanted to get him up so late at night, for it was about midnight. We were soon welcomed in and I saw that inside the screens there was a tented enclosure around which the screens formed a sort of

The Kurdish War

narrow court. We sat down in one corner of the court under an extension of the tent top. A sick man lay close to the tent wall and sat up to grin feebly and say something to which no one replied. The owner's wife came out and turned over the ashes in the fire pit until she found some glowing embers on which she laid thorns and then blew them into flames.

She was the ruler of the roost in this little family; a sharp-faced woman with a nose as pointed as an icepick, wide-set eyes that saw everything; a Gothic face from a painting by Durer, crafty, quick and a little cruel. The children came from her mould; all looked exactly like her. Even her husband looked like her, despite the softening downiness of a white moustache. I wondered if they came from the same family and were cousins. She heated the samovar and produced bread and yoghourt and flaked cheese, but I felt the first nasty rumblings of an uneasy stomach and ate nothing beyond a little yoghourt. I leaned back on my elbows and drank my tea while the escort talked and laughed with the woman, the husband butting in occasionally. A girl of about three screamed 'Ma! Ma!' until the woman took her in her lap and fed her.

'You will never catch fleas with these people,' said Amin. 'They leave them all behind when they move.'

I asked where they were going now.

'They have been in the mountains and now they have come down here for the winter.'

Not so many years ago the Kurds were largely a nomadic people. Their vast herds and as many as 3,000 families on the move across the mountains and the plains were among the great sights of the Middle East; and among its great curses too. The Herki, the largest of the nomadic tribes, ate their way across the lands of the settled tribes like locusts, feuding as they went, particularly with the Barzanis, whose grazing was hardly enough to support their own flocks. Tobacco cultivation and the changes its introduction has brought to the tribal economies may be one reason why the nomadic tribes have tended to settle. It is a good cash crop; more profitable than sheep and goats. Another reason may be the growth of population in the mountains and with it a more miserly attitude towards the grazing lands. And anyway, it is unfashionable and 'primitive' to be a nomad these days and the pressures

The Kurdish War

which ease English gypsies from their caravans into council houses are in essence much the same in Kurdistan.

At last the escort decided to sleep and a felt mat was laid on the ground for me next to the sick man who muttered in his sleep. I wrapped myself in a blanket and gave my raincoat to Amin who curled up in it. The other members of the escort relied on their several layers of clothes.

We left next morning comparatively early after tea and more bread and yoghourt. I felt ill and my stomach was definitely troublesome. The track led across grassland that had been burnt off by the government troops, past a destroyed group of huts and down to a ford. We tried to get the mule to return on its own after it had carried one of the escort across, but it plunged off a little way down stream to a green island and began to graze. Clods of earth failed to budge it and in the end one of the men had to take off his shoes and stockings and fetch it for me to ride across; then return with it and finally cross himself with the sick boy on his back.

The river ran through a stony but quite broad and grassy valley flanked by low cliffs of limestone which held somewhere the intriguingly named 'Cave of the Ravisher'. Once we heard the whirr of a jet in a valley to our right and the sound of a bomb exploding, but otherwise it was peaceful, with men working in the fields, ploughing with mules and brown cattle. In the two villages we passed through the children came out to stare at us; pale children, the offspring of the Hamawand tribe which in its day was noted for banditry and rebellion. Nearness to the Kirkuk-Sulaimaniya road and authority gave it incentive for both.

My stomach gave way at last, and I staggered greyly towards Cham-i-Razan with diarrhoea and vomiting so frequently that it was some time before I could manage to keep down an Entero-Vioform tablet. Near the gorge of Cham-i-Razan, four of the escort, including Salah who had come with me from Persia, left us for their own villages, and I rested for a while, practising a few shots at stones with Amin's pistol. My aim was not very good; but then neither was his.

The gorge was thickly wooded, with fig trees clinging on to the limestone cliffs and trees hung with the vines of wild grapes. A squirrel ran up one flat, upended table of stone and

The Kurdish War

Salah (another Salah; it is a common name) stopped and pointed it out to me. Groups of partisans washed clothes and splashed in the stream which ran through the gorge, questioning Amin and the escort as I rode past. We came out of the wood and climbed a steep track up to a cave on the hillside, following a file of Arab and Kurdish prisoners carrying firewood. Around the cave's entrance were some fifty or so partisans who watched me as I walked up the last few yards. A man who I gathered was the adjutant of the base met me and took me to the cool back of the cave where it joined another narrower tunnel along which came the voices of men talking spasmodically to one another. The acting commander, who was on top of the mountain, would soon be down to see me, said the adjutant. I was offered a meal but refused it and asked instead whether they had any pomegranates, a request which seemed to surprise the adjutant. On the way through the gorge I had developed a sudden and hopeless desire for oranges but had switched this to pomegranates when I noticed the skins of some on the track. The adjutant said he would send off at once to the village for some, although it was a little late in the year. I told him not to worry; it was only if they had some in their stores.... But it was a question of hospitality and the adjutant was firm. A man was sent to the village. It would be several hours before I had my pomegranates but they would certainly be there by supper time.

'Do you know what the German for pomegranate is?' asked Amin.

'*Granat* something or other,' I said.

'*Granatapfel.*' He had worked with a German construction company.

I felt the next question coming; could see it in the brightness of his eyes, the terrible urge of the born brain's truster to demonstrate his knowledge. I beat him to it, similar instincts working within me: 'The word grenade comes from it.'

'Ah.' He sat back disappointed. 'It looks like a bomb, an old-fashioned bomb.'

I felt so tired and nodded so often that the adjutant offered to make up a bed for me in the quietness of one of the smaller caves. I could feel the eyes of the partisans watching me over their rice and stew lunches and braced my back

The Kurdish War

to prevent my eyes closing. The blue of the sky at the cave entrance seemed very far away and the line of squatting, eating men remote despite their curiosity. The back of the cave was cool and shadowy and I sat in a sort of trance broken by my belches and stomach rumbles.

6 *Partisans at the Democratic Party headquarters near Malouma*

On the summit of Mount Sarband

7 *Refugee children outside their cave*

Inside the cave

CHAPTER VIII

The commander of the base, Jelal Talabani, a member of the DPK's political bureau, and his second-in-command were away on a tour of the front. A few months later Talabani was to rise to greater prominence when he headed the Kurdish negotiating team which went to Baghdad after the death of Kassem. After the collapse of the talks and the resumption of the war in the summer he lived in Europe, joining the group of Kurdish exiles and expatriates who shuttle a little mysteriously between the capitals and major cities of Western Europe until recalled in the autumn of 1963.

The third in seniority at Cham-i-Razan was Mustafa Karadaghi, a large, loose-limbed and kindly man of about forty. A peaked fatigue cap a littly awry on his head, a light Russian-made automatic slung under his left armpit, he came down the cave to welcome me and apologize for his delay. Before joining the rebels some six months earlier, Karadaghi had been a member of the Iraqi diplomatic service, holding the posts of Consul at Prague (where in Kassem's leftward days there were a great many Iraqi students) and then at Lagos. It was at Lagos he decided to defect and visit London, Bonn and Rome to see if he could muster any official support in those capitals for Kurdistan. He was politely received, but nothing more. An intelligent realist, he was not surprised.

As I had gone without lunch, Karadaghi decided that he would not bother with his but would take me on a tour of the camp. I protested (thinking as much about delaying clambering up the sides of the gorge as about his stomach) that he shouldn't go without his food on my account, but he insisted and we set off. Although the prisoners were making and improving tracks, to get from one cave or hut to another meant lurching, leaning and scrabbling along the rockfaces. I was surprised how agile Karadaghi was despite his weight.

The Kurdish War

Puffing and cramped by sickness I followed him towards a much vaster cave with a whalebone curved mouth that must have been fifty or sixty feet high. A small group of men had collected to watch us as we approached, leaning on their sticks, their rifles slung over their shoulders. It struck some chord from school Bible lessons, or it may have been a recollection of a painting in the Ashmolean Museum in Oxford; David's Cave of Adullam, except that the partisan's membership standards might have excluded the debtors who followed David. The caves ran for miles. No one had ever traced them to their ends, although some of the more adventurous partisans had walked far into them. There were hieroglyphs on the walls in places and some Englishman had carved 'Sarah' on one of the smaller caves.

Behind some unroofed huts in the great cave's mouth, the cooks were still busy with their pots. Near them in the cool and comforting shadows where the cave became quite shallow sat a number of partisans drinking tea and smoking. It was these I had heard talking while I sat resting in the first cave. The partisans spent much of their time sitting around and smoking cigarettes which were smuggled out on donkeys from Sulaimaniya. With the prisoners to do the chores, they could lead a comparatively gentlemanly life; but this had its disadvantages: they were often bored. Some could go home to their villages for a spell after a month or so on duty, but for others there was little to break the monotony except the patrols. Karadaghi dispatched as many of these as he could, for he found that after a fortnight of inactivity the young men began to fight among themselves.

The caves were all about 200 feet above the stream at the bottom of the gorge; safe from attack up the gorge or from above. Aircraft would have found them difficult to bomb and practically impossible to machine gun. The only course of attack would have been from the top of the far side, but Karadaghi said that the government troops had never managed to establish themselves there or tried to send raiding parties through on surprise attacks, although they knew that the partisans had established a strong regional headquarters in the gorge. He took me to the armoury, stacked with ancient Lee-Enfields and Brnos, some of them partly dismembered, cases

The Kurdish War

of ammunition, British hand-grenades and two-inch mortars and mortar bombs.

Another small cave had been turned into a hospital in which lay the victims of skirmishes in a comparatively important battle in September when nine partisans had been killed. It was clean and the patients were cheerful, and the 'doctor', a medical student who had joined the rebels in his fourth year, said they were all doing well. He was not short of anything, he added a little proudly; they had antibiotics, analgesics and dressings. How many doctors were there among the rebels? I asked. None who was qualified, answered the student. He in fact was the nearest thing they had to one. But, he went on, in case I should think this was serious, the partisans' health was very good: they had fresh air and good water and their diet gave them all they needed to maintain sound constitutions. It was surprising how well wounds healed and the sick recovered. To prove it they perked up and had their photographs taken.

Why, I asked Amin, had no doctors joined them? There must be plenty in the towns. Amin did not know. It may possibly have been something to do with the doctors' political leanings. After the ending of the Kassem régime and the persecution of the communists by its successor, a number of doctors, Arab and Kurdish, fled to the mountains.

We walked a little way down the mountain to a ledge where some three-inch flexible piping ended beside a group of men tinkering with a small generating plant which, a label on it announced, had been made in Glasgow. Sixteen men had carried it on poles, like a potentate in his palanquin, for sixty miles over the mountains. Beside it lay a pump and the roses and pipes for showerbaths. The water would be pumped up from the chilly stream below in which they now washed and they would be able to have daily showers; one has to be tough to enjoy the amenities of partisan life.

We moved down past the commander's hut, outside which the clerk was typing a news-sheet, down to the prisoners' quarters, a cleft between the strata of the rock, with the wide slot of the entrance three-quarter walled to keep out the wind and the rain. The prisoners—alleged spies, Kurdish *Jash* and Arab troops—had finished their midday meals and were resting inside. In one grotto a barber was shaving a client and in another, larger one, sat a second group of prisoners, among them a Turkish Kurd with a green turban: a spy, said Karadaghi. The man had a crinkled, toadlike appearance, and looked as if he could have gone on sitting there for centuries, implacable and not greatly perturbed.

Karadaghi was anxious that I should miss nothing and we began to scale the side of the gorge to reach the top. We had with us as escort an ex-police sergeant of the Iraq Petroleum Company who had brought with him a water bottle and mug to keep down our thirst as we sweated our way upwards. My stomach was settling down but my mouth felt dry as a kiln. On top the hill levelled off quite smoothly into a down of long, yellow grass which had not been grazed, and was studded with clumps of thorn like stunted holly. In the distance was a huddle of small mound-like hills, marking the farthest point reached by the government tanks in their attack in September. It was near there that the nine Kurds had been killed. The partisans, said Karadaghi, had managed to destroy two tanks by digging traps, but the government troops had grown wiser and learnt to fill them in with armoured bulldozers. Below a crest nearby a detachment of partisans were digging an observation post. It was quite deep and they were putting on a flimsy roof of thin poles and branches. The winter was cold and protection had to be given to those on watch, but it looked a bit of a death trap to me: too large and inadequately covered for safety from aircraft or artillery.

It seems curious to think of the Kurds as naïve about war, but they are; and I often found myself wondering after the full-blooded renewal of the fighting in the summer of 1963 how the partisans of Cham-i-Razan were faring and hoping that the hospital in the cave was not full of their mangled and ill-defended bodies. There was nothing in the way of natural obstacles on the grassland above their caves to stop determined infantry supported by tanks and aircraft; and there was nothing in the Kurds' armoury that could help them. Nor had they much idea of what weapons were needed. They talked vaguely of anti-tank rifles, not seeming to realize that these had ceased to be effective before the last war. They talked of adopting the formations of modern armies, with sections, platoons,

The Kurdish War

companies and even battalions, yet seemed to know nothing of modern infantry tactics and had avoided creating ranks within their army by giving their leaders 'responsibilities' rather than commands; a loose and democratic system, but I wondered how it worked when the fighting was really hard.[1]

The truth was that they understood only one sort of war: the defensive war fought from the edge of the mountains against the soldiers in the plains. In that sort of fight the tribesman with his rifle was the master of the day. The government forces impelled forward by authority's need to assert itself or perish, advanced, were shot down and finally the remnants retreated to lick their wounds in well-fortified camps. But how to follow up this initial victory was something the Kurds did not know. They talked about spreading the war from the mountains to first Arbil and then Kirkuk, both of which they claimed to control at night. After that would come the liberation of Sulaimaniya, which was theirs most of the time already, despite the government forces camped in and around it. In the winter of 1962 they were already bringing out prisoners and killing those whom they considered traitors. Some fifty men had been executed, most of them in Sulaimaniya. 'You have only to name someone in Sulaimaniya and we will bring him out to you,' Ibrahim Ahmed had said. But while to move into the cities would have shown their power, it might also have led to reprisals; the cutting off of food and other supplies and the bombing of the cities by aircraft. Would they be justified in exposing the people to this and might not the reaction among the people be against rather than for them?

The Kurds are not a ruthless people, despite their reputation. In their tradition wars have always been fought for gain. When the losses grew too heavy, then the fighting ceased;

[1] The rebels were in fact forced out of Cham-i-Razan in the late autumn of 1963 by a well-organized government attack. It was retaken in November but whether as a result of a counter-attack or because of the withdrawal of a division to Baghdad is not clear. Shortly afterward, in December, the rebels started to form several battalions (they had by this time about seventy Kurdish army officers including a brigadier serving with them), and established a 'military academy' near Mahvout to train platoon commanders. They also decided to have officer ranks rather than 'responsibilities' in the rebel army. Their weakness in the face of tanks was remedied to some extent by the purchase of bazookas.

The Kurdish War

when the loot had been divided, then the tribesmen returned to their villages. A certain element of this thinking remained in the Kurds' revolutionary army. What was the point of destroying valuable property to win a war? That way you won nothing but ashes and ruins. They applied that reasoning to the Iraq Petroleum Company, combining with it an almost genteel desire not to offend Western shareholders. The West had to be *persuaded* that their cause was a good one, not blackmailed into pressing for a settlement. But when they did change their tactics and blew up a few lengths of pipelines they were not very successful; their skill with explosives was poor and the most vital and vulnerable source of the country's wealth was hardly affected. Even the raids on the Ain Zallah oilfields near the Turkish and Syrian borders did not involve the wholesale destruction which might have been expected: a few policemen killed, some buildings burnt down and an English official kidnapped for a tour of rebel territory.

I walked with Karadaghi along the top of the ridge and was surprised to learn that he was not a member of the party; nor were many of those who accepted its control over some 75 per cent of an army which I estimated at between 8,000 and 12,000 men. No exact figure was ever given to me and it is quite possible the commanders did not know how many men they had.

To our left lay Kirkuk; to our right the ground sloped away from the ridge towards the low, tawny hills and the plains of the Arbil *liwa*. Ahead of us, quite exposed on the hilltop, was a wireless station, its aerial strung between two high poles. Outside a bunker covered with earth and vaguely camouflaged with sprigs of thorn sat the operator, tapping away in morse on his key. Nothing of much consequence seemed to be happening, although there was a fairly steady stream of messages coming in and going out. All messages were sent in morse because it was clearer, could be coded easily and also sent over a greater radius than voice signals. Inside the bunker the sides were stacked with captured Russian, British and American sets. The operator preferred, he said, the American.

Karadaghi had mentioned that while he was in London he had inquired about buying a radio station and found that it was possible to get hold of a powerful secondhand transmitter. The Kurds had for some time been anxious to buy one so that they could broadcast to their own people and also let the outside world know what they were doing. He asked whether I would be prepared to help and I said I would certainly be prepared to make inquiries in London about price and availability, but how he would move it into Kurdistan I did not know. It seemed to me that there were enormous technical problems in the way of operating a transmitter even if they could get into their territory; the absence of skilled technicians and generating plant capable of high voltage being first among them. But Karadaghi thought it could be done. I suggested that it might be better if they had a number of small transmitters with limited range but which could be operated by batteries and carried around on mules. Eventually the Kurds did get a quite powerful transmitter into the country at an estimated cost of £5,000 including bribes. It was never very successful and when I revisited Iraqi Kurdistan in December 1963 it was not working.

They were all immensely proud of their camp and Karadaghi insisted that I should enjoy its amenities to the full and have a bath before supper. And if I handed over my khaki shirt and underwear, he would see that they were washed for me by a prisoner. It was dusk when the bath was ready and I was led along the side of the gorge to a cave with an entrance about eight feet high—the one in which Karadaghi had said someone had written in English the name 'Sarah'. The water was being heated over a roaring fire in a great witches' cauldron, the flames leaping up white against its smoky blackness. A Kurdish prisoner in a khaki greatcoat too big for him ladled the water into a large dish some six inches deep, placed beside it an open-topped oilcan full of cold water and left without looking at me. I cooled the water to a bearable temperature and then sat in it. The far side of the gorge was vanishing in the dark and a prowling jackal howled. I thought that I would have looked very strange indeed to anyone who came along the far side: a pale man seated cross-legged in a bath beside a fire in a uterine cave called Sarah; a seldom seen ceremony of rebirth perhaps. It was warm and lulling; from outside came the quiet voices of Amin and a sentry who had

The Kurdish War

been sent to see that I was not shot by a patrolling Arab while I was at my most vulnerable.

Supper, for which in the spirit of things I wore a clean white shirt, was in the commander's hut. A peppery broth had been prepared to guard me against ill-effects from bathing in hot water. Amin told me that he preferred cold water as he believed hot baths to be dangerous; they brought on fevers. He would wash in the river later. Bathing, in fact, was always surrounded with slightly Victorian ritual. One had to be guarded against after-effects, kept warm inside and out and usually the bather had a sleep afterwards.

Apart from Karadaghi, his clerk, Amin and myself, there were at supper a teacher, a judge and the medical student. The three last were all young; none, I should have thought, more than twenty-four, and all spoke some English and read it quite well. The last became obvious when I gave them a copy of a *New Statesman* article on the Kurds which I had brought thinking that it would show that their cause was not entirely unknown in Britain. The medical student looked up suddenly when they were half-way through and shook his head sadly. Rereading it rapidly, I had not noticed that it described Ibrahim Ahmed as a communist who had been dismissed from the Secretary-Generalship of the Democratic Party. It was a curious mistake, the source of which was to be revealed more clearly later on. Karadaghi thought, however, that suitably amended it would be suitable for reproduction in his news-sheets and on behalf of the editor of the *New Statesman* and its author, Mr Roelofsma, whom I had met, I gave him permission. I doubted whether they would expect payment in dinars.

They were all mild and curiously attentive people, like other similarly educated Kurds I have met in Europe; a little diffident and cautious, feeling their way forward through half-familiar situations, learning and always aware of their own nationality; usually politely withdrawn as if measuring themselves against you and discovering in the process their own identities and the points which mark them off from others. Karadaghi, for all his modesty, was a clever and successful man who had given up his career to join the fight. He had lived in America, had graduated in economics at the University

The Kurdish War

of California and had many friends in the United States, but as a country it held few attractions for him and he had no wish to live there again. Nor, having spent so many years in the clock-powered societies of America and Europe, had he any wish to see a version of them introduced into Kurdistan. There were many virtues in their own society, he thought, and he hoped it would remain predominantly an agricultural one. The question of economic viability, which is inevitably raised whenever Kurdish autonomy or independence is discussed, was not, he thought, of major importance. The country was largely self-supporting, admittedly at a fairly low level but richer than most of the rest of Iraq. His attitude was undoctrinaire and hopeful. Problems should be dealt with as they appeared.

The teacher, the judge and the medical student sat together opposite me. The teacher thought I was brave to come to Kurdistan and asked me what I thought of the *pishmurga*. It was a new word to me and I asked what it meant. Ah! they said in surprise, wondering why I did not know the Kurdish word for patriot, or literally, one who sheds his blood for his country. They were all *pishmurga*, or prepared to be. Why, then, did not the United Nations or Britain and the Western powers help them? Were they not fighting against a colonial power, like many other races which had received outside support? They seemed to have no friends. I tried to explain that the United Nations could not intervene in the internal affairs of a nation which had not asked it to do so; and there was little that Britain could do, even if she wanted to. But they were not convinced by all this.

The judge, who wore a dark brown, almost chocolate-coloured uniform, with a Sam Browne strapped across it, talked less than the others, perhaps because his English was less ready. He had a circuit and dealt mainly with land and grazing disputes in the villages. He was kept busy, he said, although crime seemed to be more a matter these days for village and tribal leaders. Whole areas had, with the collapse of the central government's authority, gone back to tribal law. Murders were cancelled out by blood money and intermarriage between the families concerned, although in the case of repeated murder or banditry the culprit was executed. The situation was remedied in the south in 1963-64 by establishing proper courts and a civil administration.

We had almost come to the end of supper when the clerk, who had arranged it, produced his triumph: the pomegranates. He almost quivered with nervous pride as he produced them: ox-blood fruits split to show their rows of ruby seeds. They were delicious, better than any pomegranates I had ever tasted in Europe.

The teacher, the judge and the medical student excused themselves early so that I could go to bed as I was a bit worn after my sickness. I slept dreamlessly and in the morning woke to the transistor playing morning music and found the clerk lighting a fire in the centre of the room, over which he warmed my clean shirt and underpants before handing them to me.

We set off at mid-morning in the direction of Bettwahta, another important headquarters over halfway towards Mullah Mustafa's main stamping ground. The escort was a strong one of six men. Karadaghi, with his gift for public relations, had hoped to provide six men armed with British Lee-Enfields, but it had not been possible. I had told him not to worry as I was not chauvinistic about my escort's arms. He walked a little way down the gorge with me, my horse being led ahead of us on the slippery track. The prisoners drew aside to let us pass, except for the Turkish spy in his green turban who came forward to make sure that Karadaghi saw his polite salute. Whenever people ask doubtfully about the ability of the Kurds to run their own country, I think of men like Karadaghi with their calm and humane commonsense and wonder where you would find better people.

We left Cham-i-Razan and entered an even steeper gorge with a broad and deep stream at the bottom that ran to the Lesser Zab. On the far side from our track, on the top of high cliffs, was the ancient city of Julindi. 'Look,' said Amin, 'there is the king's chair and there is his gate.' From below one could see a square entrance in the reddish rock on the crest and what looked like a wall. The Medes, I believe, built a fortress town in this easily defendable spot; as had a later Kurdish emir his castle a few miles farther on, but right beside the stream into which the stones had tumbled. It had been a substantial build-

The Kurdish War

ing, much grander than anything built by the mountain Kurds these days.

The stream below us was a pale, glacial green on which myriads of little fish lay motionless like fallen willow leaves. I have never seen so many fish. I could see no sign of the brushwood and wicker fish-traps one finds in the bigger rivers and I wondered whether the refugees living in caves by the water's edge caught them to supplement their diet.

Once an Iraqi army helicopter flew across the gorge a mile ahead of us on its way to Ranya or the Dukan Dam. Someone was apprehensive lest its crew had seen us and called up fighters, but it seemed unlikely and we went on, crossing a smelly sulphurous stream that came out of the rocks and made its way through bamboo thickets, until we emerged from the gorge and rested under a tree on the smooth, grassy top.

It was so smooth that I even managed to canter the horse briefly across a hollow when we continued on our way to the Lesser Zab. I stopped the horse on the crest of the final ridge before the hills dipped down to Arbil. It was a fine and empty view yellowed by the sunlight like old paper; I turned and rocked back to Amin and the escort who, looking neither to right or left, were marching rhythmically on, heads slightly bent, moving at the fast, soft-treading Kurdish pace of about three miles an hour. The saddle was vastly uncomfortable, even though I followed Kurdish style and hooped my legs round it like a cycle clip, throwing my knees out at right-angles. I handed the horse over when we came down to the Lesser Zab and watched the man who cantered it through the tobacco fields posting comfortably in the saddle, his main purchase on the animal coming from his calves. The ex-sergeant of the IPC understood my explanation of the differences in saddles and style and nodded sympathetically.

The Lesser Zab looked black and unkind, although there was agricultural land on its bank; it was treeless land without any luxuriousness even on the edges of the river itself. We came down to where a ferry wire stretched across the stream which was a hundred or so yards across and shouted for the ferryman. A small village lay a quarter of a mile away on the far side and soon he and an assistant came and pulled themselves across to us on a raft of planks and tin cans. The assistant took the horse down to a point where it could ford the river, plunging and straining its head and neck up to keep clear of the water, which swirled about it quite fast. The water was good, according to Amin, and I washed and cleaned my teeth in it (thinking I should drink it anyway in the village) while I waited for the raft to go back and fetch the rest of the party. A man with a donkey wanted to cross to the side we had just come from and the ferryman and the owner pushed and heaved the animal on, forcing it to lie on its side so that it could be tied down safely.

My horse was brought to me by the assistant, a big, dour man, who galloped it across the stony ground and dismounted like a Cossack to hand it over with a flourish of the reins. I decided to enter the village in style and raced it up to the tawdry walls, shouting my *salaam alekums* to unsmiling and anxious-looking villagers who murmured polite *Berkherbeys*.

We were entertained in the fly-ridden upstairs room of a farmhouse, the owner and the village leaders sitting in a deferential huddle near the door opposite Amin and myself. Amin and one of the escort, a burly, quick-witted young man nicknamed Castro because he had once grown a beard, held court. They were the only two members of the Democratic Party and therefore assumed a sort of seniority. The villagers asked what they should do to escape bombing. There seemed to be no solution offered apart from taking to the fields. Amin launched into what sounded like a eulogy of the party and the villagers' eyes became more and more glazed. It was not the first time I was to see evidence of a weary retirement when faced by the warriors. What was in it for them? Nothing very much in a material sense; possibly nothing at all. Nationalist wars were fought by the proud, the brave and the ambitious to vindicate and preserve themselves; for aesthetic reasons which may have their roots in glory and produce exotic flowers but butter no buns.

I was glad to leave the depressing upstairs room and ride out on a broad track which led through bare fields in which men ploughed with cattle and donkeys. White ibises flew along the black course of the Lesser Zab and autumn crocuses that had somehow escaped the feet of men and animals grew

The Kurdish War

in the track. I thought, with only vague appropriateness, of Soane's translation from the Kurdish:

> From out the turf, the narcissus seems like a scar
> Upon the ground of winter—who still has not passed far.

More prosaically, I asked Amin whether they used the autumn crocus bulbs to make saffron for dyeing and flavouring. 'No.' But there was a bulb of some sort which they ate in the north. It sounded much the same as the English earth-nut.

We marched obliquely away from the river towards a range of mountains. The river sank lower into its valley below us until I could see the town of Taqtaq lying beside it some ten or twelve miles away. Soon, an hour or so before dark, we came to a substantial village dominated by a ruined Turkish fort on a mound and riding up the steep main street were met by a group of villagers who unlike those at the last village seemed glad to see us. The ex-sergeant, who had taken me under his wing, led me to a pleasant house owned by an old man; a well-built and cheerful house with a courtyard full of fowl and a balcony outside the main room. The householder's wife played a part in looking after us. Cheerful, one-toothed, and with all but one eye, the tip of her nose and her mouth hidden by her baggy headdress, she raked the fire into life, popped glowing wood into the samovar and made tea; and later, with much cheerful but unaimed and unprovoked cackling laughter, brought a large supper of the inevitable rice and rubbery chicken.

CHAPTER IX

We turned even more directly north towards the mountain range the following morning. Speckled grey and brown birds perched on rocks and clods of mud and watched us pass. Once the ex-sergeant cadged some large white radishes from a farmer who was taking them in a donkey cart from his fields to a village. He cut them into segments and shared them out; they had a bitter, turnipy taste. After only a few days on a diet of mainly rice and chicken I longed for vegetables and fruit, and when the ex-sergeant found some small yellow berries lying among the gravestones under a large tree I gathered a pocketful and chewed them throughout the day. They were *qansum* berries, said Amin. The flesh was sour and refreshing; the pip, according to Amin, was eaten by women to improve their hair.

A deep gully formed by flood water from the ridge of the mountains crossed the plain towards the Lesser Zab and we turned up it into a ravine that became a pass. Donkeys slithering and lurching almost to their knees under loads of faggots came down blindly, forcing us to jump out of their way. Near the top of the pass was a branch headquarters of the partisans, unseen despite the bareness of the mountain until we suddenly came on a party of *Jash* widening the track under the supervision of two guards. The prisoners wore a British type of battledress and had crossed rifle badges in their berets. The post consisted mainly of a small cave with a narrow entrance and a scooped out hollow in the rock which commanded the track. They had made a smooth and comfortable terrace with a low parapet of rocks over which I could see the town of Koi Sanjaq, the farthest point reached by the Turks in 1922 when they drove south of their present border and struggled with the British for possession of the Mosul *Vilayet*, drawing some of the tribes to their support with promises of self-government but facing hostility from others who had suffered

The Kurdish War

too much under their rule to trust them again. I borrowed the commander's field-glasses and looked at the town's grey police fort.

The police no longer bothered them, he said; did not try to prevent smuggling or the movement of armed men. In the evening the town became theirs. How much they had achieved! Last winter they were on the ridge behind, on the other side of the road from Koi Sanjaq to Ranya and now here they were, only thirty miles west of Arbil.

How long was it, I asked, since a convoy had passed along the road to the garrison at Ranya? Two months, he said. Everything had to reach the police by helicopter. The police fort on the road, which I would see when I crossed the ridge, had stayed untaken only because they lacked heavy weapons to breach the stone walls. Their prisoners had been captured while trying to return by convoy from Ranya for leave. I looked across at their quarters under some projecting rocks. The weekend cases which they had brought with them were stacked neatly together. I wondered why they did not try to escape when they were so near to Koi Sanjaq where they could surely seek refuge with the police; but the commander said they would have no chance of crossing the plain unnoticed. Someone would spot them and pop! that would be the end of another little donkey. He despised them and trusted them less than he would an Arab. For a Kurdish traitor he had no time at all.

Amin and Castro laughed as he said this. They knew of two traitors who had had their ears and noses cut off. And when they went back to their villages the villagers asked:

'But what has happened to your nose?'

'I have had an accident.'

'And your ears? What has happened to them? Were they lost in the accident too?'

A hated police chief was shot down in a Sulaimaniya street by two small boys and another man had his throat cut during a festival when he was embraced by his killer. Amin showed me how it was done: the killer placed his hands at arms length on the other's shoulders and then, with a snatch, drew a knife from the folds of his waist-sash and sliced it across the man's throat.

The Kurdish War

'Would you kill someone if the party ordered you to?' I asked Amin.

'Believe me, Mr Adamson, I could not kill anyone.' He looked at me sideways, embarrassed and not quite sure whether I would take this as a confession of weakness or as evidence of his humanity.

Was I a good shot? the commander asked. I shrugged my shoulders modestly. It was about fifteen years since I had fired a rifle at the Royal Marine small arms school at Browndown, near Gosport. The commander handed me a Brno that looked as long and felt as heavy as a Brown Bess.

'Mind the kick,' said Amin anxiously. He did not really like guns.

I aimed at a rock on top of a ridge, snatched the trigger and saw no dust from my bullet.

'A very powerful rifle,' I said, patting the stock and hoping that was all.

But the commander looked sly and said he would like me to aim at a mark which he chose. There was a small white blaze on a rock some 200 yards away. Perhaps I would have a shot at that.

I fired and saw my bullet hit the rock six feet low and left. The commander laughed cheerfully. I tried again and through the glasses saw I was about three feet nearer.

The commander laughed even louder and tried with the rifle, which was his, missing the blaze by about a foot.

Castro fired with his Brno carbine, missing by about the same distance.

I had been defeated by their saddlery, but I refused to be defeated by their rifles, and I asked for a Lee-Enfield. One of the snub-nosed 1914-18 variety was brought and I knelt like a figure from the front rank of a thin red line. Dreadful things were done to the sights of rifles by the Kurds. Adjustable peep-sights were removed and replaced by locally manufactured ones and sometimes the whole foresight and muzzle of the gun was altered to give it a more handsome appearance, like that of the much admired Brno. I steadied the rifle as well as I could, carefully took the first pressure of the trigger and fired, hitting the mark exactly.

'That's enough, I think,' said Amin, looking towards Koi

The Kurdish War

Sanjaq and half expecting a detachment to come pouring out of the town towards us. The commander looked a little sour, as if by hitting the mark I had trespassed into an exclusively Kurdish domain.

I had taken a number of photographs, trusting to the semi-automation of the 35 mm. camera to make up for what I lacked in skill. But disaster came near when I opened the camera to change the film and found that the used one had slipped when I tried to roll it back, exposing some of the shots. Amin, who had worked as a photographer, seized the camera from me and took it to the cave, which had a narrow entrance and was dark. It was very hot and apparently stayed that way throughout the year, never becoming cool enough to sleep in. With the camera under his jacket he worked blind to roll the film and then place it in the metal container. I did not expect many shots to be saved, but, thanks to Amin, only a very few were lost.

We left the cave to sit on the terrace overlooking Koi Sanjaq and found a newcomer had arrived from Bettwahta, where we were going, bearing the news that there was a foreign prisoner there. A Belgian, he thought, but he was not sure.

We waited until almost dusk before we left as there was a slight element of risk in crossing the road on the other side of the ridge in the daylight. Armoured patrols occasionally moved along it. The ridge of the mountain was surprisingly wet, with marshy springs which in winter must have erupted into torrents to pour down the ravine past the partisans' outpost. The far side was steep and I got off the horse, thinking that I would rest it, for despite the hours spent at the outpost it was jaded. But Castro, after leading it for a while and asking whether I would ride, jumped into the saddle. There were patches of high grass and thickets of small trees and bushes on this, the lusher side, of the mountain. Flocks of sheep grazed over it and once, seeing something grey slink through the bushes on our left I thought I had spotted a wolf and shouted out, sending Castro trotting off, his rifle held across his saddle bow. But it turned out to be only a shepherd dog getting out of our way without barking, which was unusual.

There was no sign of life at the police post mentioned by

the commander and we turned left on the metalled road in the valley and walked casually along it in the brilliant dusk. There were ruined cars and lorries, one of which had belonged to Castro, and burnt out houses. No one seemed to live by the road any longer and only once did we see any lights, those of a village some quarter or half a mile back.

The night was so cold and clear that I decided to continue walking rather than freeze and get bored on the horse. Castro, Amin had told me, was famed as a walker; so had Amin been in the days before the fever debilitated him. They prided themselves on what they called the 'Partisans' walk', keeping up a fast four to five miles an hour for long periods. Castro dismounted to stretch his limbs and I kept up with him, a tall man with a stride far longer than mine. We swopped words:

Arom, to walk; *mang* (or *mon* according to others), the moon; *estera*, star; *asman*, sky; exclaiming in surprise to one another at the similarity of our words. Did *arom* and roam come from the same stem? And *estera*, so like the Spanish *estrella*.

We waited for the others at a point where the road began to swing more abruptly towards Koi Sanjaq and then turned away north in pitch black, for the sky had suddenly clouded, over extremely rocky ground, losing the way repeatedly and spreading out over the ground searching for the trail and often only keeping in touch by shouting or hearing the horse as it stumbled and snorted. We found the path in the end, no more than a slight paleness twisting through a cleft down to a ford in a wide but shallow stream. We splashed through it and after a few minutes of argument about the way set off westward. There was, said Amin, a *chai-khaneh* on the road for which we were heading, but no one knew whether the proprietor was still in business. Before long we saw the glow and flicker of a large bonfire and found as we got closer that it was burning on the verandah of the *chai-khaneh*, the flames leaping up to the wooden roof. An abandoned steam-roller leaned dangerously into a ditch on the far side of the road and from inside the building came the sound of someone tearing up

The Kurdish War

seats and woodwork for the bonfire. Beside the fire stood a man with calm, oriental features—not so uncommon in Kurdistan where the Mongol invaders spread their seed liberally among the widowed and unwidowed Kurdish women. He wore his double-breasted blue tunic buttoned up to the neck and, curiously, had no headdress of any sort. It was an intelligent face, watchful and subtle; elsewhere, perhaps, that of a renegade seminarist who had discovered himself too successful as devil's advocate. To me, since the character of its owner had no bearing on my affairs, it was merely an interesting face which seemed to have been shaped by influences and pressures outside the run of Kurdish experience, but in the escort it caused suspicion and distrust. Amin questioned him, warming his hands while he looked at him obliquely, his voice careful, and the rest of the escort stared non-committally into the fire. The man who had been tearing away at the woodwork inside came out with an arm-load which he threw on to the fire. We stood beside the bareheaded one and watched the small flames spread across it like yellow lichen until they broke into high, leaping tongues.

Our group moved off down the road away from Koi Sanjaq taking the two men with us and was soon overtaken by a large party of villagers returning with their mules and donkeys from the town. The mules were hurrying home, heads down and striding, despite their loads, and after them the donkeys trotted like worried children. A woman in a cape rode in the middle, laughing and shouting in a high pitched voice whenever her donkey broke into a fast trot, bumping her loosely in the saddle. I walked, finding the fast movement of the animals and the bulky loads brushing against me oddly exciting and stimulating. It was very dark and the villagers seemed not to see me, but talked across and around me, the men moving fast to keep up with the animals, all bound together by the common desire to get home.

The escort, thwarted of their tea at the abandoned *chaikhaneh*, decided to turn off to a village beyond a little meadow. The first building was a large and substantial farmhouse with a tractor standing in front of it. Beside, but detached from it, was a storehouse with a room above to which we were taken, a little grudgingly, I thought, by the owner, who then had to leave us in the cold by the door for several minutes while he went to look for the key. Inside, when we had lit the oil lamps, I saw that the room was presided over by a large picture of General Kassem, no patron saint of ours, but oddly no one mentioned it to the owner or even joked about it much among themselves. It made them uneasy, not angry. In other civil wars, men have been shot for having the wrong photograph on their walls. The two men were questioned by Amin and Castro and answered with much polite use of the comradely *kaka*, or big brother. They produced papers deferentially, the bareheaded one's delicately sensual mouth twisted at the corners by anxiety despite his impassivity. There was something about the manner of Amin and Castro that irritated me: a bit bullying and arrogant. There was nothing to prove that they were spies: one was going to see his cousin, the other his brother-in-law; the bareheaded one was different and aroused their suspicions but nineteen times out of twenty suspicions are baseless.

Amin eventually and rather grudgingly decided they could go and with many more polite and grateful remarks the two men left rapidly before they had had time to drink more than one glass of tea. A meal of sorts was brought to us, of bread and yoghourt and cheese for there was no time for anything more elaborate. And if there had been, I wondered whether it would have been very willingly given. In the no-man's land close to the roads people were naturally guarded about their commitments, and here, under the patronage of Kassem's smile, the rebels' writ did not run very strong.

We left for another and safer village well off the road where we could sleep in safety. It was past midnight and the village slept until the dogs heard us cross the stream and then came out to bark and howl as we stumbled through the soft steaminess of a large dunghill towards a hut which served as the headquarters of the local branch of the Democratic Party. There were five men sleeping there and they left their warm quilts, rubbing their eyes and groping for their rifles, to fetch us tea and food before joining their no doubt grateful wives. The escort, with the usual Kurdish unwillingness to go to bed, sat up and talked and slopped yoghourt on to bread. Amin urged me to lie down and sleep but in a mood of sulkiness and

The Kurdish War

irritation which embarrassed them, I refused until they made signs of settling down. 'If you sit up, then so shall I,' I said and immediately felt like a bad-mannered child.

In the morning as I washed in a runnel under a plum tree, Amin said the villagers knew of the prisoners at Bettwahta. They had seen him riding a mule a few days before. Why he was a prisoner, they did not know, but we imagined he had been captured in a raid near a city.

A long, wedge-shaped valley pointed towards Mount Sarband where Bettwahta was. It looked from the village in the clear morning air as if it would be only a short march, but the hours and the valley stretched on. Villages huddled like muddy landslips at the foot of the mountain ridges. It was an area which had completely passed into Kurdish control; the large police post on the north side of the valley had been abandoned. A buzzard came down from the mountains to search for snakes and mice and one of the escort aimed at it as it perched on a bank. The bullet sent up a spray of dust from below its feet and it flapped off back to the mountains.

We reached Bettwahta after three hours, our party having strung out so that we extended for about half a mile. A herd of horses grazed in a green-rock-bordered paddock beside a stream which came rushing down the mountainside through the village itself. It was a handsome place, with well-built two-storeyed houses of stone, some of them badly damaged by cannon fire. There seemed to be no tracks through it, and we made our way up the stream bed and across walls, hedges and fields of tobacco until we came to a narrow path on top of the bank of a water-course above the fields.

The Bettwahta base lay in the grey dolomite rocks of a shallow gorge that plunged into a high and ragged mountain. Fruit trees grew among the fields that had wedged themselves into the gorge and the place had a pleasant and calm air. The headquarters hut was a long one-storeyed mud building with two rooms side by side and pointed, almost Gothic windows. The deputy commander (for once again the first- and second-in-command were away) had a fierce, Mongolian face that did not match his grave and courteous manner. I had only just been ushered into the hut and, buttressed with cushions, seated myself for tea, when a young man in European dress was

The Kurdish War

brought in. I thought at first he was the 'Belgian', but he looked very dark and he told me in excellent English that he was an Arab, Adnan Ismail, a geologist, who with an Englishman, Frank Gosling, of the Iraq Petroleum Company, and three others, Arabs and an Assyrian, had been captured in the hills between Kirkuk and the Tigris by a Kurdish patrol and then brought to Bettwahta. The Kurds, with comparatively few ways of making their successes and their case known to the outside world, believed that by taking the odd European on an enforced tour of their strongholds they would at least occasionally make an appearance in the headlines. A few months earlier they had captured another Englishman at the oilfield of Ain Zallah, near the Syrian border, and kept him for five weeks. Why they had also taken prisoner on this latest occasion the Arab geologist and the three others I could not understand, but presumably they thought it best not to let them spread a warning of what had happened before they got Gosling safely behind the 'lines'.

Gosling, who came in shortly afterwards, was a large, blond and patiently good-humoured man of thirty-eight. He looked the worse for wear after his trip by jeep and on mule back across the mountains, with five or six days' growth of beard and lips that had been cracked by fatigue and a changed diet. He seemed vague and rather cut-off in manner, but this I found was because he suffered from deafness. He had been well treated and it was stressed to him continually that he was the Kurds' guest, not their prisoner. They had agreed to take a letter to his wife at their house near Kirkuk, he told me, but it might take some time to deliver, might never be delivered (it wasn't) and she would worry. 'I shall be back in half an hour,' he had told his wife before his disappearance. It would have been lamb cutlets for dinner.

I asked the deputy commander whether it would be possible to take Gosling with me and see him across the Persian frontier, but he said he was unable to authorize this without permission from Mullah Mustafa, who wanted to talk to him. It was rumoured that the leader would soon be coming south and would pass through Bettwahta. Although it was obvious that Gosling would not be kept for more than five or six weeks, it annoyed me that he was kept there at all. It would

The Kurdish War

have been easy enough for a wireless message or a courier to have been sent to Mullah Mustafa asking whether he could go with me, but there is a certain rigidity in the Kurdish character, and besides, a few weeks meant nothing to them and, as I was to find out for myself later, the difference between 'guest' and detainee is a loose one. I found it disturbing that one of my own nationality should be held a virtual prisoner, a position which carried the undertone that he came from a hostile nation.

All I could do was promise Gosling that I would do my best when I saw Mullah Mustafa and urge him to let him go as soon as possible. We walked round the base together, looking at caves which housed stores, a cobbler and even a white horse, his head deep in a nose bag. Where the wall of the gorge began to turn away to face the plain there were a number of caves which refugees had taken over, stacking them with boxes and tins and sacks. The women were difficult to photograph, either turning their heads away and pulling down their headdresses, or running away and giggling, but the base's storekeeper, a fat man in a modish suede jacket, managed to persuade them to stay still and not hide their faces; and after a while they were confident enough to look at the camera and pose to be photographed while they carded wool and made bread.

Gosling, who is a knowledgeable photographer, discovered how to adjust the camera to the right ASA number, a technicality which had defeated Amin and me, and one more problem was overcome. All that I needed now was the right sort of film, for the film I had bought in London was low speed and not the high speed sort which everyone told me I should have.

It was obvious that there were very many fewer men drifting around the Bettwahta base doing nothing than there were at the other places I had visited. Fighting had been going on, near Shoqlawah, twenty miles north-east of Arbil and on the road to the Persian frontier. The town had considerable importance as a military base for the Iraqi army and also because it guarded the way to Arbil, the first on the rebels' list of three major towns which they were considering moving into in the spring.

The Kurdish War

The commander of the base, Omar 'Dababa' Mustafa, another member of the Political Bureau, was near Rowanduz talking to Mullah Mustafa, and the battle was in the hands of his second-in-command, who returned later that evening, pale and fatigued. They had killed twenty *Jash* and taken twelve new Russian rifles for the loss of three partisans in one of the small but bloody skirmishes which characterized the war. He apologized for not being able to talk for longer but he had to discuss plans in private with his staff.

What with returning troops, my escort and the prisoners, the room in which we all slept that night was crowded. 'A Blackpool landlady couldn't do better in Wakes Week,' said Gosling, a Lancashireman, as we crammed ourselves in. It was stuffy and I was glad to get up before it was fully daylight and walk down to where I had noticed water pouring down from a pipe into the irrigation stream. One of the partisans who was up followed me, whether to protect me from possible attack or because he thought that I too was some sort of prisoner, I was not sure.

I splashed in the chilly water and attempted to shave and then gave up. Other partisans came and slapped water on themselves nearby as it grew lighter, and Amin appeared and sat smoking on a rock. A brown land crab scuttled along the rocks. They never ate them, said Amin, knowing my interest in questions of that sort. Why he did not know, but perhaps it was because of the off-putting colour.

The Mongolian-looking Kurd who had been in charge of the base when I arrived had shaken his head rebukingly over Gosling's growth of beard, which he seemed to feel was some sort of protest against his detention and thus a rebuke to Kurdish hospitality. So I lent my razor and shaving brush to Gosling who obligingly shaved himself clean. He had had a kidney operation a few weeks before his capture, complained of pains now and was obviously worried lest the trouble flare up again. I did not depress him further by telling him there was not one doctor in the whole rebel territory. He suffered later not from kidney trouble but from a serious attack of dysentry which struck him just before he crossed the frontier into Persia.

It was doubtful whether anyone knew for certain what had

The Kurdish War

happened to Gosling's party after it disappeared (nothing definite was in fact known in Kirkuk) and I promised Gosling that I would let his wife and the Iraq Petroleum Company know he was safe, if I got out before he did. I took down, too, the name of his driver and those of the Arab geologist and the other two men, who worked for a British firm of irrigation engineers, whose London office did not seem to have even heard of the men's disappearance when I rang them.

I felt particularly sorry for the Arab geologist who feared that he would be imprisoned by the secret police when he was released for no reason other than he had spent some time in Kurdish hands and was therefore of doubtful loyalty. He opposed Kassem, he said, but not actively. 'But then almost everyone would like to see him gone.'

I said goodbye to my escort from Cham-i-Razan and they padded off in their rubber-soled moccasins without looking back: the Kurds never looked back after they had said their goodbyes, I had noticed. Perhaps like the Greeks they considered it unlucky to do so. The animal which was to carry me to Mullah Mustafa was slow in arriving and I stood with Gosling in the bright sunlight and discussed whether Iraqi Kurdistan really possessed the mineral riches the Kurds were so sure lay under their feet. There were the main oilfields, of course, but not everyone agreed that these were in Kurdistan. Gosling did not think there was very much else, although dolomite rocks, like those around us, were often associated with oil. Otherwise, there were the staples of their economy, such as tobacco and their flocks; and one day perhaps they might develop a tourist trade and grow more fruit and vegetables in their well-watered valleys.

The Mongolian-looking deputy gave me an anemone with grave oriental courtesy, and I pushed the stem through the mesh of my sweater and wore it like a button-hole. A mule arrived at last, dispelling hopes of one of the sleek horses I had seen in the meadow on the edge of the village. It was a russet, immensely lanky and half-starved animal, obviously the most dispensable animal in the village. I clambered on to its stirrupless, straw-filled saddle, said again to Gosling that I would ask for his immediate release and set off up the mountain with Amin and one guide. The animal seemed as tall as a camel.

The mountain was higher and bigger than it looked from the gorge and the trail twisted up and up, from false crest to false crest. On the far side of a ravine *Jash* prisoners were working on an improved, broadened trail. It was an exhausting climb for Amin on foot and a taxing one for the frail mule, on which I sat enjoying the bright sunlight which created deep pits and splashes of shadow around the grey pinnacles of of dolomite. Between the rocks were scrubby bushes and clumps of *ghewun*, the gum Arabic plant, around which flocks of sheep and black goats chewed their way under guard of yellow dogs and vacant-eyed shepherd boys. It took us two and a half hours to reach the summit, from which, as we came under the final crest, we heard the sound of a rifle. It turned out to be a returning patrol practising with a new Russian rifle, making the target, a red and white Barzani turban, fly into the air. We waited with them until our escort, which had followed us, caught up at the top. Among them was another of the fair-haired strain of Kurd, this one so gingery and blue-eyed that he might have been a Scot and his name Hamish instead of Hamid. They are very proud of this survival of ancient genes (which crop up among other Asian mountain races; the Pathans, for instance) and say it fortifies their claim to kinship with Europeans. It is, I suppose, a Bronze Age streak, a reminder of some submerged, forgotten race which unlike its Hellenic twin has (so far as I am aware) left no myths.

We moved through spectacular mountain country, more savage and difficult than any I had seen so far. I could understand why the Iraqi army had been unable to break the Barzani and other tribesmen, into whose feudal region we were now entering. Behind us lay Mount Sarband, its 'frontier'; ahead, slightly to the left, Betarkhan, and on our right front Bardarhesh and Beramga, all of them about 8,000 feet high, the tops a wilderness on which the Kurds went only in search of ibex and wild goats. The game was seldom seen from below, said Amin; once he had photographed two deer coupling in the mountains near Sulaimaniya.

We lunched in a pretty village with huge walnut trees

The Kurdish War

growing over the lanes and beside the fields; then climbed towards the cliffs edging the south-eastern face of Mount Betarkhan. A black donkey watched us pass; a stray perhaps, for it brayed and brayed sorrowfully until as if it could stand solitude no longer, it ran away down the mountainside towards the village, bucking its heels in the air as it went.

It was warm climbing down the mountain in the afternoon and we looked forward thirstily to a spring in a tussocky re-entrant, but the water was too slimy and stagnant for me and several of the escort, though some drank it, and we pressed on to a second spring a few miles farther on. This was clear and fell from some mossy rocks into a little pool, with an ancient wooden ladle beside it. After I had drunk I sat down to smoke a cigarette and saw coming up the track from the valley a party of men moving fast. Two were on horseback, the first a bulky man who smothered his white horse. This, said Amin, was Omar 'Dababa' Mustafa, the commander of the Bettwahta base, Mullah Mustafa's military heir apparent, and an important member of the Democratic Party. He had a strong, formidably vigorous face and a direct manner; spoke some English and was able to tell me more than anyone else so far about the government forces disposed against the Kurds, but when I asked him what forces the Kurds had, he refused to answer, giving me a direct, rather quizzical look as if he was a little puzzled by me.

'We heard that you were coming,' he said, but did not say how. I presumed at the time that they had received a wireless message over their own communications system or a courier had brought a message.

Omar 'Dababa' was in a hurry which may have been connected with the meeting of the Central Committee. This, I imagine, was the subject of his visit to Mullah Mustafa, who was soon to start moving south himself.

A lawyer who had practised in Baghdad, Omar 'Dababa' had earned the nickname 'Dababa', or 'Tank', in his student days. During a riot after the war, when a large group of rioting students were chased through the streets of Baghdad by tanks, he leapt on one of the tanks and killed the driver. Looking at him, I felt a twinge of sympathy for the tank driver.

Omar 'Dababa', I noticed, carried a camera and I explained

The Kurdish War

to him my problems over film. He could solve that, he said, and walking over to his horse he untied a large case and brought out from the bottom of it two rolls of German high-speed film. I offered him low-speed ones as replacements, but he declined them, although I imagine film was not very easy to obtain despite efficient smuggling. He had to hurry on to get back over the mountain into Bettwahta before dark and mounting his horse he rode off at a fast pace, his men striding along behind him.

Obviously a considerable amount of military as well as other traffic used the trail and it surprised me that the government troops did not place ambushes or try to control it from the air. Rowanduz and the big military camp of Ziwah were not far away on the other side of the mountain, and reasonably enterprising patrols could have made their way across unseen. The army sent out patrols occasionally, but they were never very determined and were usually content with a hit-and-run raid on a village. Aircraft, too, bombed and machine-gunned, but even these raids were less frequent than they had been and some suggested that they were running out of ammunition as neither Britain, nor anyone else, was anxious to supply Kassem. We were caught by the darkness as we came to the top of a ridge where we searched for the trail, which was lost among small stones; then, finding it again, walked along the ridge before descending among the large boulders of what looked like a torrent bed. My rickety mule suddenly slipped on a boulder, lurched forward and pitched me over its head on to the stones. I curled up as I fell and got away with a mildly bruised arm. But I had enough of riding and decided to walk, leaving the animal to the escort, who bickered among themselves in a tired, dispirited way over who should ride. We travelled for a few more hours through woods of sizeable trees before we came to a large, straggling village. Beside a stream was a mosque where we were to spend the night. A fire burned under its high porch and the flames reflected on a table-load of large medicine bottles as mysterious and unconvincing as those in an old-fashioned pharmacist's. Above them was pinned a coloured print of Mohammad's birthplace at Mecca.

CHAPTER X

The mosque was used as a hospital and patients and staff were asleep when we entered. I wondered whether anyone would question an infidel sleeping in a mosque, but the mullah had long since gone from the village and no one seemed to have any religious objections to me. The orderly in charge of the hospital rose wearily from his blankets and ordered yoghourt and bread, and a large tea chest of walnuts was brought out and the shells cracked with a little hammer. We sat close to the stove in the light of an oil lamp which threw enough light to show that the roof was supported on large wooden supports in two lines like the columns of a nave, but I could see little more. Even in daylight it was difficult to see, for the shutters on the windows were kept closed.

The orderly drooped beside the stove but answered questions. There were, unseen in the darkness near the wall, seven sick and wounded. Typhoid was the main health problem; which didn't surprise me, as the Kurds were never very careful where they drew their drinking water from. I asked him how he managed with the seriously wounded, and he said that if they were seriously wounded they usually died on the way to hospital, since there were no roads and it was a slow and exhausting journey over mule trails. If they were alive when they reached him they were usually going to live anyway. Contradicting the medical student at Cham-i-Razan, he said they were short of antibiotics and some drugs.

The patients were very quiet during the night, although once I woke to see the orderly and a helper, who held an oil lamp, bending over a restless man.

The weather changed and it was grey and drizzly in the morning, making it impossible to see the mountains. Amin said that the winter was really starting and soon the snow would fall heavily and the villages become cut off and isolated

The Kurdish War

in their valleys. When the mist cleared and the clouds rose I would see that the snow had come farther down the mountains. It was December 5th and the worst weather would soon be on us.

I splashed out into the middle of the stream and washed myself from a stone, telling Amin, who asked how typhoid was caught, that he should fear poison in standing water. It was a fast, thigh-deep stream, quite broad in parts; a stream to delight a trout fisherman's heart.

On the porch a group of walking wounded, including a little boy with a bandaged arm, sat round the fire drinking tea. A large cardboard box on the table with the medicine jars and bottles contained hundreds of packets of Ex-lax, but I could not think that purgatives were much needed in these hectic parts. Inside—the sick lying so still that I wondered if some had died—the orderly and his assistant were doing their rounds, dressing a gaping thigh wound caused by a bomb or shell splinter. I wished that I had used my imagination and brought some penicillin with me.

The walk to reach the hamlet where Mullah Mustafa was staying was a short one. The track followed the stream and then edged a slim and sloping way round a shoulder of a narrow gorge. Beyond was agricultural land backed by Mount Karokh, whose plateau top was covered (for the clouds were lifting and one could see) with thick snow.

We were welcomed at the hamlet by a grave, pleasant man who spoke limited English with an excellent and educated accent. He had learnt English, he said, while serving as a soldier under British officers. We sat in the upstairs room of a large hut, one corner of which, between the stove and the door, was occupied by an old man of eighty. It was very stuffy and after first sitting in the favoured place at the back, I moved closer to the door where there was a slight draught to shift the heat and stale air.

Amin said that Mullah Mustafa was somewhere near, perhaps in the same hamlet. A young man who spoke broken French came and sat beside me and asked who I was. He was very good-looking, with a long face, large brown eyes and a manner that I found too smooth and ingratiating. I was reserved with him in my answers to his questions and he empha-

The Kurdish War

sized that he had been sent by Mullah Mustafa to find out who I was. Kak' Mohammad showed no resentment of my slightly hostile manner then or later; I only once saw him ruffled. He was a person of considerable shrewdness and control; friendless but admired in a way. Like Ishmael in Istanbul, he had a political face of the sort that sets vibrating every nerve in a secret policeman's body. And I was not surprised to learn that he was wanted, under various names, by the police of three countries. The Democratic Party also wanted to get their hands on him, for he was alleged to have embezzled 500 dinars given to him to set up in Persia a printing press which somehow never materialized. 'The party would shoot him if they got their hands on him,' Amin confided, but with exaggeration, I hope. In fairness to Kak' Mohammad, all the time I was with Mullah Mustafa, and later, he was unfailingly kind and helpful.

I had expected, following the protocol-free ways of the party strongholds, that I would at least be taken in and introduced to Mullah Mustafa, even if he was too busy to talk to me at length. But I was told he would not send for me before the evening, and even that seemed a bit doubtful.

The rain drizzled sullenly outside and small creatures ran through the open brushwood of the roof, dislodging bits of twig and mud. Two men of about forty came inside to shelter, one of them carrying a brief-case as well as the inevitable Brno rifle. They were both former officers of the Iraq army who had deserted and attached themselves to Mullah Mustafa, one a major and the other a colonel, Assiz Akrawi, who six months earlier had left his unit south of Baghdad and made a dangerous journey across the country to join the rebels. His wife and a baby he had never seen were imprisoned in the capital as a reprisal and a deterrent to other would-be deserters. As Akrawi had trained in Britain and Russia and held commands in Iraq, he was a natural choice as field commander for the rebels in the Rowanduz area. His task was a difficult one since there was no real military organization among the tribal units, nor had they all that much inclination to be welded into the revolutionary army with sections, platoons and so on similar to those of the Democratic Party. Another problem was that the new structure cut across the men's tribal affiliations; nor was there any established headquarters for their commanders to work from.

The Kurdish War

The nucleus of Mullah Mustafa's forces were some fifty or so Barzani tribesmen who moved with him from one village or group of huts to the next to avoid the government's bombers and forces. The government had tried hard to kill Mullah Mustafa, and he, remembering how the RAF had broken up previous rebellions by air bombardment, had a great, perhaps excessive, respect for aircraft.

Akrawi told me that he had tried to get the tribesmen to accept the principle of company attack, in which a third of the force provides heavy covering fire while the rest move in on the enemy. But this had been unacceptable.

'No,' said the tribesmen, 'either we all go into the attack together or not at all.'

Fighting a defensive war on their own terms, their methods had been remarkably successful. They would hold a ridge against infantry attack until the aircraft came in low to bomb and gun them. Then they would retire from the ridge, leaving look-outs who would call the rest back to the top when the aircraft had finished and the infantry had begun to struggle up the mountain again. From the top the Kurds would pour in fire at close range; extremely heavy casualties were inflicted on the government troops by very small groups of Kurds before the army, too weary and lacking in enthusiasm to think up new tactics, decided it was better to stay in their fortified camps.

I would have thought that Akrawi with his military background would have found it difficult to fit himself to the unmethodical ways of the tribesmen. But he seemed to have grasped that in this army there was no such thing as an order; everything had to be done by consent. He had too, I suppose, to prove himself a better man. And this may have explained why whereas the tribesmen, like all Kurds, kept their chests covered with layer upon layer of jackets, shirts and pullovers, he never wore more than a khaki shirt beneath his bandolier. He had to learn to withstand the cold and the weather, he explained. But I saw him looking cold and shivering on several occasions and I hoped he did not catch pneumonia before his stamina had reached the right level.

The owner of the huts—the man who had learnt his English in the army—was well known as a successful shot and hunter, and we lunched on partridges. Afterwards, as the afternoon

The Kurdish War

dragged on, Kak' Mohammad took me for a walk a few hundred yards outside the hamlet, where there was a small encampment; a shallow cave screened by bushes. This was the temporary home of Abbas Mahmand, *agha* of the Arkou tribe, and the one who at Ranya, some forty miles south, had in September 1961 touched off the revolt. He was a big St Bernard of a man, six feet three or four inches tall, with red, watery eyes, unsmiling, and his face and jaw wrapped round as if he suffered from toothache. He had little to say, and when I asked him about the start of the war he looked at me suspiciously and said that all questions of that nature should be put to the leader. I was uncovering zones of sensitivity about which I knew little, I realized, and I was treading clumsily; so that a question on the relations between the Democratic Party and himself made him even more uncommunicative. We were about to lapse into Kurdish dourness when a plump young man in brown costume held by a black *pishten*, or waist-sash, at the middle and with a brown *klow* that looked a bit like a fez (so that he might have been some relic of the Ottoman Empire, a pasha stranded by the outgoing tide) interrupted eloquently to say that whatever their affiliations, tribal or political, they were fighting for their rights as Kurds. They were all soldiers of the Kurdish people.

'Ah,' said Amin, relieved, 'this man has the right answer.'

Abbas Mahmand was very proud of his son Swahrah (which means knight) who was only twelve but carried a Brno taller than his shoulders as well as a bandolier, and insisted that I take a photograph of him; and as I did so a solitary man on a white horse rode in: Hamsah Agha, chief of the Manghor. He turned his horse obediently for me to photograph him, its feet feeling delicately for the stones as he held its head high. His forebear, also Hamsah Agha, had allied himself with Sheikh Ubeidullah in the great Kurdish revolt against the Persians in 1880. With the sheikh he had ridden as far as Maragegh and shared in his victories until the revolt had collapsed at Rezaieh. He was killed in an ambush at Mahabad, that ill-omened town for Kurdish rebels. To see the present Hamsah Agha here, not far from Rowanduz, was certainly proof that some of the tribal leaders from across the frontier were giving the Iraqi Kurds assistance, for though the Manghor spread into Iraq they are usually regarded as Persian Kurds. There were, I found, quite a number of Kurds from the Persian side who had slipped across the frontier to fight, as the French-speaking Kak' Mohammad had done. The 'Persian heroes' was Amin's derisory term for them.

My summons to Mullah Mustafa came when it was dark, after much waiting and to-ing and fro-ing by Kak' Mohammad. His hut was very close, less than a hundred yards away, and he sat at the end of it, one arm resting on a cushion like a packed kitbag. He rose stiffly to shake hands with me and waited patiently standing while I returned to the door to take off my shoes, having forgotten to do so when I entered. A fierce walnut-coloured man of fifty-nine, with straight black eyebrows that almost met across an eagle's bill of a nose; a tough, obstinate old warrior who might or might not have much heart left in him after so much campaigning and struggling. He stood with his head a little on one side, smiling a rather forbidding smile that was both quizzical and defensively mocking. His shirt and jacket were open at the top, showing hairs thick and black as a horse's tail on his barrel of a chest. His trousers were in the Barzani style, wide and bell-bottomed as a Victorian sailor's, and covered his feet. He wore, like all of them, a bandolier, and his Brno rifle was propped in a corner within reach. Right beside him was his transistor radio, its aerial extended. Once that evening he listened to Baghdad Radio and on other occasions to the BBC Arabic Service, Israel, the Persian and Russian Kurdish programmes and news broadcasts from various Arab countries.

The room was quite full: there were Mullah Mustafa's two bodyguards who went with him from Mahabad to Russia and never leave him now, Col. Akrawi, Kak' Mohammad, an ex-police inspector who was the chief wireless operator (and spoke good English) and various others. There were no courteous inquiries from Mullah Mustafa about my health or my journey, but I gathered that that was his way. A whetstone was on the floor in front of him and he took out a small penknife and began to sharpen the larger of the two blades. The ex-police inspector said they knew that I was coming because they had picked up a coded Iraqi army message sent urgently from Pinjwin, in the south, to the Ministry of the Interior in Bagh-

The Kurdish War

dad, saying an American journalist with two men in the employ of the Persian Government had crossed the border. It seemed obvious that news about me had trickled down to Pinjwin from one of the villages I had stopped at on the Iraqi side and that the two men were the guides Ahmed and Salah. I explained through Amin, and Mullah Mustafa listened, nodding, his head bent well down over his whetstone.

Since there seemed to be no room for an exchange of pleasantries, I asked him a few questions about the war and how it was going, and he replied non-committally without looking at me; so I turned to what he meant by autonomy for Kurdistan, a subject on which I felt he would have to answer directly and could also be more closely questioned.

He envisaged, he said, a Kurdistan which would take one-third of Iraq's oil revenues—a share proportionate to Kurdistan's population—and a similar share of the seats in a new assembly in Baghdad. Local government, the region's own finances and development and education would be in the hands of the government of the autonomous state, as would be the police and her own defence forces. The central government's powers, it seemed, would be limited to foreign policy.

What would happen, I asked, if the central government wanted to move troops across Kurdistan either to defend its own borders or to help a neighbour and the Kurdish regional government was not in agreement?

'They would have to get our permission,' he said.

I said that I thought that what he was proposing sounded to me more like independence than autonomy. What did he see as the difference between the two things?

I gained a quick look for my bluntness; he evaded the question and repeated that what they wanted was autonomy.

If it came about that there was a Kurdish government with powers of the sort he had described, would it not, I asked, provide a stimulus to Kurds in the neighbouring countries to revolt, either to set up their own autonomous states or to join the Iraqi Kurds? If so, would he encourage or discourage them?

I had phrased the question a little too carefully as I guessed it would be one which would be judged delicate, and Amin, who was flustered and nervous, did not appear to understand

The Kurdish War

precisely what I was saying. The ex-inspector, however, did, and from now on I relied on him to interpret, since he understood the political content of what I was saying better than did Amin, who for all his sharpness was not very good on these matters.

The leader (he did not like, I was told, being called 'General') raised himself straight from his whetstone. His mouth stretched out wide over his perfect, white teeth and his back was very straight for a man of fifty-nine. He spoke very firmly, almost angrily, nodding his eagle's bill first at the inspector and then at me, as if we were mountaineers who had come too close to his nest. He was living in Iraq. They were living in Turkey, Persia, Syria, Russia. What did he mean to them or they to him? He had no interest whatsoever in them. How had they helped him or the Iraqi Kurds in their struggle? They had done nothing except smuggle.

That seemed to me a little ungrateful, since I had seen the chief of the Manghor ride into camp that morning, but I questioned him on his reaction to 'Mr Medes'' remark in Istanbul that when Mullah Mustafa had established himself, then the Turkish Kurds would consider whether they should rise.

'That is their affair,' he said. 'I cannot stop them.'

He had nodded his head so emphatically that his red and white Barzani turban, which in the style of his people he wore piled thick and high like a dowager's hat instead of loose and floppy in the way of the Sulaimaniya and other Kurds, had slipped forward over his eyes. There is no reason to think that he does not mean what he says when he claims that he has no interest in the Kurds outside Iraq, for he is no great idealist and his main loyalties are to the Barzanis and his family. But in the light of the little I knew at that time, it seemed to me he was being dishonest or at best evasive. For as the President of the Democratic Party of Kurdistan, he must have known that his party had links with Kurds in the neighbouring countries; must have met them at times since the war began.

I put this to him and he said sullenly, getting down to his penknife sharpening again: 'I am not the President of the Democratic Party.'

This seemed so odd and surprising that I checked that what he had said had been translated correctly. The inspector and

The Kurdish War

Kak' Mohammad grinned while Amin looked uneasy, his mouth screwed up and his glaucous eye seeming to swivel uncontrollably. But the interpreter was correct.

How, I asked, feeling thoroughly lost, could the misunderstanding have arisen?

'I was forced to become President by Kassem.'

Then it seemed very odd that Ibrahim Ahmed and others at the Democratic Party of Kurdistan's headquarters should have referred certain questions on future policy to 'our President'? Why should they have done this if he was not President?

'Because they are too lazy to take responsibility themselves.'

At that rate, then, he no longer considered himself leader of the Iraqi Kurds, much less President of the Kurdistan Democratic Party? He thought about this for a few seconds before saying, again without answering directly, that he was not necessarily against the policy of the party; he was not against any party which worked for the people's interests. He was only against those who sought to injure the Kurdish people. It seemed to me fairly obvious that he included Ibrahim Ahmed and the rest of the leadership of the party in this last category. I skirted round the personalities and asked him a loose question on his view of the policies of the party.

The translation was unclear, which may well have been a reflection of Mullah Mustafa's original Kurdish, but the gist was that the party had yet to show that it was working for the people. They had not proved that they could shoulder the responsibility of the nation.

What did they have to do to show they were, in his view, working in the interests of the nation? Would land reform, for instance, be in its interests?

That must be left to the will of the people.

What were his views then as, presumably, the leader of the Iraqi Kurds, on what constituted the interests of the people?

He was not the leader of the revolution, merely the expression of the will of the people. It began to seem that it was not an eagle on its nest that I was interviewing but a Delphic Cheshire cat. Surely, I said, hurrying up a few clichés to save the day, he was at least the physical embodiment of the people's aspirations, their hunger after liberty and the right to express and identify themselves as Kurds?

The Kurdish War

The translation came back ponderously: 'I am not the body of the revolution. The body and the brain of the revolution is the people. It is their blood which is splashed across the mountains.'

He summoned up dinner at this point and we settled down silently to eating. He ate very fast and had finished and was washing his hands and rinsing his mouth before any of the rest was more than two-thirds through.

I wondered whether he found me a terrible bore, continually thinking up tiresome questions. He seemed a weary, enclosed man, for all his vigour.

I rinsed and washed away the grease of yet another chicken supper and dutifully got back into my stride. What lessons had he learnt from the collapse of the Mahabad Republic? I had asked Ibrahim Ahmed the same question and I thought it would be interesting to compare answers.

'That there are a great many cowards in this world.'

I told him that people said he was a communist because he had gone to Russia after the collapse of the Mahabad Republic. He laughed sourly and said that people would apply labels whatever one did. 'I had an invitation to come to England, from Mr Churchill, but I preferred the Russian invitation.'

For a moment I was not quite sure whether he was joking or referring to some real invitation, for although 1947 was during Mr Attlee's premiership, Mullah Mustafa had been in close touch with the British in Tehran before the fall of the republic and it was just possible some sort of qualified asylum had been offered. But it was a joke and he was looking at me and smiling because I had taken him seriously.

Since it was the lack of support from the tribal chiefs that had been one of the main reasons why the Mahabad Republic had folded so suddenly, I asked him about the start of the present rebellion and which tribes supported him, but he refused point-blank to discuss it.

It seemed that his whole attitude was one of calculated evasion and I could not see why he should so clumsily and without apology refuse a question of this sort. So I sat staring angrily at the quilt under my crossed legs, temporarily out of questions. A long pause followed until I said to Amin that perhaps it would be as well if we went, as Mullah Mustafa was

The Kurdish War

probably tired and obviously unwilling to answer me directly.

But Amin said nervously that it was not yet time to go; these things always took a long time. I had noticed that Mullah Mustafa himself had looked faintly perturbed by my reactions and I wondered whether I was not being stupid, misjudging an oriental need for circumlocution and indirectness; mistaking diffidence and lack of confidence and knowledge of the outside world for rudeness. So we stayed and there was an easing of the atmosphere. I smoked my way through a pile of Kurdish cigarettes that had been placed in front of me and questioned more inconsequentially. He depended a lot on the opposition among the Arabs to Kassem, who now, he said (quite accurately, as was made clear three months later when Kassem was killed), stood alone without friends. But nevertheless the Kurdish position was not strong, although they had driven the enemy back and often defeated them. They had no heavy weapons of any sort. Who would let him have them?

It seemed tactless to answer 'no one' and I asked him whether the absence of anti-tank weapons would prevent him moving into Arbil or Kirkuk in the spring? He thought it would be wrong to try and move forward before they had managed to take places like Rowanduz. They should move step by step.

We had sat and talked together for over two hours and he was still sharpening his penknife. By this time he had moved on to the small blade. The intensity with which he sharpened was alarmingly purposeful, as if he had some minor but especially enjoyable execution in mind. He put great pressure on the blade against the whetstone and bent his whole body over it. He would pause only to straighten and look at me, or to blow a finished cigarette from his foot-long cane holder into the hearth and light a new one. It seemed as good a time as any to ask for the release of Gosling, but the request merely produced some boisterous good humour. This was a case where I was at a disadvantage and he could show his powers and also make me feel uncomfortable.

Mr Gosling could spend Christmas with him. Why should we not all have Christmas together? It would be very pleasant and we would have turkey. They had lots of turkeys in Kurdistan (they have, and they are extremely tough).

The Kurdish War

I countered feebly by saying that Christmas trees were necessary to make me feel I was really enjoying Christmas.

Ha! he said, really enjoying himself. They had lots of Christmas trees farther north; and Amin, who had seen Christmas trees and jolly, drunken Christmas routs at Habbaniyah base, nodded wisely in agreement. It began to seem like one of those ambassadorial cocktail parties in Moscow where Mr Khrushchev suddenly arrives to deliver a few intimidating jokes that strike ambassadors between the eyes as gently as cannon balls.

With desperate whimsicality—for I felt that, like Mr Khrushchev, he tended to find his jokes a good idea after a bit of reflection—I said there were, alas, no reindeer to bring the presents which I should undoubtedly feel were Mullah Mustafa's due. Even Amin did not know what reindeer were and the idea of a deer drawing a sledge carrying parcels was beyond their grasp. So I brought the subject back to seriousness and said that really there was not much to be gained by capturing odd Britons and making them walk all over the country when they would rather be at home. Instead of doing the Kurdish cause good it might make people think they were nothing but a lot of bandits.

But Mullah Mustafa shook his head and said dourly: 'Let him spend Christmas with us.' It was, I gathered from Akrawi, the first British prisoner who had given him the idea that Christmas was a great and unmissable Anglo-Saxon festival. He had shown great despondency over the prospect of having to spend his Yuletide in a mud hut with a festive Mullah Mustafa.

What were my plans? asked the leader. I said I would like to go tomorrow and have a look at the 'front line' and the government camp at Ziwah, near Rowanduz; the day after that I would like to talk to him again; and on the next day I should like to leave. I apologized for my haste and explained that I had taken five weeks to get into Iraqi-Kurdistan and it was obviously my duty to get out as quickly as I could and report on what was happening. He nodded and said it would be all right for me to go to Ziwah; and Akrawi got out some British army maps of the district and we planned the trip.

Akrawi, who had more knowledge of the outside world and its ways than the rest of those in the hut, was obliquely sympa-

The Kurdish War

thetic with me in my difficulties with Mullah Mustafa. 'A great Kurdish leader but not a politician,' he said.

My new English walking shoes had given out on the mountains and the soles were coming away from the uppers. I had thought that there were bound to be some spare ones in the stores or possibly a shoemaker in Wartey, the village where we had slept in the mosque. I had rather set my heart on a pair of comfortable moccasins. But there appeared to be no stores, no shoemaker and no one had even a second pair of shoes to lend me. In the end, one of Mullah Mustafa's 'gorillas' whose feet were about the same size as mine offered to let me have his galoshes. They were very thin-soled and split on one side, but they were better than nothing; and while I wore them my own shoes could be taken to the small town of Gallala and repaired.

I must have spent three hours with the leader and I got up to go. 'Why have you come here?' asked the inspector.

His tone was not unfriendly but I was surprised. 'To report for my paper.'

'I think you have come here to look for Mr Gosling.' I laughed and pointed out that I had not known of Mr Gosling's capture until I was well into Iraq, and anyway I would hardly have come all the way I had for that. But ludicrous or not, the inspector's remarks made me feel uneasy as they seemed to voice a certain suspicion. That this existed was, I think, due in large part to the mere fact I was British. The British, who had done so much behind the scenes at the time of the Mahabad Republic, were the only European power in CENTO, who had such a stake in Iraq which was once their protectorate, would sooner or later send someone into Kurdistan to find out what was happening; and lo! here he was! He might seem to be a reporter, but that wouldn't prevent him being an agent (and, in the light of the Philby scandal, it certainly would not). The British were always up to this sort of thing, pretending to be one thing while actually being another.

I asked Amin as we settled down on our quilts in the hut whether he, a good party man, had been surprised by Mullah Mustafa's denial of the presidency. No, not altogether, he said. He would tell Ibrahim Ahmed all about it when he got back. He had been uneasy and ill-mannered all day since we had arrived and made it plain that he disliked the strong air of feudalism and old-thinking that hung over Mullah Mustafa's retinue, muttering about 'these *aghas*'; an urban sparrow among tattered hawks. They to him were men who owned all the land and made men work for nothing.

It was a dreadful night. A battalion of fleas, carefree in a world without DDT, marched on their bellies over me. The old man near the door muttered in a curiously vibrant voice, a sort of broken alto, and every hour or so got up either to relieve himself outside or to stoke a fire that was already so hot that it had parched my mouth and throat to the texture of tinsel.

CHAPTER XI

My shoes were taken by one of Abbas Mahmand's men, who trudged off across the wet hills to Gallala in a belted overcoat. I was indebted to the *agha* again for the loan of a dark bay horse which, like all the Kurdish horses in my experience, walked at only three-quarters of a marching speed and had to be continually kicked and lashed to make him keep up. Amin had decided to stay in the hamlet as he saw no point in spending an exhausting day on the mountains where his services as an interpreter would not be needed, since both Colonel Akrawi and Kak' Mohammad would be with me. He had an old soldier's distaste for anything which unnecessarily took him away from his billets.

We followed the river until we came to a clumsy bridge of logs which, leaving the horse behind us, we scrambled across. Mustafa Agha, whose men manned the outposts I was going to see, came out of a group of huts to greet us, apologizing that they were not better furnished. He had a pointed face of squirrel-like brightness and was eager to ask and answer questions; and this I found pleasant, since politeness and pride so often in Kurdish circles limited genuine curiosity about one another. Not far from Mustafa Agha's huts we joined a jeep track which had been abandoned at the beginning of the rebellion, with the fist-sized stones still uncovered, and followed it until we reached the main road: Tabriz and Tehran to our right; Damascus, Aleppo and Beirut to our left. The British had made the section we were on, between Arbil and the Persian frontier, in 1928-32, metalling and re-contouring the old caravan trail which followed the Rowanduz river through the mountains. They had in mind its strategic importance as a link between Mesopotamia and the north of Persia, its usefulness as a means of opening up a difficult bit of rebellious Kurdistan and also trade. For the Iraqi Government

The Kurdish War

and the Kurds its strategic importance has been that it cuts Iraqi Kurdistan in half; so, much of the fighting has been on its length. For the government it proved a trap because of the difficulty of keeping open communications with the forward troops. The steep mountains on either side provide safe cover for ambushes by the Kurds in the type of fighting they like best. Troops and police on the high and comparatively flat uplands around Ryat, on the Persian frontier, were forced to surrender when neither relief nor supplies could reach them. Parachute drops of ammunition and food drifted into Kurdish hands; and troops who attempted to fight their way through along the road and the mountain tops were shot down in hundreds before they gave up and decided to withdraw to the safety of Ziwah camp, near Rowanduz.

The building of the road has been described by Mr A. M. Hamilton in his book *Road Through Kurdistan*. Mr Hamilton would be shocked to see his road today: fine metal bridges hang awry from their foundations and are impassable to vehicles, and his road is pitted with bomb and shell holes and much of the rest of it littered with fallen rocks from the mountainsides as well as the barriers built by the Kurds against armoured cars and tanks.

We crossed a skew-whiff bridge and turned along a narrow track at the top of which it became too steep for the horse, and I left it cropping the bushes. Above us was a cave where men were roasting goat's meat skewered on twigs. They shot most of their meat in the mountains and there was usually a man out on the mountain tops looking for wild goat or ibex. The outpost we were going to was on the very top of a peak of just over 5,000 feet not far away, and we started to climb up a long and wearying re-entrant. By the time we reached a saddle which joined it with another and higher peak I was drenched with sweat. There were two ways to continue the journey to the top, said the tough Akrawi. I could take a zig-zag track which would take me to a ridge which provided a comparatively gentle approach to the top, or I could climb straight up, the way he intended to go. Empires have stood or fallen on choices of that sort. We all went straight up; men old enough to be my father setting a pace that I—and, I suspected, Akrawi too—found killing. On the top the tribes-

The Kurdish War

men had built two stone sangars and naturally, being Kurds, they had lit a fire in a hollow on the sheltered side of the top. From the sangars I could see the whole of the Ziwah camp: neat rows of white tents spread out in the misty greyness of the day like some old photograph of the Crimean War. In the heart of the camp were the stationary trucks and tanks. And far out, surrounded by low stone walls, were the white tents of outposts. I looked through a tribesman's glasses and saw no signs of anyone moving. Only the top of one khaki beret.

'Do they ever send out patrols?' I asked Akrawi.

He wished they would, but they never moved out. 'No one wants to die for Kassem.'

He hoped to cut the road into the camp farther down as the snow fell; and in fact he did cut it a week later. His principle was attack, always attack, he said. It did not appear to have been the principle of other Kurdish field commanders; the camp's calm and lack of concealment looked almost smug. Cutting and clearing the road to Ziwah kept both sides busy during 1963, the Kurds falling back under heavy shellfire at one stage and then (according to their representatives in Europe) advancing to control it again.

I asked Akrawi whether he had been in touch with any of the officers in the camp. Presumably he was known to many of them.

'That would be telling,' he said mysteriously.

There may have been some sort of gentleman's agreement on that part of the front too, the Kurds doing their best to strangle the camp but avoiding unnecessary bloodshed. After Colonel Aref's régime had begun to make things too hot for the supporters of Kassem and the communists, some 100 men, led by a colonel, deserted from Ziwah to the Kurds.

One of the Kurds fired over the sangar at the nearest outpost. I looked at the outpost through the glasses and saw no reaction. I had a strong feeling that most of the lookouts were asleep.

It was extremely cold on the mountain top and Akrawi, his sweat-drenched shirt already dried by the wind, was obviously feeling it badly. So we slipped, jumped and ran down the mountain, Akrawi bowling along far ahead, moving extremely fast for a man of nearly forty. The rocks cut through my

The Kurdish War

borrowed galoshes and I looked forward to getting back to the road. We cut short the journey along the road by fording the Rowanduz river, I going dry-shod on the horse with Kak' Mohammad riding pillion behind me, while the rest took off their shoes, socks and trousers, pulled the white under-drawers which they all wore above their knees and splashed through the icy water. It was soon a grey-dark night and we ate and dried the Scotch mist out of our clothes by a fire inside a hut by a bridge, with Mustafa Agha as our host. He walked back ahead of us, one of his men shining a torch on the rocky ground, and partly because of our haste to get back to the hamlet we had started from and partly because of sheer laziness, I said goodbye to him without dismounting, and then felt ashamed of what must have seemed to him rudeness.

We did not, as it happened, reach our hamlet but slept in a large room in a village to which Amin came carrying my rucksack. My shoes had come back, the soles tacked on with broadheaded nails. It was a roomy and comfortable place by comparison with the other; and in the morning I shaved myself, drank a glass of hot goat's milk, and listened to Akrawi's transistor radio, which he thoughtfully tuned in to the BBC so that I heard about a rebellion in Brunei and listened to the young ladies of Loughton and Cheltenham High Schools quizzing one another in a general knowledge contest; while the rest ate their bread and yoghourt and cleaned their rifles. Amin, whose own store of general knowledge was always surprising, was impressed by the cleverness of English schoolgirls.

That morning we moved back to Wartey, as Mullah Mustafa had shifted his headquarters there. I had hoped to see him during the day and arrange my departure, which Kak' Mohammad thought would be a simple matter, but once more he was not available. We spent the day in the best house in the village, although whether this was through Mullah Mustafa's kindness or because he did not wish to climb the steep mountain path to get to it, I am not sure. He himself stayed in a simpler one near the river, some 300 feet below. The house was almost a villa, with a large room with a praying niche (which was used only once) in the south wall and, outside, a verandah and a terrace of sorts with a concrete tank into which water dripped from a pipe. The 'pasha' from Abbas Mah-

The Kurdish War

man's retinue joined us: a likeable, good-humoured man who did not carry a gun. His rôle was that of scribe and he spent most of the day making out long-hand copies of Schmidt's reports in the *New York Times*. Even Amin, who had at first spoken of 'pasha' Ahmed as 'one of the *aghas*' men' (there was no worse abuse than that), came to like him and laughed at his jokes.

Akrawi came and talked with me in the afternoon. He had a book on the Mahabad Republic, printed in Arabic script and with a photograph of the hanged President, Qazi Mohammad, on the gallows in the Chwar Chira circle of Mahabad. The face was swollen and twisted to one side by the rope, yet still the face of a man who had led a dedicated and principled life. Mullah Mustafa lived deep within the shadow of the hanged man, I thought. So did they all to some extent.

Kak' Mohammad invited me to go for a walk with him and we strolled—as well as one could stroll among the rocks of the mountainside—while he told me that Ibrahim Ahmed and many of the Democratic Party were communists. It was Kak' Mohammad (together with another, at that time in a Democratic Party prison camp in the south) who was alleged to have spread the story that Ibrahim Ahmed had been dismissed for his communism by Mullah Mustafa; a reflection, perhaps, of the dispute over communist infiltration of the party in 1960 and Mullah Mustafa's part in purging it.

Kak' Mohammad had visited Czechoslovakia, Switzerland and France as well as several Middle Eastern countries and was anxious to see more of the world. Did I not agree that it would be an excellent thing if the Kurds sent a delegation to the United Nations? I agreed with him. Perhaps, he suggested, I would say as much to Mullah Mustafa? 'There is a good question for you,' he said in a tone which suggested that I should be grateful. I laughed and said no doubt he would like to go to New York with it, but he kept a very straight face.

He was about thirty, I judged, and unmarried. He could be forgiven for wanting to escape into the excitement and brightness of the western world, which started full blast at Beirut; although neither he nor any of the Kurds ever complained about discomfort or the lack of women. Theirs is not a society which lays much stress on sexuality; virginity is the most important thing that a man demands from a girl on marriage. If someone else has had that, then she is shot by the husband or handed back to the family to be shot by her father or one of her brothers. Murders of this sort are traditionally treated lightly and even in the days of Baghdad's authority were punished with no more than nine months' or a year's imprisonment. A husband is also entitled to avenge his honour when he is the victim of adultery. Most prefer virtue and a long life. Despite the low status of women which this brutal emphasis on chastity implies, they were not as a rule inclined, so far as I could see, to homosexuality. That, like drinking coffee, was an attribute of the despised Arabs.

('They are all homosexuals,' said Amin. 'An Arab will take a young boy into his house and when he is too old and ugly for him, he will marry him off to one of his daughters. Aaagh!')

As delicately as I could, I asked Kak' Mohammad whether he missed having available women around, but he laughed and said that up here in the mountains there was no temptation: the women were well wrapped up in their clothes, often ugly and usually unobtrusive. The girls were married at twelve or thirteen to village men of eighteen or twenty. *Il n'est pas comme Beirut—la, il n'est possible va dormir,*' he said in his curious French.

There are few pretty girls in the mountains. Soane, that man of mystery, was lucky with his Gulchin who blushed and ran away after she had torn a piece from her skirt to mend his shirt and exposed her thigh. Even the 'Rose of Kurdistan', a mid-nineteenth-century beauty, would have been welcome. She was shown to a restrainedly lustful European officer in the Ottoman army after he had asked to be shown the most beautiful girl in Kurdistan. He was kept at a considerable distance while she was paraded. Dried, rattling pomegranates hung on spiky, leafless trees like symbols of frustration and we returned to the house where the others were stretched out sleeping.

Mullah Mustafa sent for me that evening and we had a long, rather rambling discussion during which he fashioned the wooden pegs for quail traps with his well-sharpened pen-knife. The oak sticks from which these were made were brought by one of his attendants for him to look at cursorily and approve;

The Kurdish War

then he would settle down to whittling them one after another. The finished results were extremely smooth, about three inches long with a notch like that of a tent peg in the side near the top, across which there was a narrow groove. They gave him both satisfaction and insulation. While he carved he did not have to look at those talking to him or answer other than briefly and noncommittally; and yet his absorption kept our eyes on him. It was his only escape from his followers.

I wondered whether he hated the position which circumstances had forced on him perhaps more than he had sought it and asked what he would do after the war, presuming tactfully that the Kurds would get their way. Would he want to become President or Prime Minister of an autonomous state? He would retire, he said.

Then he would hand over control to the Democratic Party?

There was no need for parties, he answered, giving me one of his quick looks.

Then who had he in mind to guide the country?

It would depend on the will of the people.

We were back to base again. But none of them wanted parties; even Colonel Akrawi said firmly that they could rule without them. And who were 'they'?

When there was peace there would be an election and the will of the people could manifest itself.

I was still intrigued by why they did so little to interfere directly with the camp at Ziwah; why, for instance, they did not concentrate the three-inch mortars they talked about so often for an attack on it. I wondered whether the mortars were all held by units of the Democratic Party and if it was jealousy which prevented co-operation. But Mullah Mustafa said there was too much danger of them being destroyed by aircraft if they were brought together. He worried a great deal about the air attacks and the effects on the villagers, many of whom had been killed in onslaughts aimed at him. He seemed to be admitting a trace of fear himself and I asked him directly whether the bombing made him afraid.

'Every man feels fear when the aircraft come in to attack,' he said rebukingly.

He knew a word or two of English such as 'Good morning', 'How are you?' and 'Speak!'. This last was used when I fell into a silence, baffled by the 'will of the people' or some such Kurdish nebulosity. He had his little jokes, I felt, and I wondered as he turned once again to 'Klistmas' and 'Meester Gosling' whether I wasn't one of them. I countered his repeated suggestion that we should all spend Christmas together by inviting him to cross into Persia and spend it with me.

'But who would look after Kurdistan?' he asked.

'Mr Gosling,' I said; and they all laughed cheerfully.

Mullah Mustafa came to the door with me when I left and sniffed the night air. I said I would like to take a few photographs of him before I started for the frontier; and he gave me one of his fierce smiles, looking at me sideways, and said he thought I should spend ten days with him. It was a joke, I was sure, but when we got back to the villa Kak' Mohammad and Amin said he was being serious. I raged at them all quite uselessly. It was Mullah Mustafa's evasiveness and the language barrier that was the problem. Why should I not spend ten days with them? asked Kak' Mohammad defensively. Others had done so. Others, I said, had not had to spend five weeks in getting into the country after making a long and expensive journey from London. Nor had they had to face the problem of crossing the frontier mountains before the snow made them impassable. Moreover, what right had Mullah Mustafa to tell me when I should leave?

I knew that in the morning Mullah Mustafa would leave Wartey and make his way a little farther south towards the territory of the Democratic Party. He had heard of the meeting of the Central Committee and wanted to be within earshot of it. There were questions which worried him: why were they not more aggressive? Was there some sort of pact which he did not know of?

I spent a seething, sleepless night and in the morning got the others out of their quilts early and led them reluctantly down the hill to Mullah Mustafa's hut before the mists had cleared, but he had left already. I waited while Kak' Mohammad went across to another hut to make inquiries. I had threatened to leave on my own, even if it meant walking without guides or a horse, but it was a hollow threat.

Kak' Mohammad came back and said that Mullah Mustafa

The Kurdish War

had started on his way south, but he would like me to follow him. It was only a kilometre and a half and he wanted me to watch the first stages of a military plan of attack he was setting in motion. I doubted whether there was any plan at all, but Amin said he had heard rumours that fifty men had gone south and were planning to cut off Rowanduz, as Colonel Akrawi had said they would.

The way was very muddy and it was clear that quite a large number of men and animals had travelled on it shortly before. The whole headquarters was on its way south.

The one and a half kilometres turned out to be seven or nine miles. 'The Leader's' red turbanned men were sitting on the barren shale of a dry water course on which they had lit a number of little fires of thorn and twigs. Mullah Mustafa himself was hidden from sight by a shoulder of slate and rock and I and my party sat round one of the fires and drank tea.

The summons came and accompanied only by Amin I walked across the shoulder to the far side of the ravine where I could see Mullah Mustafa sitting alone in a cleft in the rocks beneath a leafless thorn bush. He was surprised, as they say in eighteenth-century plays, reading Omar Khayyam; a very fine, new looking edition with coloured pictures and the text in English, German, French, Farsi and Arabic. It looked virgin but he said he liked Omar Khayyam and often read him for relaxation. Indeed all Kurds with any pretentions to learning know their Khayyam. He asked Amin to take our pictures together after I had taken his and we sat on his brown, wide-checked travelling rug. He wore his raincoat. His rifle, shepherd's walking stick and overnight bag were behind us.

I said politely that my newspaper would be very happy to be able to print a picture of him. He smiled a sceptical, sideways smile; and I said 'What do you think I am?'

'Something in my mind tells me you are not a journalist,' he said.

'I am not a spy,' I said.

'No,' he said, 'I did not think that.'

I thought it was time to get matters absolutely straight and speaking very slowly and without taking my eyes from his said that I was a newspaper correspondent and nothing else: certainly not an emissary of the Foreign Office come to release

The Kurdish War

Gosling. I wanted only to write as accurately as I could about the Kurdish war and be able to leave as soon as I could before the snow made it difficult. I said all this at some length and very emphatically, and in the end he said: 'I know you are telling the truth; you have a pure heart.'

I thought he looked disappointed. How much more satisfactory for him if I had been some scion of the Foreign Office, heavily disguised with camera and loose-leaf reporter's notebooks. Britain's power had been paramount in his youth and middle-age. She had broken his people's rebellions; with the Americans, forced the Russians to withdraw from northern Persia after the last war (a point which had impressed him deeply) and so caused the collapse of the Mahabad Republic. In the past he had frequently written to British officials. 'Look upon us as a father looks upon his son. Our interests, opinions and plans depend on Britain's decision. This is the substance of my heart's desire.' Like many Arabs and Asiatics he had been unnerved by the cold reserve with which British officialdom disguised the slenderness of British power. They were always the hidden hand; paternalistic as long as one went their way, treacherous if one did not. This illusion of British power continued for long after the reality had gone.[1]

We sat and drank tea which his servants brought us and he asked me if I would stay with him for two or three days while he went south. He knew that I wanted to be away but he would like me to have what Amin translated as 'a memory'.

---

[1] Not such an illusion as I imagined. The following year, after the death of Kassem, the British agreed to support the Baathist government against the Kurds. The supply of aircraft and arms including armoured troop carriers was agreed in principle (although little apart from six Hawker Hunter fighters and aircraft rockets appeared to have been delivered by the end of 1963) and British officials negotiated a secret 'gentlemen's agreement' whereby Turkey and Persia agreed to take stricter measures to isolate the Iraqi Kurds. The Turks arrested a number of Iraqi Kurdish students suspected of being nationalists, the Persians took some measures to tighten up their control of the border and the British refused a visa for Britain to Jelal Talabani, the Kurds' 'roving ambassador'. For the British, who hoped to stabilize the political situation in Iraq and the Persian Gulf, there was a satisfactory *quid pro quo* in the dropping by the Iraqis of their claim to Kuwait. So far as Britain was concerned, the policy was still in force at the end of 1963: the Foreign Office refused a visa to Ibrahim Ahmed, the Secretary-General of the DPK, when following visits to West Germany and France (where he attempted to win support for the rebels) he wanted to visit Britain.

The Kurdish War

I took this to mean no more than the pleasure of travelling with him on his stately progress south and I weakened, thought it would be churlish to say 'no' and instead said I would be very pleased to walk and ride with him for three days and observe him among his followers.

It began to rain and we had to move to the mouth of a shallow cave some ten feet above the bottom of the gully. His men lit a fire in front of us while he questioned me for a change. We sat cross-legged and close together, the smoke rising slowly into the damp air. A red squirrel scampered across a grey rock. He wanted to know whether I thought there was any chance of the United Nations intervening to stop the war. I said bluntly that there was none. The United Nations could not intervene without a request from the government of Iraq and I hardly imagined that would happen. They had no power to interfere otherwise.

'But they did in the Congo.'

I explained that the United Nations had intervened in the Congo at the request of its government to prevent secession not to aid it, but he was unconvinced. Thousands had been killed and thousands more would die in Kurdistan if nothing were done. He was in a sad, pessimistic mood; full of weariness. All he wanted to do now was to retire to his home in the mountains of Barzan and spend his old age peacefully. When had he first become a nationalist? I asked him. When he was a few months old, he said with sour mockery: he had been imprisoned with his mother when he was only eighteen months old. That was because his brother Sheikh Abdul Salem (hanged by the Turks in 1916) had led a rebellion of the Barzanis. This present war, like all the wars, had been forced upon them. They were struggling for their lives and needed heavy weapons and guns to fight the tanks and aircraft. Would the Persians let these weapons through? he asked. I said I doubted it, not with Mahabad as part of their history.

They had no friends, he agreed. Everything that happened in the Middle East was blamed on the Kurds: and he told me an anecdote:

'In a household the family and the guests were sitting together when one of the guests farted loudly and the father of the family turned round and blamed the youngest son of the

The Kurdish War

family and beat him, although it was not him. Is not that little boy Kurdistan?'

He was, I said.

Everyone believed that the Kurds would drift towards the communist bloc if they won their autonomy, Mullah Mustafa went on, but he could guarantee that if they received tokens of friendship in the shape of heavy weapons, then the Kurds would side *with* the West. I said nothing, although I suppose I might have asked how a retired President sitting in his village could guarantee anything; and he went on to ask if I would take a message to the Foreign Office. This was a declaration of friendship for the West and a request to Britain to put pressure on Persia to allow heavy weapons suitable for dealing with tanks and aircraft to cross the border to the rebels. He repeated the message several times and rambled round the idea in a distracted, rather depressed way; then asked whether I thought the British Government would react favourably.

It was quite certain that they would not, and I said so, adding that the Kurds should not delude themselves that anyone would help them. No one had ever helped them in the past, apart from Russia, and she had given them very faint, self-interested friendship which had proved unreliable when put to the test. If they wanted to win the right to self-government they could only do so through their own strength and subtlety when it came to negotiations. As for the British, their main interests in the Middle East were oil and the containment of Russian influence. The British might want to see Kassem gone, but I doubted whether a Kurdish State was a price they were prepared to pay. And also, he should ask himself whether he thought the Persian Government really wanted him to win, however much it too disliked Kassem and his Left-wing government.

He added to his guarantee of friendship another not to support or try to stimulate Kurdish rebellions in Turkey or Persia. He even said at one time that if it proved impossible to come to an arrangement with the Iraqi Arabs, he might try to join the Iraqi Kurds to the 'Shah's Persia'; but he shied off this delicate subject when I questioned him. 'We might even think of joining Turkey,' he said ingenuously, although I could think of nothing more unlikely.

The Kurdish War

It was becoming a conversation that went round in hopeless circles. His solutions lay in fighting and negotiations with the Arabs, and I could tell him nothing useful on those matters; or nothing that would not have seemed impertinence.

I wondered as I thought about his message to the Foreign Office how much of his anxiety was due to the armoured equipment of the government forces and how much to a desire to strengthen his own military position *vis-à-vis* the Democratic Party. A mixture of both no doubt. I have mentioned before his brother Sheikh Ahmed, some ten years older than Mullah Mustafa and the nominal leader of the Barzani sheikhdom. The sheikh never joined the revolt (except briefly in the autumn of 1963) but lived for most of the time in Baghdad. Some have suggested that one reason for the dispute with the Democratic Party was their refusal to hand over 600 rifles to the Barzanis so that Shiekh Ahmed and his followers could arm and join the revolt. The Sheikh, unreliable and according to some a bit mad, has never been trusted, not even by the tribal leaders. He succeeded to the sheikhdom as far back as 1916, when Sheikh Abdul Salem was hanged, and from then on his career was a series of miscalculations, the most serious of them a claim by himself and his followers that he was an incarnation of god; a heresy (some said it was Christianity and that his followers ate pork) which was too much for his co-religionists of the Sufi order in other tribes. All this has not lessened Mullah Mustafa's regard for the brother from whom he took over as effective leader of the Barzanis in the tribal fighting which followed; a reflection of the strength of his family ties and a deeply religious nature which holds in awe the godly attributes of sheikhs.

Written messages were brought to him and he put on his spectacles to read. It was news from the lethargic south where there had been skirmishing with the government forces. 'Ha!' he exclaimed. 'They are beginning to fight now they can see our red turbans.'

The servants had cleared away the samovar, glasses and the sugar bowl, like waiters hinting to later diners that their time is up. It was very grey and drizzly; we had had no lunch apart from a bit of bread and yoghourt and it was obviously best to get on to the next village before it became too dark.

The Kurdish War

Mullah Mustafa preferred to walk rather than ride his mule and politely I walked with him, letting Kak' Mohammad ride. The leader wore his belted raincoat, trousers flapping over his black rubber shoes, rifle aslant his back and shepherd's stick prodding the rocky ground. He walked fairly slowly; an immensely stately man, but pleased with himself as I ran ahead to photograph him.

'Speak!' he said to me in English, smiling in his formidable way as he came abreast of me. But my world seemed miles away and I was incapable of recalling it then in any interesting way, particularly through an interpreter on a narrow and muddy mule trail. So I excused myself and said perhaps we could talk again tomorrow.

Kak' Mohammed galloped ahead of us into the village where we were to stay the night, brandishing his rifle and shouting war-cries like some Kurdish wolf descending on an Arab fold. His horse's hooves cracked the tobacco stalks with their few purple flowers and flung up the mud of the field. He enjoyed, I had noticed, the narcissistic self-portrait of himself as an old-fashioned Kurdish warrior and took great trouble shaping his turban, which he wore with an oriental panache worthy of one of Saladin's bodyguards.

CHAPTER XII

In the morning a man with the pleased, anxious-to-be-off air of someone who is about to escape from routine chores for a few days squatted by the stove while Kak' Mohammad counted several large wads of dinars into his hands.

'What is that for?' I asked Amin.

One of Abbas Mahmand's brothers, a thin-legged man with a weary face, asked Amin what I had said and then told him to tell me it was for clothes and shoes.

After the man had gone, Kak' Mohammad said that Mullah Mustafa would be travelling during the day to the village of Birdanga, at the foot of Mount Sarband. We would go ahead and I would see him there. So we walked and rode beside a pleasant stream with graceful trees that looked like planes beside it. The rain poured down soaking through my trousers and jacket. Amin clung to my old raincoat, which I had lent him. It was a very good coat he said to me on several occasions, looking at me carefully to see what my reactions were. It was rather long for him, but in a way that was all the better. He had thought it a bit short for me. Kak' Mohammad's felt *pestek*, a sort of waistcoat worn over rather than under the jacket, hung soddenly to his back.

The village of Birdanga was charming, even in the rain. Tall trees lined its stream and the walls of well-cultivated fields. Above, Mount Sarband rose into the mists. Our new host suffered from an eye disease like Amin and so many of them; he was very—almost deferentially—polite and led us anxiously through his kitchen where the women were making bread behind a foreground of chickens and pale children, the girls with hennaed hair. The stove in our room was stoked up and my drenched trousers were hung up to dry on a wire, while I wore a pair of baggy Kurdish ones of very good quality which the owner of the house lent me. Throughout the day

The Kurdish War

it poured with rain, great swirling clouds coming down like whipped up avalanches from Mount Sarband. In the intervals of storm the host rolled the roof with a wooden roller to seal up any cracks through which the rain might trickle. Once I went out with Amin for some fresh air and walked up the little hill behind the house. A drift of voices chanting and singing came from somewhere lower down the valley and Amin said he thought they were Assyrians, some of whom had moved into the mountains. It sounded very mysterious and wild; I asked him if he knew the song, but he said he did not. It might be a Christian hymn in Syriac.

I wondered whether in his journey along the northern frontier of Iraq he had passed through the Yezidi tribe and he said he had seen them once, all dressed in white, at one of their religious services. They were devil worshippers, he said, reflecting the conventional view of the Yezidis, who propitiate rather than worship the powers of evil. No one was allowed to use any word that begins with *sh* for that was the first syllable of *Shaitan*, the devil. Nor were outsiders allowed to attend their services and they were very secretive, but they were very kind and good people.

On the way back to the hut he mentioned that Mullah Mustafa intended to give me a present of a carpet worth 180 dinars. That was what the man had been given money for that morning. He had gone with a mule to fetch the carpet and would be back in about five days. I said I had no intention of waiting; but, said Amin, surely I had realized what Mullah Mustafa had meant when he spoke of a 'memory'? It was time more than ethics which worried me, although if it was the Kurdish custom to count out the money for the guests' presents in front of them, it seemed to contain some nasty assumptions about the real purpose of 'presents'. I thought of storming into the hut and making a strong protest to Kak' Mohammad and demanding to see Mullah Mustafa, but Amin said he was not supposed to tell me about the carpet; and I wondered whether they would not consider a protest as merely part of the form, a *de rigueur* bit of hypocrisy. When they talk about honour count the spoons into their hands.

Back in the hut I approached Kak' Mohammad circumspectly about the carpet and he admitted that one had been

The Kurdish War

sent for. I said that I could not possibly accept it. 'Ah! That is because your heart is pure,' he said. 'The leader will be very angry if you refuse. Everyone else has had a gift.'

I felt too full of rectitude for comfort but insisted that I could not take it or wait; besides, I said, searching for practical reasons that might appeal to them more, the customs duty on carpets was extremely high in Britain. I would be unable to get a carpet through without paying a vast sum the equivalent of its worth. They understood that as a real problem.

Changing the subject to my departure, I said I was determined to leave tomorrow. The weather was getting worse and soon the high mountains on the frontier would be impassable. I insisted that Kak' Mohammad should do some thinking about my route which we could then agree with Mullah Mustafa. He thought it would be best if I headed towards Mahabad, in Persia, which I should be able to reach in one night's ride. This seemed preposterous, for even as the crow flies it was a good forty miles from the frontier; and the others agreed that by night through the mountains, which reached over 7,000 feet, it might take two or three days.

'Pasha' Ahmed, the scribe, could see I was angry and made various soothing remarks to get me back into a good temper. And when I asked Amin to leave the transistor radio tuned in to Radio Sanandaj, in Persia, so that I could listen to the long narrative poems which seem to go on all day, he came and sat beside me and asked whether I was interested in poetry. A good secondary education and a relatively leisured career as manager of a dairy products factory had enabled him to study and appreciate Kurdish and Persian literature. The narrative poems, whose lugubrious vowel sounds and lamenting music I found soothing, were all in the same melancholy mood. Two or more voices, one of them usually a woman's, would recite, sharing the verses. 'Ow, ow, ow,' they went; or that was the impression I got from the frequency with which that sound cropped up. Every so often there would be a break for music by a flautist or a man playing a *zitar*. One poem was about a man who had lost his son and mourned over the gravestone until the poem became a duologue with the dead son. Another was about a man in prison, a Kurdish hero who gets a letter from his daughter. He reflects on her and his misery

The Kurdish War

and also the impossibility of communication, not only because he is in prison but because of the differences in experience. This was a poem which they all considered very satisfactory and Amin translated as best he could from 'Pasha' Ahmed's recitation:

> 'O, What are you trying to tell me, sweet face on the photograph?
> 'O, What is your message, O frame?
> 'And you, O gum arabic, what is your message?'

There were obviously limitations to translations of this sort and I did not try to record them. Not all the poems are so melancholy. Some are about love; full of rather obvious sentiments but sometimes charming: 'Ah! Dear one, do not sit in the sun that your rose-coloured cheeks be not reddened by the sun....'

'Pasha' Ahmed asked me to recite something to them, which alarmed me as I have a dreadfully bad memory for poetry. I thought of A. E. Housman as being their meat, but could not remember any of those sad, worm-riddled verses about soldiers going off to war and had to resort to a version of:

> 'In valleys green and still
> Where lovers wander maying....'

mixed with a verse about 'by Ony and Teme and Clun'. Shakespeare was too complicated and abstract for them to appreciate let alone for Amin to translate. I tried Auden's 'Lay your sleeping head, my love, human on my faithless arm,' but it merely bewildered them. So I turned to poetry with strong rhythms such as Chesterton's 'Before the Roman came to Rye' and Belloc's 'Do you remember an inn, Miranda', which they seemed to like a little better.

'All our poets,' said the 'pasha', 'are against life. Who are your poets of that type?'

I tried hard but could not think of any, which is not surprising since conquest came too early in our history for it to be expressed in generally recorded literature, unless one counts the Irish. But I couldn't remember Yeats's 'Easter, 1916' or any

The Kurdish War

other poem by Yeats for that matter. I turned, in an attempt to match some aspect of our experience with theirs, to the poets of underdoggery, but all I could think of was 'It's the poor wot gets the blame' and the hanged men of Villon, who wasn't English. Their faces, expressing a sort of anxiety as well as a desire to understand, were turned towards me in the lamp-light as I struggled, and I felt, quite appallingly and sadly, a gap between us which only I could bridge and somehow, even in this small instance, was failing to bridge. In the end I quoted, from a mixture of vanity and despair, a poem written by myself. I had never recited it to anyone and I don't suppose I ever will again. On one level, as they say, it is about an old-age pensioner in a park watching a small girl dancing upon a lawn which is marked 'Keep off the grass'. Both the idea of an old-age pensioner and bits of grass on which one was not supposed to walk were a bit beyond the experience of my audience, but the line which really defeated them and Amin, who was translating, went (it was an appeal by a chorus of pensioners to the child): 'Don't you know your legs are strumpets to tulips doing penance in the sun?' Amin thought that strumpets were musical instruments and found it even more bewildering when I explained that they were whores. We gave up poetry at that point and turned to stories.

'Pasha' Ahmed had a great fund of these, mainly, if not solely, from Persian and Arabic sources I imagine, some of them cheerfully bawdy. Kak' Mohammad told a more sophisticated one about a Kurd bewildered by the lavatory in a Swiss hotel. Kak' Mohammad could hardly stop laughing as he told the story and all the others enjoyed it immensely.

The 'Pasha' asked me to tell some typical English jokes, so I told them a shaggy dog story, wondering whether despite the fact that it dealt with dogs and alcohol (two subjects which do not figure in their joke repertoire) they might find it grotesquely amusing. They laughed tolerantly and I added a Victorian dirty joke about a cook and a policeman but that was completely beyond them. 'I am afraid some jokes do not translate,' said 'Pasha' Ahmed sadly.

He launched into the Mullah stories, which meant we had to have seven of them, since whoever tells one Mullah story has to tell seven. These are very weak stories of the back-of-a-matchbox variety but curiously, through their idiocy and obviousness, at times very funny. The surprising thing to me was that they still existed in current use. It was rather like hearing the merry jests of Til Eulenspiegel, or Howleglas, being recited in a remote part of the Yorkshire Dales. In fact, the only time I had come across the Mullah tales before was in a work on medieval joke books. Mullah is a silly lad of great naïvety, everybody's fool, in fact. Curiously some of the literalities on which the jokes turn are translatable into English, such as: 'One day Mullah's mother wanted to leave the house. So she told Mullah to guard the door; which he did, standing by it. Some friends passed by and asked Mullah to join them. Mullah at first said he could not, but then after a while said to himself, "My mother only told me to guard the door." So he took it off its hinges and took it with him to where his friends had gone. When his mother came back she found the house open to any robber who passed by, so she waited until Mullah returned and beat him. But he protested and said, "Why, mother, you only told me to guard the door and see, that is what I have done."'

Another turned on Mullah being told to hold the horse's head, which is the only part of the horse he is left with by the end of the story.

On the far side of the room next to Abbas Mahmand's brother, sat a Barzani soldier with a gold tooth and a long, well brushed moustache which made him look faintly like Sir Gerald Nabarro. He told this story:

'Once there was a boy and his mother who were very poor; so poor that the boy decided to move to another village. He sat his mother on a donkey and they set off. But on the way they crossed a river where the mother fell off and was drowned. The boy brought her out of the river and wondered what to do. A plan came to his mind. He sat his mother on the donkey again and managed to keep her upright, with a piece of bread in one hand and a cucumber in the other. Leading the donkey, he came to a field where a man had cut some hay. The boy turned the donkey into a field and hid while the donkey, still with the boy's mother on its back,

The Kurdish War

began to eat the hay. Shortly, the owner of the field came and shouted at the woman to take the donkey away and when there was no answer picked up a stone and threw it, knocking the dead woman off the donkey. At this, the boy came out of hiding and claimed the man had killed his mother with the stone. The man believed him and agreed to pay 200 dinars in blood money. So the poor boy was rich—and the donkey had the hay as well.'

The soldier laughed rather excessively at this. Amin leaned towards me and said for my guidance: 'It's supposed to be funny.'

I told one final story, and knowing my audience by now, I made it 'The Merchant's Tale', Chaucer's story of wicked young May married to old and trusting January. When I had finished Amin said, 'Ah! We tell that story in Sulaimaniya. There, the teller is a very silly old man who breaks the line of people praying in a mosque and is made to tell a story.'

We played over supper a game with a chicken's wishbone. The Kurds do not wish after breaking it; instead the ends are kept by the two who broke it. Each then has to try to persuade the other to accept something from him. The first to accept loses. Kak' Mohammad had an enormous gift for winning games as I was to discover a few days later and he soon won this one by handing me my camera which I absent-mindedly accepted.

Information gained over supper: if a woman puts too much salt in the food it's a sign she wants intercourse: and if a man and a woman make love very frequently they produce daughters rather than sons. I could see a conflict of Kurdish psychologies, male and female, somewhere between those two assertions.

After supper I wrote my diary with the lamp beside me, my shirt and underpants, which had been washed in the river, drying on a wire strung between the chimney of the stove and a pile of boxes next to the wall. I still wore the comfortable trousers which had been lent to me. Someone had suggested during the day that I should have my photograph taken in full Kurdish dress as a memento, but it seemed to me that this would have been an oddly patronizing and very phoney bit of

The Kurdish War

posturing on my part and I said no; I had my sort of dress and they had theirs. I hoped that they did not think I was being ill-mannered. Their costume was too much a part of them to be worn in the spirit of fancy-dress by a visiting European with romantic ideas.

Amin had spoken to me several times about the possibility of him leaving the country. He had taught himself to use a camera well enough to enable him to earn an extra income by photography before the rebellion (and he had certainly proved very efficient and knowledgeable when he had my camera problems to deal with) and if he could get out of Iraq to Beirut he had the promise of a job with a German camera team working in the Middle East. The trouble was he had no passport and could not obtain one. The British would not help him, although he had worked for years at the Habbaniyah base. If he could enter Persia and live there for a while he would be able to apply for a Persian passport. But how would he be able to earn any money to keep himself and his wife and three children (who were receiving the equivalent of £7 10s. a month from party funds) in Sulaimaniya and also pay his fare to Beirut? He had asked Mullah Mustafa about it but he had, as always, been non-committal. He was thirty-seven and his was 'a wasted life'. He repeated the phrase several times, too bitterly to be self-pitying. His father had died when he was young and his stepfather had not liked him. When he was thirteen and a half he had left school in Sulaimaniya and gone to work for the RAF at Habbaniyah. He had all sorts of jobs there, including kennelman and houseboy; then he had worked as a 5s. a day messenger at Khanaquin, the frontier town on the road carrying supplies to Russia from the gulf and later he was a checker with a German construction firm building the Dukan dam. He preferred the Germans to the English, who had not always been kind to him. 'They treated us very badly, some of them,' he said, shaking his head. His last job had earned him 50 dinars a month, about £45, a very good wage. He learnt languages quickly; could speak several dialects of Arabic as well as Farsi, English and a few words of German and French. He had taught himself mathematics and amazed me by knowing all about troy weight, rods, poles and perches, and how to change metric weight into avoir-

The Kurdish War

dupois, and a whole host of similar things I knew little about. I wondered what he would make of his life if the revolution succeeded. It would hardly be a rich country, for the terms on which they wanted autonomy would be bound to mean the breaking of many ties, commercial and economic as well as political, with the Arabs. And if it failed, there was not very much to hope for. The firing squads and the gaols would claim many of them. I told Amin that he could come with me into Persia if he could get permission to leave from Mullah Mustafa.

'Pasha' Ahmed called across the room before we went to bed: 'You are feeling happier now, Kak' Adamson?' and I said 'yes' obligingly. I thought to myself that I would wait until tomorrow and then demand to see Mullah Mustafa. Kak' Mohammad looked his usual suave self, although the leader was still not in Birdanga despite his repeated assurances during the day that he was on his way. He would be here early in the morning, he said.

Amin said as he settled down to sleep: 'Tomorrow I shall ask Mullah Mustafa whether I can leave. I shall say, "My Master, may I go with Mister Adamson".'

CHAPTER XIII

Of course, Mullah Mustafa did not appear in the village next morning. He was 'on his way' said Kak' Mohammad defensively. I challenged this and said perhaps it would be best if we went to meet him but 'Pasha' Ahmed, alarmed at the thought of a muddy walk through the rain back the way we had come, put his hand on his heart and asked if I would take it from him that Mullah Mustafa would be in the village by 9.30. I said I would, with a sideways glance at Kak' Mohammad. Nine-thirty came and went, but I decided to let matters lie for a while and I asked Amin, who had an excellent memory, to give me some dates and facts about the beginning of the rebellion so far as it affected the tribes, not the Democratic Party. He did, rattling off dates and names until suddenly there was a sharp interruption from Kak' Mohammad seconded by Abbas Mahmand's brother, who was sitting next to him.

Amin stopped and looked down sulkily and when I asked him what was the matter said, nodding at Kak' Mohammad, 'He tells me not to say any more.'

'Why not?' I asked. 'If I ask you to tell me something no one here has any right to interrupt.'

I realized that I had been tactless in questioning Amin, a member of the DPK, on such delicate tribal matters but it seemed better than laborious and probably useless attempts to get the answers from the assembly at large. But I was in no mood to back down and I told Amin to translate to them what I had said, which he did.

Kak' Mohammad, ruffled and heated for the first time in my knowledge of him, said of Amin that I should not ask him questions of that sort. *'Il n'est pas un diplomate.'*

'You have some diplomats here?' I inquired with heavy sarcasm. Perhaps we could go and see them so I could ask

The Kurdish War

them the questions. 'It would be better if you asked this gentleman here about that sort of matter,' said Kak' Mohammad, meaning Abbas Mahmand's brother who sat hunched and uncomfortable beside him.

I said that I would be delighted to, but then Amin refused to put the question in Kurdish. 'How can I talk to a man like that, an *agha* who can neither read nor write?' he asked in a righteous huff. But I insisted furiously and he did so. There was a change of front then, an agitated moment or two in Kurdish before Kak' Mohammad said that all questions of this nature must be put to Mullah Mustafa.

At that I was really angry, closed my notebook and slapped it on my knee. 'I have asked your leader and he would not answer. Very well. We will go to him now and I shall ask him again.' I stood up and put on my jacket, packed my rucksack and ordered the horse to be got ready.

They sat taken by surprise for a while, discussing the situation among themselves, before getting slowly to their feet. Would I not wait a minute, they pleaded. Mullah Mustafa would be in Birdanga soon. I decided I would walk as it was a quicker and more independent method of leading the way, and I told 'Pasha' Ahmed, who was too fat to enjoy walking, that he could have the horse. He said sadly that I should not have worn Kurdish trousers. They had made me as hot-headed as a Kurd. For most of the three-mile walk I was a good thirty yards ahead, hoping I was following the right mule track. Amin came abreast of me once to say that he was afraid of what they would do to him, these *aghas* and their men.

'What will they do to you?' I asked sceptically.

'I don't know quite, Mister David.'

We came in sight of the village and Kak' Mohammad asked me to wait as Mullah Mustafa might have moved on to another village. If that were so, I pointed out, there was not much point in waiting here. We would go into the village and find out where he was.

The owner of the house where we had stayed two nights before came out and invited me into his house, but I declined emphasizing that it was only because I expected to see Mullah Mustafa in a few minutes and it was hardly worth disturbing his household for so brief a time. Kak' Mohammad wanted me

The Kurdish War

to go inside, but I told him I would wait where I was while he went and arranged for me to see Mullah Mustafa. Some twenty minutes passed, while I drank tea which the owner of the house brought, before Kak' Mohammad returned and I was taken to Mullah Mustafa.

He was sitting in a dark and dingy little house with an enclosed and muddy forecourt in front of it. As usual he was whittling quail traps, which lay in a pile white as bones beside him. What did I want? he asked.

I told him that my question on the origins of the rebellion had been referred to him.

'I have already said that I cannot answer questions on that.'

I saw a psychological advantage in the discourtesy of his refusal and said that I had also come to see him because I intended to leave tomorrow and I would be grateful if he would arrange an escort. He would agree there was little point in my staying on.

'Your present is coming.'

I thanked him for his intention of giving me one and said that in the circumstances I could not accept anything so expensive. It was wrong to give such gifts while his people were often homeless and in need of many things which his money could buy. And besides I did not expect gifts. If I had accepted it out of politeness it would only have been because I intended to sell it in Europe on behalf of the Kurds. This must have sounded unconvincing for he said he would insist of me accepting a gift of money.

'Everyone who comes here must take a gift. It is the custom.'

The most suitable gift, I suggested, would be some personal object of his. Something small and not of tremendous importance to him, I added quickly.

'But what have I got that I can give you?' he asked pathetically. 'Do you think I carry signed photographs with me?'

I wanted him to give me one of his quail traps, but he said it would be too insignificant. He turned, wearily and almost obsessively, to the question of heavy arms; and then said suddenly: 'I don't trust the interpreter.'

Amin as he said this looked, even in the dim light, an un-

The Kurdish War

healthy shade of grey. His bad eye swivelled almost independently, like the white eye of a frightened horse, to look at me as he interpreted.

'I have full trust in Amin,' I said.

'I haven't any trust in interpreters,' said Mullah Mustafa. 'Many of the things in Mr Schmidt's report (in the *New York Times*) were not what I said.'

That, I pointed out, was not Amin's fault, since he had not interpreted on that occasion. I had taken great care with Amin, making sure that he fully understood my questions and sometimes making him repeat them before he put them; and often going over the replies very thoroughly to sift away ambiguities.

We said no more on this subject but mounted our merry-go-round of question and answer on UN intervention, British policy and the possibility of borrowing heavy arms. He repeated his message to the Foreign Office and I said once more that British policy was cynical, opportunist and self-interested, like the foreign policy of any country. The possibility of overthrowing Kassem was not sufficient to influence the British in his favour. I would deliver his message but I did not think he had anything to hope for. Many Arabs, I went on, thought the British had sent encouragement to the Kurds, but I doubted whether that was true. He admitted that he had not heard of any agents; it would have been the first step if the British had wanted to help him.

For hours, it seemed, we went round and round on these matters. Once I suggested to him that it would be best if he sent emissaries to Tehran and tried to negotiate directly there on the questions of arms and supplies. He replied in a tone of moody, hopeless anger:

'We have sent messages to the Persians, but we have had no answer. Do you think we are children not to have tried that?'

Was there any country in the Middle East, I asked, which he thought could be any ally of the Kurds? Russia? He spent many years of exile there, speaks Russian, but was never very happy there and is no communist. All his loyalties and his background are against such a creed. Israel? Whenever I mentioned this possibility to Kurds in Iraq they looked faintly shocked. Israel was a creation of Western capitalism, which they too had opposed in Iraq. In Mullah Mustafa's view any such link would completely alienate the Arabs and unite the whole Arab world against them. But the Kurds in Europe take a different view. They see Israel as a country which has struggled against 'Arab imperialism' and succeeded.

'Enough of these serious matters,' he said after a while, a glum heaviness pressing on both of us. As I had talked to him the day before about hunting in the mountains, he asked me whether I did any shooting in England. I said 'no'. There were not many opportunities for pastimes of that sort in south-eastern England.

He had often hunted in the mountains. He had shot partridge with Captain Lyons, a British political officer in Iraqi-Kurdistan. 'Once Captain Lyons shot only one bird with two cartridges while I brought down nine in two shots.'

I asked him about the bears which the sheikh in Rezaieh had said were so dangerous. I must have sounded sceptical for he looked reproving and said they were extremely dangerous and he knew of many cases where men had been savaged by them. He described two cases which he had seen personally. In one, a man with whom he was hunting was leapt on by a she-bear and badly mauled.

We had lunch and although the meeting had not been a very propitious one from Amin's point of view, he decided to put his question and ask whether he could leave the country and take up the offer of a job in Beirut. He would, he said, be of more use to the Kurdish cause outside the country than in it. Mullah Mustafa, predictably enough, said no; he wanted Amin to stay with him for a while. I wondered whether he merely wanted Amin's services as an interpreter or was keeping him because he did not want him to report too soon to Ibrahim Ahmed on what he had said about his relations with the party or recount the message he had given me. Relations between the politicians and Mullah Mustafa and the tribal leaders were obviously very bad. In the hut there had been a discussion about the steps to be taken to release Kak' Mohammad's former colleague in Beirut who had been imprisoned by the Democratic Party in the south; and also talk of the 'flight' from his tribe of the guide Ahmed who had brought

The Kurdish War

me across the frontier. He, before joining the party organization, had been one of Abbas Mahmand's men.

The march back to Birdanga began soon after lunch. I paddled out through the mud of the forecourt, the waiting Barzanis rising politely from where they had squatted in the semi-shelter of the eaves. Mullah Mustafa rode a plump grey mule; I walked on ahead, soon outdistancing his party. Before entering Birdanga village the track crosses a grassy whale-backed hill; I paused on top with a group of Barzanis to wait for Mullah Mustafa.

It had been a frustrating, wearisome morning. I still did not know whether I would get the guides and help I needed to leave. Moreover I felt I had mishandled the whole episode. The western informality of Ibrahim Ahmed's headquarters had misled me into thinking that the same untortuous ease of relationships, the same surface attunement would prevail in the supposed core of the movement here. I cursed my lack of knowledge of the Middle East and the deep, prevailing rhythms of Oriental manners and gave a hard, exasperated lunge with my foot against a boulder. It shifted, toppled slowly and began to roll down the hill as Mullah Mustafa rode up the zig-zag trail below, and while I do not think it would have struck the leader, he might have wondered what I was up to if a large rock dislodged by me had rushed past his mule's nose. So I had to run after and grapple with it until I managed to stop it, the Barzanis on the summit laughing delightedly.

I asked Amin what would be the fate of a British journalist who struck Mullah Mustafa down with a rock, even accidentally.

'They would not do anything to you, Mr David. Perhaps Mullah Mustafa would say with his last words: "That is my life." Believe me, Mister David, it is never worth losing your temper.'

I walked behind Mullah Mustafa to a pleasant two-storeyed house on the other side of the river from where I had stayed before. It was quite late and he invited me to have supper with him and talk. His good humour had returned after a grey morning and he laughed as I tried unobtrusively to scratch the flea-bites which covered most of me from the neck down. Tea was brewed and after four sugarless glasses (I found they made it so sugary as to be undrinkable, unless I insisted on no sugar) I put my glass on its side as a sign I wanted no more; but I heard Mullah Mustafa whispering to the servant to ignore it and bring another glass. I drank it and again put the glass on its side. Another glass was brought and I sensed a little cheerful speculation on how many unwanted glasses they could get down me. In some parts of the country the sign for 'no more' is a completely upturned glass, so this time as the servant came I reversed the glass and said 'Besser' (enough) very firmly, at which Mullah Mustafa placed his hands on his knees and threw his head back with a laugh he had been suppressing for some time.

'Well,' he said later, 'you are determined to leave?'

I said that tomorrow was the day I had fixed.

He was sorry that I felt unable to wait a little longer and I explained that I had to leave as soon as possible and not risk the snow and bad weather blocking the mountains on the frontier. So be it, he said, you can leave tomorrow; and we turned to discussing the route. Amin had told me that Ibrahim Ahmed had suggested I should return more or less the way I had entered, but that would have meant returning to his headquarters and I thought it might be undiplomatic to do so, for Mullah Mustafa might have proposed that as he was making his way in that direction I should accompany him. He might also have resented the fact that I would be leaving through the stronghold of his rival. The best route looked like being through the town of Qal'a Dizeh and across the frontier to the Persian town of Sardasht and then either to Mahabad or Saqez. But an elder of the Arkou tribe said that tribes on that route were unfriendly to the rebels and the road out of Sardasht might well be blocked by snow at this time of year. So it was agreed that I should take a more northern route, where the tribesmen were more agreeable and the snow unlikely to be so bad.

Mullah Mustafa invited me to stay the night at his house, but I refused on the grounds that he would have people to see and a great many things to talk about: I would call on him in the morning and say goodbye. He, too, was leaving Birdanga, to go to Bettwahta and Gosling. I put in a final suggestion that he should arrange his public relations so that he would not

The Kurdish War

need to take people like Gosling prisoner. 'Why not?' he said cheerfully. 'The exercise is good for them.'

Amin, 'Pasha' Ahmed and I lost our way as we searched for our house by the stream, but there was a moon and we struggled over brushwood fences and walls until we found the stream and a track.

No more had been said about the present but Amin said Mullah Mustafa intended to give me a sum of money. He would be very angry if I refused.

'I shall give it to Ismet Cherif, in Lausanne, if he insists on me having it,' I said, exhausted by the whole business.

'Even if you don't want it there are others who would like some,' said Amin pointedly.

And in the morning when I went to say goodbye Mullah Mustafa ordered the room to be cleared of all except himself, Amin and me. And then after we had talked for a while about this and that he sent Amin to the door to call in a man who handed Mullah Mustafa a small but bulging blue envelope.

'I do not want you to regard this as in any way a bribe,' he said handing it to me. 'We have little we can offer you in the way of comfort or hospitality and we are grateful to you for having come here to see us and write about the sufferings of our people. I would like you to use it to buy a present for your wife and children.'

I did not open the envelope but passed it to Amin to hold. My speech of thanks was diplomatic, ambiguous and, I hope, dignified. 'I accept the gift in the spirit in which it is given,' I said, with a grave bow of the head in acknowledgment. And, to be honest, I am still not quite sure what that spirit was; an essence of several conflicting emotions and motives, I suppose.

Amin opened the envelope and took out a wad of dinars tied together with a piece of rubberized string and began to count them. I signalled him to stop, but Mullah Mustafa, who said the wad contained 100 dinars, thought it would be best if they were counted. So we sat staring at our knees while Amin went through them slowly, wetting his right forefinger to help flick them back. They were all there, and he put them back in the envelope and handed it to me. I slid it deep into my left-hand trouser pocket. It was no time to talk about ethics.

The Kurdish War

Mullah Mustafa looked relieved that I had not made a fuss, and I felt a deep, wicked desire to laugh. One should never miss the chance of an unusual experience. I walked outside with Mullah Mustafa. My horse, another wretched animal, was waiting for me below the verandah. Mullah Mustafa's way led straight up the mountain from the house.

We said goodbye and I told him that I should always be grateful for what he had taught me about the Kurds. I understood a great deal more than when I arrived, and most of it was pleasant. He started to walk up the mountain alone, his followers still tying gear on to a mule and wrapping their own little parcels.

'*Qa hafeece!*' I shouted after him, suddenly feeling emotional. Perhaps it was his solitariness on the steep mountainside that affected me. He paused and turned round, an unKurdish thing to do, looked surprised and called back to me, '*Qa hafeece!*'

We turned towards Wartey and the Rowanduz road with home somewhere at the end of it, Amin riding ahead of me on a mule with ears folded wickedly back. I wondered whether patriotism would ever have any rewards for Mullah Mustafa and rather doubted it; the only rewards would be those of a proud, obstinate and bloody-minded integrity. He would never learn anything and perhaps, which was sadder, knew it. There was his diffidence, a curious and marked trait; the result of having been knocked about by events and cleverer men. It came out in odd ways. For instance I had asked him whether he had ever travelled in Western Europe and he had said no. Yet during our talk in the little cave he had suddenly referred to a visit he had made to Prague and Switzerland. Why, I asked Amin, had he lied to me in the first place? 'He did not know you very well, when you first asked him,' said Amin, as if that explained everything. Possibly he feared he would be trapped by some sticky, sophisticated question which he would not understand, as he did not seem to understand any on the political structure of an autonomous Kurdistan or its economy; although that may have been a diplomatic evasion.

It would have taken months to get to know him well and hold his confidence. After six days I felt a mixture of affectionate sympathy and pity when I thought of him. His virtues were such courageous, archaic ones that one admired them as to a certain degree noble, yet found also something destructive and negative in his nature. This, it seemed to me, was because his traditions and his loyalties did not allow him to reach out for a wider, more complex system of principles, or perhaps compromises. He was fighting a modern revolution in the manner of a tribal chief; honourably but without ends other than pride and independence. That is a bit harsh as an assessment of a man who has become the symbol of his people's resistance, but I think it should be understood that his rôle has been given him by chance as much as by his character. The wars in which he was bred were tribal wars tinged with nationalism. With Mahabad he found himself as the commander of 3,000 exiled riflemen in a state without an army to defend it. Circumstances thus made him a general in a nationalist war tinged with tribalism. His life has been a recurrent pattern of war, defeat, exile; the pattern of life of many Kurds and one which has led to a strong and perhaps dangerous charcteristic of the Kurds: their melancholy fatalism. That characteristic was apparent in Mullah Mustafa.

I said I felt pity for him as well as sympathy. No one who has fought for what is, looked at broadly, a justifiable and honourable cause deserves the life he has led; although to talk about 'deserving' in such circumstances is sentimental. Whether deserving or undeserving the hard truth is one *gets* one's fate. But one can still feel pity for an old man on a treadmill of rebellion, and I wished later that I had been less 'professional' and more sympathetic and sensitive in my dealings with him. I had been misled, as I have said, by the westernized informality of Ibrahim Ahmed's headquarters and the base at Cham-i-Razan into thinking that the same spirit ran through the whole of the rebel movement. But with Mullah Mustafa I came in touch with an oriental world whose manners, suspicions and codes I did not appreciate until too late. My only courtesy, the only gesture which I made at the end, was to accept his money. That at least made *me* understandable.

It was stony going on the track and after a while I dismounted and walked. The weather was better and the mountains showed white against patches of blue. Where the

The Kurdish War

ravine closed in, two shepherd boys sat opposite one another on the clifftops and carried on a conversation overhead, their voices level and uninterrupted by our journey below.

'What would you do if you had the money?' I asked Amin.

'Keep it,' he said, looking at me as if I were mad.

We went through Wartey and reached the hamlet where I had stayed before, in the hut with the muttering old man. The English-speaking owner had been out in the mountains hunting ibex but had only brought back partridge which we ate followed by beakers of vinegary pomegranate juice. He said wolves had come down from the mountains that day and carried off a goat.

He had several well-fed and surprisingly good-tempered dogs, large, creamy-white animals with cropped ears. He was the only Kurd I met who admitted to being fond of dogs, although they will put a high money value on a good one. They are, too, the only animals they name. Flower-names are popular for them. Horses, mules and donkeys are regarded unsentimentally and worked until their death, when they are left for the dogs to eat. A good mule, according to Amin, could cost 70 dinars; a donkey perhaps 30 and a horse as little as 20. A horse was no use for work and riding was a luxury.

Several more soldiers joined our escort at the hamlet, including two Persian Kurds—two of the 'Persian heroes' about whom Amin spoke so scathingly. Kak' Mohammad went off to sleep in another hut, taking my rucksack with him so that he could send it on ahead as my horse was *près du mort* and any lightening of its load would be important. I was surprised at this, since my rucksack weighed only a few pounds. I was not very keen on letting my notebooks, diary and map out of my sight, but it struck me it did not matter very much whether he or anyone else read, or tried to read them and I let him take it. Throughout the night two of the escort sat on guard. As they did not go outside the door I presumed it was to see that no one attempted to steal the 100 dinars while I was asleep. I thought of telling them to lie down and forget about it but such a conflict of orders would only have embarrassed them and I decided to talk to Kak' Mohammad when I saw him in the morning.

The sentries, when I thanked them over breakfast and

apologized for being the cause of lost sleep, placed their right hands on their hearts and said it was their duty.

The tributary running into the Rowanduz river had to be crossed on our way to the little town of Gallala, where we were to have lunch, and I kicked the horse through it alone while the escort went farther downstream to a bridge. I lost them for a while and cantered backwards and forwards across some fields before I saw them plodding up a hill and waving to me. The country had been badly eroded in parts by overgrazing and trees hung on by their roots to gullies ugly as wounds. Partridges scurried here and there in coveys, reluctant to fly, running then standing still sideways on to us, heads nervously erect, one eye on us. Kak' Mohammad stalked one covey, but went too fast, so that the birds were in flight when he fired with his Brno.

On the first steep hill one of the sentries, the older of the two, a man of about forty, fell far behind and we had to wait for him on the summit. I told Kak' Mohammad that I did not think it necessary for them to guard me, but he said he had been told to take great care of me in the villages. The man caught us up, bent with stomach pains and looking so grey that I put him on the horse and went slithering and leaping on foot down the muddy side of the hill towards the Rowanduz to Persia road. I felt very fit and robust that morning and I set the pace for Gallala which we reached about midday. In the town's main street the people drifted about aimlessly or stood at the doors watching us. Trade had virtually stopped and there seemed to have been little attempt to set up any sort of administration to look after the running of the town and roads. It surprised me that no one had been set to work sweeping away the stones and mud that had fallen along the main road we had come along; and in Gallala no one had made any attempt to restore the school and rest house, both of which had been badly damaged not by fighting but by hooligans.

Were there no teachers for the children? I asked.

None.

Why had they all gone, even the Kurdish ones?

Because the State no longer paid them.

I was invited to sit in a shop which existed on smuggled matches, yellow packets of Persian cigarettes, rubber shoes, bales of blue and pink cotton, Nacet razor blades and even diminutive bottles of violet perfume. Kak' Mohammad went to a nearby house to arrange a bath, which meant waiting for an hour or so while the water was heated. It was my first real wash since the bath in the cave at Cham-i-Razan and I was grateful for it. Afterwards Kak' Mohammad suggested I should rest for an hour since it was often dangerous to move about after a hot bath, but I snorted at this and said I was ready for lunch. Colonel Akrawi, looking tired and still wearing only his stained khaki shirt over his chest, arrived and sat and talked for a while. Messages were coming through on the wireless that the Kurds had managed to cut the road below the Rowanduz camp so that the garrison was now completely isolated, except from the air.

We ate, sitting at a table for once, in a house next door to the gutted remains of the town's police station. I was left alone for a while with Amin and I gave him twenty dinars for his services as an interpreter and said I hoped they would help his wife and children. He gave a quick 'thank you' and the notes vanished into a pocket somewhere as if they had never been.

I suppose I had better end the story of Mullah Mustafa's dinars with my accounts; ten I kept and spent on a present for my family, as Mullah Mustafa had requested, and the rest I divided among three separate envelopes (in case the Swiss customs questioned one bulky packet containing so much foreign currency) and sent to Ismet Cherif Vanly, as I had said I would.

It was getting late when we left for Darban, the village where we were to sleep, but the air and the sunlight were as sharp as diamonds and the light lasted for a long time. The *agha* of a village just off the road walked and rode with us for some time and invited me to come to his village where they grew very good fruit. My enjoyment of fruit, particularly the hard, round wild pears which grew on the mountains, had been noticed. But even that enticement was not enough to deflect me from the frontier. The road climbed and it grew cold and frosty. Day gave way to brilliant moonlight, with the shining snow peaks of Hellgirt on our left and that of Candiley (which means 'lamp') on our right. An aloof moun-

The Kurdish War

tain which we saw only occasionally between other peaks, like another moon among clouds, Hellgirt had caught Amin's imagination with a mixture of mystery and mathematics. It was the highest mountain in Iraqi Kurdistan, over 12,000 feet, and on the summit there was a spring. The nomads came in the summer with their flocks and tents and camped there; there were no trees but the grass was tall.

The road had been popular with motorized escapists from the cities before the war. They came to avoid the heat of the summer on the plains and camped on the cropped grass beside the road. The temperature never went over 90 degrees in the mountains, even in the hottest months of summer.

Beside a bridge there was a *chai-kaneh* owned by a man who had once been a communist but had learnt better after a spell in a rebel prison. He was now, according to Kak' Mohammad, *avec nous*. His family were eating their chicken and rice supper when we entered and went on doing so while we sat on wooden benches close to the wall and waited for the samovar to boil. An idiot boy of about eight in a black and yellow striped shirt and skirt, ran from one member of the family to another to be fed with kindly but detached patience. The owner of the *chai-kaneh* was a tall, thin man with a large, hooked nose that made him look more Armenian than Kurd. Not only were his politics indeterminate, but so, it seemed, was his religion: verses from the Koran alternated on the walls with pictures of the Nativity and Jesus and Mary showing their sacred hearts. I wondered whether the man was a Christian or had perhaps put up the pictures in anticipation of a mixed clientele, but Amin said he was a Moslem and the explanation was that among the Kurds all religions were venerated. It would be truer, I think, to say they were tolerated. A basically pagan open-mindedness often characterizes the Kurds, making them prone to the emotional satisfactions of religious extremism and yet free from excessive bigotry. The effect of this was felt most by their neighbours the Christian Armenians whom the Kurds often slaughtered mercilessly for a mixture of reasons, religious and secular, and yet sheltered in their villages during the Turkish massacres of the First World War.

The idiot boy picked up his father's cigarette left burning

on an ash-tray and puffed it until an elder brother told him his father would beat him unless he put it down. He scurried away to his mother, making wordless complaining noises.

We drank our tea and I noticed at the far end of the room a print of a kitten watching two quacking ducks on a pond, and I wondered why they had pinned it up and whether they liked it or even noticed it beyond the fact that it filled a space on the wall. There are not many cats in Kurdistan; and those I had seen did not look as if their kittenhoods had been particularly jolly. The whole cult of humanizing animals, or at least enfolding them in human sympathy, is outside the ken of the mountain Kurd, even the occupants of a *chai-kaneh* on the main road to Persia, or so I should imagine. So presumably it represented something more than just a picture of a kitten and two ducks; a certain level of attainment, like having a cocktail bar in the lounge. Something which brought them close to the car-owners camping on the verges or passing through on their way to the ski-slopes.

CHAPTER XIV

—o🙵o—

A party of villagers from Darban came out to meet us on the road and guide us into the village, a torch which one of them carried picking out the stones and pot-holes in the dark road under walnut trees. A great many people had gathered in a room as large as a village hall. The riff-raff and socially negligible were kept behind a low wall the height of an altar rail. I sat in the place of honour, well propped with cushions and was invited to stretch out my legs and be comfortable. With some difficulty I got Amin to translate my polite conversation (he would always attempt to answer all questions from his own enormous fund of general knowledge); and after supper faced a sort of impromptu conference with the villagers spread out across the room to ask questions about United Nations' aid and the possibility of Western support. I was honest and felt a ripple of politely suppressed disappointment pass among them. More encouragingly, I told them that their bravery was admired everywhere, particularly that of the villagers who had suffered most of the losses; and that found more approval. What was their main problem, I asked, and the majority seemed to think it was the price of smuggled tea, which now cost the equivalent of £27 10s a chest.

Among the villagers I noticed a man who was the nearest approach to a dandy I had seen in Kurdistan, a guest who was passing through to another village. He wore a bright blue Kurdish costume which looked as if it had been tailored, a fringed white turban and a silk *pishten*, delicately patterned in pink and white, round his waist. Slightly built but tough-looking, he carried a dagger with a bronze knuckleduster as a handle, and I thought at first he was probably a bandit too powerful for the other highly respectable villagers to take action against. But Amin said, after making some whispered inquiries, that he was a well-known boxer. We played games

The Kurdish War

after supper and he came and sat among the players, a kingfisher among chaffinches, very self-conscious and a bit isolated by his knuckleduster dagger, but friendly.

The first game was hunt the cartridge. Five pairs of socks were laid out in two rows of five each with the feet of the socks tucked into the legs as if they had just been washed. Two teams then faced one another across the socks. One man took a heavy Brno cartridge, held it hidden in the palm of his hand and tried to smuggle it into one of the five socks in the row nearest his team. The facing team watched closely, craning forward on their knees and barracking and teasing, while the man with the cartridge went backwards and forwards along the line of socks several times before it was thrown open to the others to guess in which one he had left it. It was impossible to see the cartridge in the sock and no movement of his hand had shown where he had dropped it. They played this a number of times, with a turkey as the prize for the team winning the most times. The soldier with the Nabarroesque moustache, who had come from Birdanga as a member of the escort, was the best at hiding the cartridge. He had a poker-face which gave away nothing. And Kak' Mohammad, with his subtle intelligence, was able to tell most times where the hider had left the cartridge. He could tell by the man's eyes, he said. They always changed when he left the cartridge.

This, like the next game, was enjoyed not so much as a straight guessing game but as a chance of teasing and exchanging jokes and argy-bargy with one another. The teams would argue and laugh for five minutes or more before a decision was made on which sock to point to as the hiding place. I was invited to join in the second game which was played by two teams of ten or more who sat facing each other across the wide room. Once again it was a guessing game, this time to discover who was sitting on a stone wrapped in a large piece of cloth. With my tight European trousers, I was at a disadvantage against the Kurds with trousers baggy and spreading enough to hide a clutch of ostrich eggs. As in the first game, one member of the team acted as the hider; a ticklish job. Black moustached men with bandoliers of cartridges strapped round their chests and daggers in their *pishtens* giggled like girls and one of the hiders became so hysterical

The Kurdish War

that he fell over. They played this game uproariously for a long time, watched by a four-deep audience behind the wall at the end of the room. I simulated extreme guilt when the opposite team questioned me and was accused wrongly four times of hiding the stone before the fifth time when they caught me with it on the first guess.

It was gone midnight before the turkey which had been the prize for the first game arrived, boiled and well salted. I lay down and went to sleep while they were still eating it.

The full coldness of the mountains hit us in the morning and I found the muddy ruts in the village streets were frozen hard. Kak' Mohammad was holding a conference of some sort with the village elders and I walked round with Amin to look at a long white streamer of a waterfall on the other side of the river and at some of the watermills. It was a nice little village, with a civilized leisureliness; it had a vine-covered tea place beside the road and a patch of ground which a concrete pond and an attempt at a layout of paths had brought close to being a public garden.

Amin, exercising his general knowledge as I stood looking at the waterfall, asked me if I knew how many tons the Dukan Dam weighed. I asked for the exact measurements, knowing how much Amin would enjoy giving me them in exact detail.

'Including road, tunnel works and foundations?' I asked, when he had finished.

'Yes.'

'Then five guesses?'

'All right.'

'Two and a half million tons.'

'Too little, Mister David.'

'Eight million?'

'Too much.'

'Seven million, then?'

'Ah, you are right.'

The Kurdish bears ambled into our conversation again as we waited for Kak' Mohammad. Amin talked sadly about the comfortable hut at Ibrahim Ahmed's headquarters where his belongings were and I asked him why he didn't walk due south and collect them before joining Mullah Mustafa, who

The Kurdish War

in any case was moving in that direction. He looked appalled. He would have to travel on his own and there were the bears to reckon with. They came up behind lonely travellers, stood upright on their hind legs and jerked their pistols out of their holsters before they realized what had happened. 'It's true, Mr David.' But it was such a ludicrous picture that he couldn't be entirely serious about it.

I grew impatient waiting and at last walked up the road to shame Kak' Mohammad out of the house where he was talking with the village leaders. He dashed out after a few minutes and we said our goodbyes and began to walk to the frontier, which was now quite near; a line of snow-covered mountains rising above a barren plateau streaked here and there with snow drifts and with two or three villages on the edge of the agricultural land. We turned off the road and along a mule track to a village where we were given tea. A young man came and stared at us from a doorway. He had, said someone, eloped with a girl from a nearby village. In this district they were famous for elopements. It surprised me that in village society any man could get to know a girl well enough to make sure that he wanted to run away with her. But Amin said there were always chances for them to meet when the girl went out to collect wood or water. After the elopement all was well if the man paid compensation to the family. If he did not, he could be killed without much blame attaching to the murderer.

Before turning north to what I hoped would be my take-off point for the border crossing I made a detour to see the Ryat police post captured by the Kurds in fighting early in the year: a strong, stonewalled fort with a turret and surrounded by barbed wire. Its garrison of 105 held out for thirty-three days before the hopelessness of their situation and a lack of food and water decided them on surrender. Parachute drops of supplies drifted into Kurdish hands and bullets whipping through the rifle slits and high steel doors killed two of their number. Their graves, as clumsily heaped and bare as those of paupers in an English churchyard, lay side by side in the courtyard of the fort next to a pile of rubble created when Iraqi aircraft machine gunned and bombed the fort after its capture. No Kurds were killed, said Kak' Mohammad, which

The Kurdish War

amazed me when I looked at the riddled metal doors and thought of the amount of ammunition that must have been expended. Perhaps the police thought it best not to enrage their enemy by firing back too often. Next to the fort was a former administrative building from which the Kurds had tunnelled in an attempt to sap the wall of the tower, as in medieval siege tactics. The room from which they had tunnelled was full of earth and I wondered how the sappers had managed to get in and out without being shot from the fort, which was only about thirty yards away.

I turned north parallel with the frontier, towards the village where Kak' Mohammad said I would be able to find guides. If I am vague about distances and times, it is because it would be undiplomatic to be precise. Those who helped me were people whose families and lands stretched across frontiers which are the contrivances of Arabs, Persian and Turks, not theirs. We eventually arrived, then, at a pleasant, well kept house where the mullah came and ate with our host and us. like the chaplain of an English squire. It was quite a good meal, and I thought, a bit guiltily—since it seemed ungrateful —that we were close to Persia where food was cooked with some art. Platters of sweet black grapes were brought to us afterwards, but Amin refused these on the grounds that black grapes had given him malaria when he last ate them.

The owner of the village was a young man whose good manners were not able to disguise altogether the fact that he was disconcerted and embarrassed by my sudden arrival. He was not, I thought, a supporter of Mullah Mustafa or the rebels. More likely a quiet-lifer who wanted to keep his peace with the Persian authorities without falling out with the rebels; an uncommitted man.

He asked me if I had visited Algeria during the war and I said 'yes'. How many Algerians died, he wanted to know; and I told him possibly 250,000. They were all amazed and perhaps shocked at the sacrifices nationalism can demand. I asked him what he thought the losses of the Kurds were. Between 3,000 and 5,000, he thought, adding bravely: 'But the Kurds would be happy to die if 250,000 was the price of liberty.'

After lunch, the owner of the village, Kak' Mohammad,

The Kurdish War

Amin and one of the village elders went off on their own to talk about my route. I sat and smoked for a quarter of an hour or so before a servant came and took me to a small garden where they were sitting. Obviously, no decision had been reached. It was not possible, said the village owner, to ride to Nagada, on the road to Mahabad, as I had suggested. There were too many troops and I would be seen, even if I travelled by night. He wanted me to go back to the main road and get in touch with the Persian authorities there; but I said I preferred to cross the frontier and make my peace with the Persian authorities later. Any other way would cause protracted negotiations and awkward explanations that might delay me for weeks. All I wanted him to do was to get me across the frontier to the village of one of his relations. From there I could send a message to some friends who would be able to help me. There was no one who would be able to help on the Persian side, he said, and suggested again that I should go along the main road. It seemed time to show some impatience, so I said that if he would not help me we would all go south and cross the mountains by the pass near Sardasht, forty to fifty miles away, through difficult country. He had only been trying me out, for he said at once that he would provide me with guides and a horse and see that I crossed the frontier that night to the village of a relation of his. No service was too great for one whom Mullah Mustafa wished him to help.

We set off soon after for the frontier village which would be my jumping off point that night. I had been given a fawn *claeatur* of goats' wool, which I pulled down over my ears against the cold. 'C'est tres chic,' said Kak' Mohammad.

It had all been arranged with such surprising speed that I felt for the first time lonely, or perhaps more accurately, alone; as if I was already outside their world. The mountains, their snow slopes waiting for me, looked austere enough to place some moral prohibition on my crossing them.

I hate saying goodbye to people, perhaps because I do not know how to say it gracefully or without some odd feeling of guilt that people with a franker, less self-examining nature can avoid. I would slip across the mountains and they would stay to fight their possibly hopeless war; Kak' Mohammad was

The Kurdish War

wanted by the police where I was going, and Amin could not get permission to leave; and even if he did, how would he ever get his family out of Iraq and into Beirut? I felt very warm to them and sorry that I had to protest and bully my way out of Mullah Mustafa's camp to the frontier; and sorry too that in an odd way I had been involved in their divisions and seen the weaknesses that ran like a fault through the rebellion. I wished I could help them or show them that I sympathized and hoped they would survive to live the decent lives they deserved. But all I could do was to leave them some soap I had in my rucksack, together with a few Entero-Vioform tablets and my raincoat for Amin. He offered me a thick slab of Aleppo soap, like fudge, which is highly valued in those parts, but I said no, I didn't want it, even 'for fun' as he put it. The only souvenir I brought out with me was a red oak apple the size of a squash ball. They litter the mountain-side under the trees and it seemed as good a reminder as any.

We ate supper and then moved to a hut a mile from the frontier. Small parties of Kurds either mounted or driving donkeys passed in the dark. Two smugglers, we heard, had been arrested and the guides Karim and Abdul went to investigate. Yoghourt and bread and honey was brought, but I did not eat much, although Kak' Mohammad urged me to, saying that the honey would keep me warm on the mountain. I wrote at his request a short bread-and-butter letter to Mullah Mustafa in which I avoided any mention of his present and said I wished him and his followers well. There was a long ride ahead and I lay down and slept until the guides returned with the news that it was all right to leave. It was eleven o'clock and every rock and shadow of a snowdrift showed in the light of a moon and stars so bright that they seemed to hang well forward of a blue-black sky. I did up the collar of my jacket, wound my scarf tighter and regretted that I had given away the blue denim trousers in which I had first crossed the frontier.

We stood together for a moment shaking hands. They would wait, said Kak' Mohammad, until they received a letter from me saying that I had arrived safely. I apologized for making them all walk so far, but Amin said it was in the

The Kurdish War

service of Kurdistan. Perhaps we would all meet again when the war was over and life more settled, I said, and they replied that they hoped so, but did not manage to sound very convinced we would. 'Goodbye, my friend,' said Amin, holding the horse's head as I mounted.

Kurdish style, we set off without looking back; three men walking and two, including myself, riding. The two men leading on foot had been conscripted to show us the way across the mountain before we reached the lower ground on the other side. The track was soon lost in snow in which the horse slipped and stumbled, breathing hard in the cold air, and finally stopping when we came to a gully. I dismounted to let the guides drag it across and walked from there on. The going was difficult not only because of the snow but because of clumps of shrubs. We lost the way once but found it soon and worked round the edge of a spur through drifts of up to two feet deep. I found it hard to keep my footing until Karim, the leader of the party, lent me his shepherd's stick. He kept a distance of about 150 yards between us and the three others, whom we could see clearly. Behind us the horse, head thrown back against the pull of the reins held by Karim, sent crumbling waves of glittering snow down the mountainside. We were well across the frontier by now and I could see miles into Persia: right across the valley to the low peaks of the mountains on the far side; rivers gleamed liked the tracks of snails and the patterns of the ploughland looked as if they had been engraved in steel. We had come well down the mountain when Karim tapped me on the arm and pointed to a party of four men with rifles coming to intercept the leading three. We moved back quickly and hid behind a hump in the mountainside. The two groups talked together for several minutes before there was a whistle and we were waved forward. I understood Karim to tell me not to stop and I walked quickly through the group, Karim pushing me sharply in the back when one of the four men with rifles said something in a surprised tone as I passed. They were Kurds, I saw, probably of the same tribe as my guides. They stood with their hands in their pockets, rifles slung over their shoulders, the local militia on patrol against smuggling. They watched us go on down the mountain, but did not follow. The two men who

The Kurdish War

had shown us the way across the mountains were reluctant to go much farther but Karim pushed them violently when they hunched their shoulders mutinously and walked slowly. He let them go only when we had left the snow some way behind and reached the edge of the ploughland.

The whole valley was silent and still. Anyone crossing it would have seen us, as we would have seen them from over a mile away. If we met anyone who might stop us, said Karim by signs, he would clap his hands and I was to follow the other horse as fast as I could go. It sounded rather dangerous advice to me and I hoped we would have an uneventful journey; which it was, slow and immensely peaceful as the horse ambled sleepily over the smooth ground. I marvelled at the difference between the mountain country we had just left and the plain, which was suddenly and unmistakably Persian in its scale and the shapes of the mountains to the east. Dogs in a village two miles to our right howled at the sound of our horses, as their hooves caught on the shale of some small hills which obtruded into the plain at one point. Beyond them a river divided into several strands which had to be crossed. One was deep but narrow enough to be jumped by the horse. He refused it once, snorting in disbelief at being asked to do such a thing. But I took him back and then whipped him over it with the end of the reins, landing with a rocking thump, but together, on a muddy bank.

I could see our village quite clearly a few miles ahead, a huddle of cubes, gold with black shadows, among its farmlands. Expectedly, its dogs barked as we came close to it, but no one came out and we skirted it to enter past the substantial house of the owner and then along a street to a house with a narrow courtyard. Its owner came out after a few minutes' knocking and took us into the room where he had been sleeping. His blankets and quilt lay on the floor beside a dead stove and he had hardly managed to get his eyes open. It was not far off dawn, but he brought out some gorse and wood and lit the stove before fetching the samovar and a bowl of yoghourt and bread. Abdul went to call the owner of the village who arrived shortly wearing a heavy blue overcoat over his pyjamas; a tall, grave man, with a sensitive and intellectual face under a white silk turban. He spoke some

The Kurdish War

English and soon grasped, with the aid of a letter from his relation on the other side of the border, why I was sitting in the middle of his village at half-past four on a Friday morning. I wrote a letter to a man who lived some forty miles away, telling him I was back in Persia and would like his help, and the owner said he would get his brother to take it as soon as it was light. A metal bed and a chair were brought for me and as soon as the owner had gone I rolled myself in a blanket and went to sleep, leaving the Kurds still eating yoghourt beside the stove.

It was after seven when I woke. The others had gone. The street outside had a mosque-going, Friday quiet and the villagers seemed to be either still in bed or sitting round their stoves. The sun shone brightly but as thin as torch-beams through three tiny windows. It was a pleasant and rather interesting room in its way. Above and beyond my toes as I lay on the bed was a shelf with a row of Pepsi-Cola and other greenish bottles, all empty; and in the middle of them two pink plastic ducks and a small but indefinable plastic animal. The walls were decorated with sheets of Farsi newspapers, several faces of girls, a print of a nineteenth-century painting of a plump, half-naked courtesan looking at a necklace, two more coloured prints dedicated to the heroism of the Persian army, with a medley of soldiers struggling hand-to-hand, firing cannons and being received into Paradise; a tactful picture to have in that well-garrisoned region. An influential sheikh figured on another poster and in a photograph taken when he was receiving a testimonial from an American general. There was a regulation portrait of the Shah, of course, and two other posters, one of a group of American Boy Scouts drinking Coca-Cola and the other of a burly, bearded soldier drinking from a water-bottle. But most intriguing were two squares of linen which were pinned below the shelf of Pepsi-Cola bottles and looked like tea-cloths. They were decorated with antique cars, I could see, despite the fact that the cloths were hung back to front; and the lettering on top was Latin. I worked it out slowly, reading from right to left and guessing where the folds hid the lettering: 'Veterans of the Road'.

Ibrahim looked in as I was getting off the bed and soon

The Kurdish War

came back with wood for the fire and the samovar. Sanitary arrangements were difficult, since I could not go outside, and I was taken through the kitchen to the cow-shed which was next to it and all part of the house. Chickens roosted around my ears and cows chumped the cud in the darkness. On the flat roof above a group of children ran about, their feet shaking down the dust. I asked for hot water as I passed through the kitchen on my way back to the room and it was brought to me in the room, where I was shaving when the owner of the village called in to tell me that his brother had set off with my message. He sat watching me as I shaved and gave discreet answers to my questions about the attitudes of the local landowners, *aghas* and peasants to the rebellion across the frontier. One sheikh—the one I had met in Rezaieh—opposed Mullah Mustafa; another supported him in principle, but not beyond that. Some men had gone across the border but the majority were uncommitted. It seemed, even from the faint whiff of village life I was getting in my room, as much Persian as Kurdish and the inhabitants no doubt like most Persian peasants unassuming and docile so long as life did not become unbearable; and moreover still, despite the changes coming from land reform, held in their places by the authority of the landlord.

With me the guide Karim had been informal, perhaps accepting me as part of the Western world along with Pepsi-Cola bottles and plastic ducks. He was a bright man, quick-witted and nobody's fool. Unusual in a Kurd, his hair was long and hung down over his collar in black curls, and this, together with a gold tooth and sharp eyes, gave him the look of a gypsy, of the romantic, Borrowesque kind. But when the landlord spoke to him he dropped back into his formal place and stood very upright, his eyes looking over our heads and his hands folded—the arms a little stiff and shoulders back—across his belly, his 'no' in answer to a gentle, teasing question a deprecatory click of the tongue against the upper front teeth combined with a quick jerk back of the head. Yet their manner was quite easy within this frame of formality, and Karim spoke at length on some subject or another. He had more real respect for the *agha* than he ever would have for any European, or for that matter any Westernized politician.

The Kurdish War

The day passed gently. I lay on the bed, slept, thought, wrote my diary and talked with the *agha*, who called to see me twice during the day and ate an early lunch with me before going to the mosque. Once a group of children burst into the room, stared at me in silence and then fled. 'It is impossible to keep anything secret in a village,' said the *agha* when I told him about this.

I find myself using words like 'gentle' and 'docile', words not all that often used in connection with the Kurds. And I suppose it is because the village seemed a long, long way in its tone of life (a vague phrase, but then what I am saying is not very much more than an impression) from the mountain villages only a few miles to the west. Kurdish nationalism is still strong in Persia, but I am not sure it is the same sort of nationalism that you find in Iraq; just as Mullah Mustafa's nationalism is not the same as Ibrahim Ahmed's. They are split in so many ways; by geography, by tribes, by custom and politics, by national frontiers and by education. Do the Kurds of Persia have more in common with those of Iraq than they have with the Persians, who come from much the same stock as the Kurds? I rather doubt it. Just as I have a feeling that in any Kurdish state in Iraq many of the politicians would find that they had more in common with the Arab socialists than with the *aghas*.

This begins to sound like a pessimistic summing up, and before I go any further I should say that I believe the Kurds have as much right as anyone else to their independence. Nationalism is often sentimental, cheap, jingoistic, based on economic and racial clap-trap, the belief of a militant few expressed over the apathy of many, often disastrous in the end, as perhaps Kurdish independence would be. But nevertheless it is valid, aesthetically perhaps more than morally. Whichever it is, it is better than the inspiration of those who oppress in the name of their own nationalism. Who would say today, that Britain was wrong to create the Irish Free State, or that the Poles are not entitled to their freedom? It is curious how countries in both Africa and Asia which have been subjected to the rule of imperial powers and whose leaders still inveigh against colonialism refuse to acknowledge very similar sins committed by themselves and cling desperately

The Kurdish War

to their imperial frontiers as if they were all they had between them and shame.

'How can we give the Kurds what they demand?' said Taleb Hussein Shabib, the Iraqi Foreign Minister, when I talked with him in London a few days before he was forced out of office in November 1963. 'We might as well create an independent state for them. It would not be a federal state.'

Who can altogether blame the Iraqi leaders and those others who are also the overlords of the Kurds? Co-operation, conciliation and compromise are meaningful only in the political vocabularies of rich and secure countries. The Middle East suffers too much from the debilities of poverty and ignorance, and the human selfishness which goes with them, to allow much latitude for generosity.

Yet in a world less bedevilled by pride and poverty, the answer for the Kurds would lie in the federal system they demand. Their official concept of it is a narrow one. They dare not seem to look beyond the frontiers of Iraq. But the idea deserves to be considered more broadly. The rigid adherence to frontiers fixed by seventeenth-century emperors and twentieth-century diplomats sitting in Lausanne after the First World War helps no one to achieve greater happiness. A loose federal system, with the existing countries keeping their present frontiers yet lowering them for the easier passage of trade, people and ideas, could provide a solution, but it would only work if it were flexible enough to avoid the tensions which have destroyed the United Arab Republic and strong enough to deter the Kurds from seeking full independence. And having said that, I then have to go on to admit that a solution on those lines is not practical politics at the moment. Neither the Turks or the Persians would admit that there is any demand for self-government among their Kurds and gauging how strongly their nationalism runs would, in the existing political set-ups, be extremely difficult. So at this stage it is best to think only of Iraq.

No one can claim that the unitary state devised by Britain has been a success. There never has been stable government in Iraq; the rival factions have been too strong. Prime ministers and régimes have come and gone as rapidly as a theatre changes its plays. Would a self-governing Kurdish state make the

The Kurdish War

country more stable? It could hardly make it less so and the freeing of the Arabs from the fallacy that Iraq is one and indivisible and entirely part of the Arab world would at least make it possible for them to think more creatively. I do not believe that the Kurds' geographic position would mean that they dominated the federation militarily (ironically, it was partly fears of Turkish military domination of Mesopotamia from the Kurdish mountains that made the British argue so determinedly for the inclusion of the Mosul *Vilayet* within Iraq); they would not necessarily have either the armoured weapons or the inclination to do so. Their conception of war is and always has been defensive rather than aggressive. The other important question is that of oil revenues and how they should be shared. Worse problems than this have been hammered into agreements and some sort of equitable agreement (not necessarily on the proportional basis demanded by the Kurds) should be possible. Far from being a disturbing element in the relations between the two races, oil could be a unifying one; both would find it in their interests that it continued to flow and was sold to the West, its only market.

Whatever happens, I believe that Kurdish nationalism has taken a permanent place among the political forces of the Middle East. It is deep-rooted and tenacious, no longer just a flower of the mountainsides but increasingly an urban phenomenon. It is the urban, middle-class Kurds who will eventually decide what happens in Kurdistan, for they have become the managers and guides of the revolt through the Democratic Party. Despite the Marxist streak which runs through the party, I do not think there is any great danger of a self-governing Kurdish State turning to the Soviet Union for help—unless it is forced to do so by the hostility of the Arabs or its other neighbours. The party is basically a battle group, its elements held together these days more by the common purpose of victory than by any identity of political belief among its members. Like similar groupings in South America—or, for that matter, the Baath Party in Iraq—once it had achieved victory it would very probably find itself faced with the problem of how to hold together the moderate and extremist wings. My opinion is that the undoctrinaire, pragmatic element in the party would dominate it.

The Kurdish War

But it is hard in such a situation to make any forecasts. So much depends on how and when a settlement is reached. A long war will favour the extremists; might even make a federal solution impossible so that the Kurds' goal inevitably became complete independence. Today, although the dispute between Kurds and Arabs is more bitter than it has ever been, it is still possible to negotiate[1] an agreement which would leave the economic framework of Iraq intact and keep the Kurds as willing and pacific partners in the State. If the Arabs think otherwise, they would do well to recall Algeria and note that in such wars neither time nor God is necessarily on the side of the big battalions.

I left the village where I had hidden on the night of the day I arrived and not long afterwards passed by the Chwar Chira circle at Mahabad where Qazi Mohammad proclaimed the first Kurdish republic in 1946 and was later hanged. It seemed a sombre little city, still overcast by its tragedy, and I was glad to leave it and drive away on the road to the railway station at Maragegh, past strings of camels going to the markets, and out of Kurdistan.

---

[1] See note at end of Appendix.

APPENDIX

During the cease-fire which followed the death of Kassem in February 1963, the Kurds sent a negotiating team to Baghdad. No headway was made but both sides put forward their proposals in some detail. The government called theirs 'decentralization'. Not altogether surprisingly decentralization was rejected by the Kurds. The following is taken from the July 1963 issue of the *Bulletin of the Republic of Iraq*.

THE IRAQI GOVERNMENT'S PROPOSALS[1]

Preamble

1. In execution of the provisions of the Phased Programme which was issued by the National Council of the Revolutionary Command on March 15, 1963, the decentralized system means the dividing of Iraq administratively into Governorates, each enjoying sufficient freedom of action for the administration of its affairs under the supervision of the Central Government.

The Governorate

2. The Governorate is an administrative unit whose borders shall be defined by law. It shall consist of one or more Liwas (provinces) whose sub-divisions shall be Qadhas, Nahiyats and Villages.

The Governorate Administrations

3. (a) The Governorate and its sub-divisions shall be administered, beginning with the villages, by Government officials and elected Councils to be called: Village Council, Nahiyat Council, Qadha Council, Liwa Council, and Governorate Council.

(b) The number of members in each of these Councils and the methods of their election shall be determined by a regulation, which will also name the officials who, by virtue of their positions, will automatically be members of these Councils.

[1] See note at end of Appendix.

Administration at Governorate Headquarters

4. The administrative organ at Governorate headquarters shall comprise:

(a) The Governor, who shall be appointed by the Central Government, be responsible to it for all governorate affairs, and be considered, by virtue of his position, Chairman of the Governorate Council.

(b) The Governorate Council, which shall comprise:
   i Members elected by direct secret ballot.
   ii Nominated members to be appointed by a Republican Decree.
   iii Heads of offices at Governorate Headquarters, who shall automatically be considered members of the Council, provided that their number, together with the appointed members, shall not exceed one-third of the elected members.

(c) The Executive Council, which shall consist of heads of departments at Governorate headquarters and whose members and chairman shall be appointed by a decree of the Council of Ministers.

Jurisdiction

5. *Governorate Council.* (a) The Governorate Council shall be a legal body having the right to dispose of both movable and immovable property. Its property shall be considered State property.

(b) The Governorate Council, exercising its powers under a special law, shall concern itself in the following matters: education, municipality and village affairs, construction, housing and communications, supplies and trading, public health, labour and social affairs, and agriculture and irrigation. It shall generally be responsible for administering the Governorate and making sure that the various administrative organs in it are functioning efficiently and in harmony with the Government's policy. It shall issue local regulations in conformity with the powers granted to it by law, these regulations to be subject to ratification by the minister concerned. It shall approve the budgets for the local administrations as well as a budget for the Governorate and submit all these to the Government for final approval. It shall prepare and present proposals to the ministers concerned regarding development projects. It shall draw up internal regulations for its sessions and conduct of work, and keep records of its proceedings.

6. *The Executive Council.* The Executive Council shall be re-

The Kurdish War

sponsible for enforcing the resolutions for the Governorate Council if not disallowed by the minister concerned, as well as for enforcing all laws and regulations and administrative directions. It shall prepare the Governorate budget, draft local regulations, control all the accounts of the Governorate and prepare them for auditing.

7. *Revenues.* The Governorate revenues shall be made up of the following: the remaining half of the net Government revenue from the land tax, the second half of the petrol duty, additions to the land tax and consumer taxes and municipality dues, special grants made by the Treasury, tolls from bridges and ferries, any share of the State revenues which the Central Government may fix by law, as well as the share fixed by the Central Government of death duties within the Governorate, donations and estates left by heirless persons, loans, allocations in the general budget for local administrations.

8. *Expenditure.* The expenditure of the decentralized administration shall be as follows: salaries and allowances of the officials and employees of the administration and allocations for its departments, allowances for the members of the Governorate Council, all expenditure required by the services and works coming within the sphere of the decentralized administration and deposited with it in accordance with the laws and regulations.

9. *General Provisions.* The Council of Ministers shall issue general directives to be followed by the Governorate Council. Should this Council fail to follow them the Council of Ministers shall suspend, cancel, or amend any decision issued by the Governorate Council, and it shall also have the power to deprive the Governorate Council of any power or jurisdiction for this purpose.

APPENDIX I

1. *The Governorates*

   Iraq shall be divided into the following Governorates:
   1. Mosul, consisting of Mosul Liwa and with the town of Mosul as its headquarters.
   2. Kirkuk, consisting of Kirkuk Liwa (excluding the Qadha of Chamchamal) and with Kirkuk town as its headquarters.
   3. Sulaimaniyah (headquarters, Sulaimaniya town) consisting of Arbil and Sulaimaniyah liwas (including the Qadha of Chamchamal), Duhoka Liwa (comprising the Qadhas of Zakho, Duhoka, Ammida, Akra, and Zaibar of Mosul Liwa).

The Kurdish War

4. Baghdad (headquarters Baghdad) comprising the liwas of Baghdad, Ramadi, Diyala, and Kut.
5. Hilla (headquarters Hilla), consisting of the liwas of Diwaniyal, Hilla and Kerbala.
6. Basrah (headquarters Basrah), consisting of the liwas of Basrah, Nassiryah, Amara.

2. *The Kurdish Language*
The Arabic and Kurdish languages shall be considered the official languages in Sulaimaniyah Governorate. Teaching shall be conducted in the Kurdish language in the primary and intermediate stages, and Arabic as a second language. Teaching shall be in Arabic in the secondary stage.

(The second Appendix gives a long list setting out in detail the specific duties of the Governorate Council under the headings of education, agriculture and irrigation, public health, etc.)

THE KURDISH COUNTER PROPOSALS

I. The Iraq Republic is a unified state consisting of the two principal nationalities, the Arab and the Kurdish, who enjoy equal rights and have expressed their will, in accordance with the right of self-determination, to live together.

II. The Iraqi Constitution shall include provisions for a higher legislative organ for the Republic, for a President of the Republic and for a Government. It shall also provide for the setting up of the national body through which the Kurdish people shall exercise its national rights in legislative, executive and judicial matters, in the region of Kurdistan.

III. The following matters shall be within the competency of the Central Government:
   1. Presidency of the State.
   2. Foreign Affairs, comprising political, consular and trade representation, international pacts and agreements, United Nations affairs, declaration of war, and conclusion of peace.
   3. National Defence (land, sea and air forces).
   4. Currency and minting.
   5. Oil affairs.
   6. Customs.
   7. International ports and airports.
   8. Posts, telegraphs, and telephones.
   9. Railways and highways.
   10. Nationality affairs.

The Kurdish War

   11. The general budget of the State.
   12. Supervision of the central radio and television services.
   13. Atomic energy.
IV 1. The Kurdish people shall exercise its national rights through an Executive Council emanating from a Legislative Council elected by residents in Kurdistan, by direct free secret ballot.
   2. The national body provided for in Article II shall have competence in the fields of justice, internal affairs, culture and education, health, agriculture, tobacco, municipalities, labour, social affairs, development, summer resorts, and all that relates to raising the living and social standards and to economic development and other matters that have not been included within the competence of the Central Government.
V The Legislative Council shall enact all the laws necessary for exercising the powers specified in Clause 2 above. The Legislative Council shall elect the President of the Executive Council and shall have the right to withdraw its confidence from him and from the other members of the Executive Council.
VI The Executive Council shall exercise the executive power within the limits of the competence of the national body as stated in Clause 2 above, and shall enforce the laws enacted by the Legislative Council as well as the laws and general regulations made by the Central Government in so far as they relate to Kurdistan. The Executive Council shall appoint the officials of the administration and other departments in the region, and shall be responsible in all its actions to the Legislative Council.
VII The finances of the national body for the Kurdistan region shall comprise the following:
   1. Local resources and taxes and dues levied inside Kurdistan.
   2. Kurdistan's share, in the proportion of its population to the population of Iraq, of the revenues of oil, customs, airports, ports, banks, railways, posts, telegraphs, and telephones, save that from this share shall be deducted, again in proportion to the population of Kurdistan as compared with the population of Iraq, Kurdistan's share of the expenditure on the Presidency, defence, foreign affairs, minting, the administration of the ministry of oil, and of posts, telegraphs, telephones, and banks, as well as a share of the expenditure on railways and public highways in proportion

to their length in Kurdistan as compared with their length in Iraq.
3. A share for Kurdistan, in the same proportion as that indicated above, of all foreign loans and grants which the Central Government may receive.
4. Internal loans and non-military forms of financial assistance to be made available to Kurdistan.
5. Revenues of tobacco, summer resorts and forests.
6. Kurdistan shall be considered as having a share, in proportion to its population as compared with the population of Iraq, in all institutions, projects, and interests of a public utility character.

VIII The Kurdistan region shall include Sulaimaniyah, Kirkuk, and Arbil Liwas and the Qadhas and Nahiyhas inhabited by a Kurdish majority in Mosul and Dyala liwas.

IX The Vice-President of the Iraq Republic shall be a Kurd, elected by the people of Kurdistan in the same way as the President of the Republic is elected.

X The constitution of the national body for the region of Kurdistan shall guarantee cultural, social, and economic rights and democratic and religious freedom for minority citizens like the Turkomans, Assyrians, Chaldeans, Armenians, and other religious sects or racial groups. It shall guarantee their complete equality in rights and duties with members of the Arab and Kurdish nationalities, and further it shall guarantee their representation, in a just proportion, in the Executive and Legislative Councils as well as in other bodies.

General Matters
1. The people of Kurdistan shall be represented in the Iraqi National Assembly by a number of deputies in proportion to the Kurdish population as compared with the population of Iraq.
2. The people of Kurdistan shall have a number of ministers in the Central Cabinet, also in the same proportion.
3. The number of Kurdish officials in the ministries of the Central Government shall also be in the same proportion.
4. The number of Kurdish students admitted to Baghdad University and other institutes of higher education, as well as the number of Kurdish students sent for education on government missions shall also be in the same proportion.
5. One of the deputies of the Iraqi army's Chief-of-Staff shall be a Kurd.

The Kurdish War

6. The Iraqi army shall keep its name, but in the event of the name being changed, the Kurdish section of the army shall be called the Kurdistan Corps, this Corps to be formed by the bringing together of all soldiers, officers, and other ranks in the Iraqi army who are inhabitants of Kurdistan.
7. The sons of Kurdistan shall do their military service in it. Officers and non-commissioned officers who have been dismissed the service for national and political reasons shall be returned to the army and posted to the units serving Kurdistan.
8. Kurdish students shall be admitted to the Military, Police, Staff, and Aviation Colleges and to other military institutions in a number proportionate to the population of Kurdistan as compared with the population of Iraq.
9. The Central Government may send additional forces to the Kurdistan regions in the event of the Iraqi Republic becoming exposed to foreign attack or if there is a real threat of such attack. In all other cases the consent of the Legislative and Executive Councils of Kurdistan must be obtained, provided that the terms of this clause shall not hinder the Iraqi army from carrying out its normal exercises and manoeuvres for a reasonable period.
10. Suppressive military operations inside Kurdistan shall be undertaken with the consent of Kurdistan's Legislative Council, or at the request of the Executive Council.
11. Any legislative provision, whatever its source may be, shall be considered null and void if its effect is to restrict the national and democratic rights of the Kurdish people or limit its opportunities of exercising these rights.
12. The proclamation of martial law in Kurdistan shall be with the consent of the Legislative Council, except in the cases of declaration of war or the existence of a real danger of foreign aggression.
13. One of the present Kurdish ministers shall be entrusted with the formation of the provisional Executive Council for exercising temporarily the powers of the Council. The elections for the Legislative Council shall take place within the period not exceeding four months from the date of its formation of the provisional Executive Council.
14. The elimination of the effects of the tyrant's (Kassem's) rule by just and speedy compensation to those who have suffered injury from Kurdistan's revolt, this to be done within a period not exceeding four months.
15. In the case of a change of Iraqi nationality into Arab nation-

The Kurdish War

ality, then shall be mentioned in the birth certificate, census registers, and passports that the bearer is a Kurdistani within the United Arab Republic, if he is a citizen from the Kurdistan region, and a Kurd if he is of Kurdish origin. If the Iraqi flag or the emblem of the Iraqi State is changed, a Kurdish sign shall be added thereto.

NOTE: The government's proposals were modified when President Aref's régime tried to establish a basis for negotiations after the second cease-fire agreement in February 1964. Although the situation was confused by contradictory statements from both sides, it was at least clear that the government had gone some way to meet the Kurdish demands. It seems to have been prepared to recognize that there was a separate Kurdish region within Iraq and to have put forward proposals for a Kurdish development board with a budget, according to one source, of about £12 million a year. There was also an offer to recompense some of those who had suffered material loss through the fighting. No demand was made for the surrender of any of the Kurdish leaders, nor for the demobilization of the Kurdish forces. However, little progress had been made by mid-March 1964 (when this note was written). The government's offer did not measure up to the Kurds' definition of autonomy. Another major difficulty lay in the boundaries of the new region as conceived by the government. They did not embrace the oilfields claimed by the Kurds as theirs. Hence, although the Kurds would probably have been prepared to drop their claim for a 30 per cent share of Iraq's oil income, they would not have had what many considered indispensable to their security and well-being: a direct hold on the country's main economic asset.

For Product Safety Concerns and Information please contact our EU
representative GPSR@taylorandfrancis.com
Taylor & Francis Verlag GmbH, Kaufingerstraße 24, 80331 München, Germany